PLAYING

WITH

FIRE

How the Bible Ignites
Change in Your Soul

Walt Russell

NAVPRESS ◐
BRINGING TRUTH TO LIFE
P.O. Box 35001, Colorado Springs, Colorado 80935

OUR GUARANTEE TO YOU

We believe so strongly in the message of our books that we are making this quality guarantee to you. If for any reason you are disappointed with the content of this book, return the title page to us with your name and address and we will refund to you the list price of the book. To help us serve you better, please briefly describe why you were disappointed. Mail your refund request to: NavPress, P.O. Box 35002, Colorado Springs, CO 80935.

The Navigators is an international Christian organization. Our mission is to reach, disciple, and equip people to know Christ and to make Him known through successive generations. We envision multitudes of diverse people in the United States and every other nation who have a passionate love for Christ, live a lifestyle of sharing Christ's love, and multiply spiritual laborers among those without Christ.

NavPress is the publishing ministry of The Navigators. NavPress publications help believers learn biblical truth and apply what they learn to their lives and ministries. Our mission is to stimulate spiritual formation among our readers.

Library of Congress Catalog Card Number: 00-025318
ISBN 1-57683-142-6

Cover design by Ray Moore
Creative Team: Steve Webb, Tom Raabe, Terry Behimer, Tim Howard, and Heather Nordyke.

Some of the anecdotal illustrations in this book are true to life and are included with the permission of the persons involved. All other illustrations are composites of real situations, and any resemblance to people living or dead is coincidental.

Unless otherwise identified, all Scripture quotations in this publication are taken from the *New American Standard Bible* (NASB), © The Lockman Foundation 1960, 1962, 1963, 1968, 1971, 1972, 1973, 1975, 1977. Other version used is the *Holy Bible: New International Version*® (NIV®). Copyright © 1973, 1978, 1984 by International Bible Society. Used by permission of Zondervan Publishing House. All rights reserved.

Russell, Walt.
    Playing with fire : how the Bible ignites change in your soul / Walt Russell.
        p. cm.
    ISBN 1-57683-142-6 (pbk.)
    1. Bible—Use. I. Title.
BS538.3 .R87 2000
220.1—dc21

          00-025318

Printed in the United States of America

1 2 3 4 5 6 7 8 9 10 11 12 13 14 15 / 05 04 03 02 01 00

FOR A FREE CATALOG OF
NAVPRESS BOOKS & BIBLE STUDIES,
CALL 1-800-366-7788 (USA)
OR 1-416-499-4615 (CANADA)

CONTENTS

THE NEED FOR THIS BOOK

The strength of the church in America is its broad-based foundation penetrating almost all segments of American society. Perhaps as many as fifty million Americans have experienced the new life that is in Jesus Christ. We are a church that is broad and wide. However, as many have noted, accompanying this great strength of a populist base is the corresponding weakness of a spiritual and intellectual shallowness. We are not a very deep church. This is due in large part to our culture not being very deep in recent generations. While we Americans may be the best in the world at entrepreneurial pragmatics, we are near the end of the line in intellectual profundities. Clearly this quality of the popular American culture has marked the populist American church. This is not necessarily something to berate ourselves about, but it is something to acknowledge and address as we seek to lead the church. We must do all we can to bolster our systemic weaknesses while continuing to manifest our inherent strengths.

There are certain grand ironies with this state of the church. On the one hand, we are sitting in the midst of the most accessible and greatest wealth of Bible study aids in the history of the world. No generation of the church of Jesus Christ has been as blessed as we are with written and electronic helps to study the Scriptures. Yet, on the other hand, we are also sitting in the midst of a church that is growing in its biblical and theological illiteracy at an accelerating rate. Ask any of us whose vocation is teaching God's people in the academy and in local churches, and we'll tell you of a remarkable decline over the last twenty-five years in basic biblical knowledge and in the ability to think and act Christianly.

Why is this so? There are probably many reasons for it, as authors like J. P. Moreland *(Love Your God with All Your Mind)* and Mark Noll *(The Scandal of the Evangelical Mind)* have noted. Let me add my voice to their incisive insights. Generally speaking, our growth in grace and truth must be preceded by our growth *in the knowledge of* what grace and truth are. If this prior growth is not happening, then meaningful life-change will not follow.

It is the premise of this book that one of the great gaps in our recent leadership of the church is this very thing: we have had a lack of dynamic emphasis on the Word of God. In other words, in the midst of a lot of talk *about* the Bible and a lot of posturing *around* the Bible, there is still a meaningful lack of emphasis on reading and studying the Bible *in an intelligent, informed manner that powerfully fuels our spiritual formation.* We have failed to equip the people of God with the most basic of silverware so that they can feast at will on the Word of God. In large part, they are dying for lack of knowledge. Therefore, what we need to help solve our problems is another book!

Obviously, the impact of yet another book is generally limited. However, if that book plows new ground and helps make some important yet neglected connections for God's people, then it may be worth the death of a few more trees. I would be so bold as to suggest that this book is of such an ilk. It is an attempt to intersect with God's people on a topic for which they may have a felt need—their spiritual formation—and help them connect it meaningfully with their reading of God's Word.

THE DISTINCTIVES OF THIS BOOK

This volume has two distinctives. *First,* it is a motivational book that seeks to equip God's people with skills that will allow them to read God's Word well and be transformed in the process. The uniqueness in this is that it foundationally ties biblical interpretation to spiritual formation. They will be essentially linked so that one informs and reinforces the other.

Second, this book seeks to bring the Bible into the spiritual growth process in an even more central manner. From my perspective, the cursory or misinterpreted use of the Scriptures is a widespread weakness of the spiritual formation tradition. Why must this be so? This book attempts to meet this need in an encouraging and winsome manner that gives both skills and motivation for reading God's Word for spiritual development.

The writing of this book, like any other book, has been a group effort. In particular, my dear wife, Marty, and two children, Elizabeth and Jonathan, have paid an exorbitant price relationally for this chunk of paper you are holding. My prolonged absence from them and perpetual distraction when with them during the many months of writing have been costly. I can only ask the Lord to remember their significant sacrifice and please compensate in their lives for the absence of Dad. Their grace toward me has been great. I pray that God's grace toward them will be even greater.

GENERAL INTRODUCTION

by Dallas Willard

The SPIRITUAL FORMATION LINE presents discipleship to Jesus Christ as the greatest opportunity individual human beings have in life and the only hope corporate mankind has of solving its insurmountable problems.

It affirms the unity of the present-day Christian with those who walked beside Jesus during His incarnation. To be His disciple then was to be with Him, to learn to be like Him. It was to be His student or apprentice in kingdom living. His disciples heard what He said and observed what He did; then, under His direction, they simply began to say and do the same things. They did so imperfectly but progressively. As He taught: "Everyone who is fully trained will be like his teacher" (Luke 6:40).

Today it is the same, except now it is the resurrected Lord who walks throughout the world. He invites us to place our confidence in Him. Those who rely on Him believe that He knows how to live and will pour His life into us as we "take His yoke . . . and learn from Him, for He is gentle and humble in heart . . . " (Matthew 11:29). To "take His yoke" means joining Him in His work, making our work His work. To trust Him is to understand that total immersion in what He is doing with our life is the best thing that could ever happen to us.

To "learn from Him" in this total-life immersion is how we "seek first his kingdom and his righteousness" (Matthew 6:33). The outcome is that we increasingly are able to do all things, speaking or acting, as if Christ were doing them (Colossians 3:17). As apprentices of Christ we are not learning how to do some special religious activity, but how to live every moment of our lives from the reality of God's kingdom. I am learning how to live my actual life as Jesus would if He were me.

If I am a plumber, clerk, bank manager, homemaker, elected official, senior citizen, or migrant worker, I am in "full-time" Christian service no less than someone who earns his or her living in a specifically religious role. Jesus stands beside me and teaches me in all I do to live in God's world. He shows me how, in every circumstance, to reside in His Word and thus be a genuine apprentice of His—His disciple indeed. This enables me to find the reality of God's world everywhere I may be, and thereby to escape from enslavement to sin and evil (John 8:31-32). We become able to do what we know to be good and right, even when it is humanly impossible. Our lives and words become constant testimony of the reality of God.

A plumber facing a difficult plumbing job must know how to integrate it into the kingdom of God as much as someone attempting to win another to Christ or preparing a lesson for a congregation. Until we are clear on this, we will have missed Jesus' connection between life and God and will automatically exclude most of our everyday lives from the domain of faith and discipleship. Jesus lived most of His life on earth as a blue-collar worker, someone we might describe today as an "independent contractor." In His vocation He practiced everything He later taught about life in the kingdom.

The "words" of Jesus I primarily reside in are those recorded in the New Testament Gospels. In His presence, I learn the goodness of His instructions and how to carry them out. It is not a matter of meriting life from above, but of receiving that life concretely in my circumstances. Grace, we must learn, is opposed to earning, not to effort.

For example, I move away from using derogatory language against others, calling them twits, jerks, or idiots (Matthew 5:22), and increasingly mesh with the respect and endearment for persons that naturally flow from God's way. This in turn transforms all of my dealings with others into tenderness and makes the usual coldness and brutality of human relations, which lays a natural foundation for abuse and murder, simply unthinkable.

Of course, the "learning of Him" is meant to occur in the context of His people. They are the ones He commissioned to make disciples, surround them in the reality of the triune name, and teach them to do "everything I have commanded you" (Matthew 28:20). But the disciples we make are His disciples, never ours. We are His apprentices along with them. If we are a little farther along the way, we can only echo the apostle Paul: "Follow my example, as I follow the example of Christ" (1 Corinthians 11:1).

It is a primary task of Christian ministry today, and of those who write for this line of books, to reestablish Christ as a living teacher in the midst of His people. He has been removed by various historical developments: assigned the role of mere sacrifice for sin or social prophet and martyr. But where there is no teacher, there can be no students or disciples.

If we cannot be His students, we have no way to learn to exist always and everywhere within the riches and power of His Word. We can only flounder along as if we were on our own so far as the actual details of our lives are concerned. That is where multitudes of well-meaning believers find themselves today. But that is not the intent of Him who says, "Come to me . . . and you will find rest for your souls" (Matthew 11:28-29).

Each book in this line is designed to contribute to this renewed vision of Christian spiritual formation and to illuminate what apprenticeship to Jesus Christ means within all the specific dimensions of human existence. The mission of these books is to form the whole person so that the nature of Christ becomes the natural expression of our souls, bodies, and spirits throughout our daily lives.

PART
ONE

Inflaming
the Soul

Chapter One

PLAYING
WITH
FIRE

"For as the rain and the snow come down from heaven,
And do not return there without watering the earth,
And making it bear and sprout,
And furnishing seed to the sower and bread to the eater;
So shall My word be which goes forth from My mouth;
It shall not return to Me empty,
Without accomplishing what I desire,
And without succeeding in the matter for which I sent it."

ISAIAH 55:10-11

"If you abide in My word, then you are truly disciples of Mine;
and you shall know the truth, and the truth shall make you free."

JOHN 8:31-32

SEVERAL YEARS AGO I CO-PLANTED A CHURCH WITH A DEAR friend. We were inseparable as best buddies for seven years as we labored together in ministry. However, I began to detect some troublesome aspects to our relationship and confronted him about them privately. Unfortunately, I was so hurt and angry that I did not do this in the kindest and most appropriate manner. Seven years of foolishly choosing to deny my pain in the relationship eventually erupted in my life through hurt and anger that I could not control or express in edifying ways.

The short story is that he eventually chose not to deal with these elements of his life after two rather stormy years of confrontation. Unfortunately, our fellow elders in the church did not see this brother in the same light I did, and they sided with him. My rampant hurt and anger seriously undercut my credibility with them. As a result, my family and I had to pack up and leave our church, our home, our community, and all the dreams of my adult life. Everything I had desired to do for God was wrapped up in this church. It was like conceiving, bearing, passionately loving, and raising a child for a while, then having to abandon it. Folding our tents and slipping out of town with a sense of disgrace was the hardest thing I ever had to do.

The next two years were the most miserable of my life. Although they followed on the heels of two years of great pain and anger, they greatly surpassed them in personal pain. I was deeply enraged and consumed by anger. Every problem I had in life I attributed to my former friend. The sadness and despair of my life was all his fault. He was the villain and I was the victim. I invested huge amounts of time pondering how angry I was at him and what an evil, malevolent person he was. I was being swallowed by my rage, growing cynicism, and bitterness. I was angry at God, the church, and anybody who crossed me.

Near the end of my two years away from our former church, my wife and two or three dear friends confronted me about the anger and bitterness that was engulfing me. They lovingly and courageously faced my rage and pointed out my sin. In particular, they pointed me to some passages of Scripture that God used to break through my emotional defenses:

> Be angry, and yet do not sin; do not let the sun go down on
> your anger, and do not give the devil an opportunity. . . .
> Let all bitterness and wrath and anger and clamor and
> slander be put away from you, along with all malice. And
> be kind to one another, tender-hearted, forgiving each other,
> just as God in Christ also has forgiven you.
> (Ephesians 4:26-27,31-32)

God used this passage and others like it to reveal the bankruptcy of my self-centered view of the world. You might even say He gave me "heartburn." He also used His Word to burn through the sophisticated, multilayered defenses and rationalizations I had been energetically fortifying for four years. He also brought His purifying grace to my soul when I realized that I needed to deal with *my sin,* and stop blaming this dear brother for his. The breakthrough came when I broke down and confessed my sin in the relationship and expressed it all in a letter to my estranged Christian brother. I came to know the truth about myself in our relationship and it truly did set me free! I began to be sanctified afresh in these deeply stained areas of my life.

Through this experience and many others, I have learned that "heartburn" is a desirable thing when it comes to Bible reading. One of your primary goals in picking up this book is to end up with a burning heart by the time you put it down. Oh, you may not experience a three-alarm fire every time you read the Scriptures, but you should feel more than a little hot spot in your midsection. You see, Christians throughout history have been inflamed when they understood God's Word and its significance for their lives. Let's observe the experience of a couple of Jesus' disciples with the Scriptures shortly after His resurrection:

> And behold, two of them were going that very day to a
> village named Emmaus, which was about seven miles
> from Jerusalem. And they were conversing with each other
> about all these things which had taken place. And it came
> about that while they were conversing and discussing,
> Jesus Himself approached and began traveling with them.
> But their eyes were prevented from recognizing Him.

[Then they described their sadness about the death of Jesus and His missing body.] And He said to them, "O foolish men and slow of heart to believe in all that the prophets have spoken! Was it not necessary for the Christ to suffer these things and to enter into His glory?" *And beginning with Moses and with all the prophets, He explained to them the things concerning Himself in all the Scriptures. . . . And they said to one another, "Were not our hearts burning within us while He was speaking to us on the road, while He was explaining the Scriptures to us?"* (Luke 24:13-16,25-27,32, emphasis mine)

A burning heart from the understood Word. That should be one of our most desired experiences as children of God. But is it? Can we say that we are regularly engulfed in spiritual flames when we imbibe God's Word? Is the Bible really that fiery in our experience? And if it is, does that fire ignite the character of Christ in us? In other words, are we more like Jesus Christ in our character today than we were last year or five years ago? Has reading the Bible made that kind of difference in our lives? Are we merely hearers of God's Word, or actual doers (see James 1:22-25)?

This book is committed to the biblical perspective that hearing or reading God's Word and applying it accurately to our lives ("doing the Word") will make us into the very thing that God ultimately created us to be: *mature human beings with character and moral qualities like those of the perfect God-man, Jesus the Messiah.* We call this transforming process *spiritual formation.* From beginning to end it is a gracious, supernatural work of our loving God. He begins the process by drawing us to Himself (John 6:44). He invests Himself in the process by giving us the Holy Spirit to dwell within us and progressively change us (Romans 8:12-14). And He culminates the process by resurrecting and perfecting us to be with Him forever in an immortal body (1 John 3:1-3). This process transforms us from sin-stained rebels to eternal showcases of God's grace (Ephesians 2:1-10)!

The main thing God uses to form us into the likeness of Jesus Christ is His Word—the Scriptures. Listen to Jesus' dear friend Peter remark about this at the end of his life:

> His divine power has given us everything we need for life
> and godliness through our knowledge of him who called us
> by his own glory and goodness. Through these he has given
> us *his very great and precious promises, so that through*
> *them* you may participate in the divine nature and escape
> the corruption in the world caused by evil desires.
> (2 Peter 1:3-4, NIV, emphasis mine)

Notice that Peter tells us we don't need to seek any special experiences or secrets to become like Jesus Christ. Why? Because "his divine power has given us *everything we need for life and godliness*"! This "everything" is given to us *through* God's "very great and precious promises"—obviously revealed only in the Bible. God has designed life so that we experience spiritual transformation and avoid sensual malformation through His Word. It is His primary means of transforming us into the likeness of Jesus Christ.

You may find that hard to believe from where you're sitting today. You may even be skeptical or hardened to that prospect. No matter how you relate to this perspective, I can only ask one thing: Will you give some of your focus and time and energy to acquire the tools and motivation necessary to experience the kind of burning-heart transformation that the two followers of Jesus encountered on the road to Emmaus? Will you see if you can experience the joy of a more passionate burning heart in response to the understood Word? Join me so that together we can get close to the flame of God's Word.

I realize I may be asking you to do something you deem onerous or boring. The general opinion of many in our culture is that reading the Bible is like tying a ball game or kissing your sister or pulling weeds from your yard! In other words, it's frustrating, unexciting, and one of those necessary but terribly mundane tasks in life. Why, even children have strong opinions on the topic.

Recently our son Jonathan, then fourteen, responded to my best efforts to introduce him to Bible study by choosing the last book of the Bible, Revelation. He picked that book because he had heard it said some cool things about the end of the world. I decided to go with this intrinsic motivation, and we proceeded. At the end of our study of chapter 1, Jonathan looked at me with furrowed brow and said, "Boy, Dad, reading the Bible is sure a lot of work!"

Not to be discouraged at the great wisdom of this teenager, I led him through the next two chapters a couple days later, pulling out all the stops obtained from my many years of graduate study to help him understand these remarkable chapters. I wanted to dazzle him with the fascinating background of the seven churches of Asia in Revelation 2–3. I was confident that I had really drawn him in with my rousing historical tidbits. As we were closing our Bibles, my ever-honest son burst out with his second opinion on reading the Bible: "Wow, I never knew reading the Bible was *like being in school!*"

There you have it. Like school and a lot of work. Not exactly a winning combination. Jonathan did not add a third aspect to reading the Bible that many would assert: there seems to be little payoff for so much hard work.

No wonder people—even Christians—are staying away from the Bible in droves. What can we do about this trend? Is it a problem with the nature of the Bible, or is it our problem? Is God's Word really that uninteresting and unexciting, or have we taken some wrong turns to arrive at this assessment? These are foundational questions with far-reaching effects on the Christian life. This book is an attempt to address these issues in an honest manner. However, I don't come from a neutral corner. I am deeply and profoundly persuaded that the Bible is the most exciting and powerful book ever written. My goal is to persuade you of that opinion and give you some basic tools to persuade yourself over the next few weeks. How? By helping you experience for yourself the fiery nature of the Word of God!

If you respond to this challenge, you will be in good company. Remember what preceded the burning hearts of Jesus' two disciples on the road to Emmaus?

And He said to them, "O foolish men and slow of heart to believe in all that the prophets have spoken! Was it not necessary for the Christ to suffer these things and to enter into His glory?" *And beginning with Moses and with all the prophets, He explained to them the things concerning Himself in all the Scriptures. . . .* And they said to one another, "Were not our hearts burning within us while He was speaking to us on the road, *while He was explaining the Scriptures to us?*" (Luke 24:25-27,32, emphasis mine)

Those burning hearts were a response to Jesus' *explanation* of the things concerning His identity as the Messiah in the Old Testament. In other words, it is not unreasonable to assume that these two believers must have expended a bit of intellectual work and mental energy in order to understand and then respond to the Scriptures. But what is encouraging is that Jesus Himself appealed to their ability to do just that. If they had been unwilling to use their abilities, their response might have been something like this: "I'm sorry, but this is just too much work, Jesus! You're using too much Scripture and going too deeply into the Bible. Can't you just give us a quick, sound-bite summary of all this stuff?"

The delightful thing about the response of Jesus' followers is that it can be our response, too. Jesus has deeded as much dignity to us as He did to these two disciples. He believed *they* were capable of digesting the Word of God, thinking about it, and responding appropriately to it. He deeds us that very same dignity. In fact, one could argue that Jesus may consider us even more capable than these two confused souls on the road to Emmaus. Why? Because He has given us even more of the Scriptures to study and understand—the Old *and* New Testaments—and He has given us the Holy Spirit to aid us in this task (see 1 John 2:26-27). God and His Son highly esteem us in our ability to understand their revelation to us.

However, the punch line is that Jesus Christ will not do for His followers what He has deemed them capable of doing for themselves. The friends of Lazarus were unable to call him forth from the dead as they stood around his tomb. Only Jesus the Messiah could do that (John 11:43). However, once Lazarus was raised, Jesus expected these dumbfounded folks to unwrap all of the burial wrappings binding Lazarus so that he could be free (John 11:44). It was not that Jesus was too lazy or proud to do this. Rather, He would not do what He deemed humans capable of doing because He respected their dignity.

In the same way, Jesus Christ will not pick up our Bibles for us or pour the truth of Scripture into our minds apart from our choice to open ourselves to that truth. This means that you and

I must *choose* to read or hear the Word of God and then *choose* to study and ponder it. Even having such a choice is a marvelous statement of our dignity as human beings. God deems us more than capable of doing this for ourselves. Of course, He meets with us in a wonderful way when we choose to do so, but He will not demean us by doing it for us. That's a part of our dignity.

This surfaces another interesting parallel to Jesus' raising of Lazarus and our reading of the Scriptures. While Jesus dignified the friends of Lazarus by directing them to unwrap his burial clothing, He also dignified them by being with them in the process. In other words, He gave them *His presence* as they fulfilled their responsibilities. So it is when we read the Word of God. Jesus Christ also freely gives us His presence through the person of the Holy Spirit to help us when we fulfill this responsibility. We know this because Jesus promised His disciples on the night He was arrested that He would not leave them as orphans. Instead, He would ask the Father to send them *another Helper* (Comforter) who would function as He did in their lives, only being with them *forever* (John 14:16-18)! Jesus identifies the Helper as the Holy Spirit who would also teach them (14:26), bear witness of Jesus (15:26), convict the world (16:7-10), and guide them into all truth (16:13-15). In other words, Jesus fully invests His ongoing presence in His people through the person of the Holy Spirit.

The apostle Paul specifically encourages us about the Holy Spirit's personal help in 1 Corinthians 2:11-13:

> For who among men knows the thoughts of a man except the spirit of the man, which is in him? Even so the thoughts of God no one knows except the Spirit of God. *Now we have received, not the spirit of the world, but the Spirit who is from God, that we might know the things freely given to us by God,* which things we also speak, not in words taught by human wisdom, but in those taught by the Spirit, combining spiritual thoughts with spiritual words. (emphasis mine)

While we'll speak more fully about this in chapter 3, one point is timely here. We are not alone as we read the Bible! Jesus

Christ manifests Himself to us through the person of the Holy Spirit during the process. As we read, Jesus brings about the changes He wants in our lives through the Holy Spirit driving home the truths from Scripture. Jesus transforms us as our will directs our mind to interact with the thoughts of God's Word while our spirit submits to the person of the Holy Spirit. The Holy Spirit then teaches us "the things freely given to us by God." These things re-form our souls and cause our hearts to burn with renewed love for our God.

What this means is that if you want some life-changing "heartburn," you must take and eat the Word of God *for yourself.* A burning heart comes from the *understood* Word. May I challenge you to exercise your great God-given dignity and join me in the exciting but exacting process of studying and understanding the Bible? It really is a fiery flame that God will use to transform us. Come join me so that together we can be warmed by the flame.

THE FIERY NATURE OF THE BIBLE

It is ironic that so many nonChristians and even Christians have such a tame, domesticated view of the Bible. Nothing could be further from the truth. Because this book of writings contains the very words of the Creator of the universe, its power is almost beyond comprehension. However, the power of the Word of God is not raw, unfocused, and diffused power. Quite the contrary. The Bible has very sharpened, focused, and targeted power. Its very nature is *fire-like,* similar to a cosmic blowtorch! However, God's Word is friendly fire that enlightens and warms us instead of cooking us. Specifically, reading the Bible will reveal its fiery nature in our lives in two basic areas.

Getting a New Pair of "Glasses"

First, the Word of God torches the human-centered view of the world and the fixation on individual happiness and fulfillment so common in the West. We see a classic example of this torchlike quality in Jesus' confrontation with Simon Peter shortly after Peter declared that Jesus was the Messiah (Matthew 16:13-20). Building on Peter's great confession, the Lord adds that, as the Messiah, He would also have to suffer many things in Jerusalem, be killed, and be raised on the third day (16:21). Peter's knee-jerk response is one of rebuke: "God forbid it, Lord! This shall never happen to You" (16:22). Jesus' response to Peter identifies *the worldview cause* of his attack: "Get behind Me, Satan! You are a stumbling block to Me; *for you are not setting your mind on God's interests, but man's"* (16:23, emphasis mine).

Like Peter, we have this kind of inappropriate knee-jerk response to many incidents in life because we have set our minds on human-only interests. However, the Word of God directly confronts this pair of glasses—our worldview—and puts a better one in its place.

Each of us has a worldview—some call it a world and life view, or a philosophy of life—that we use to interpret the reality around us. This worldview is a set of assumptions or answers we hold about certain big issues: Does God exist? Is the world knowable? Can science help us? Are humans good or evil in their basic nature? How do we determine right and wrong choices (ethics)? Does history (and life) have any purpose or direction? The answers to these questions form a set of assumptions—an interpretive framework, if you will—through which we view life and make decisions. This framework is like a pair of glasses that tints our perspective on most everything we encounter in life. The diagram on the next page attempts to picture this pair of glasses—this worldview—through which many of us in the West peer.

Notice that this diagram pictures the individual person as his or her own self-contained world. In other words, in the West we have come to view a person's identity as an individual thing. Believe it or not, this is a fairly recent phenomenon. Most people throughout history have derived their identity from the family, ethnic, or religious group in which they were embedded. However, we have recently subverted this with our radically individualistic emphasis. Now anthropologists tell us that most Westerners literally view each person as his or her own universe.

This diagram also illustrates that most of us in the West are seeking meaning and purpose as our central goal in life. We desperately aim at personal fulfillment and individual satisfaction as our primary target. The modern worldview, called existentialism, has said that because identity is primarily an individual thing, then finding a meaningful identity is also an individual quest. We have accepted this as fact. Modern existentialism has said that as an individual, we must juggle and manipulate all of the various aspects of life to try to create a meaningful personal mix. This, too, we have accepted as fact. Modern existentialism has also said that our basic criterion for doing or not doing something is whether it has potential to satisfy or fulfill us as an individual and give our life meaning and purpose. Often unknowingly, we have also accepted this as fact.

Our Existential Worldview

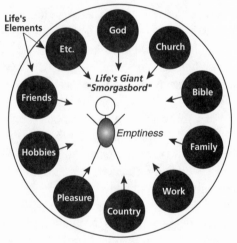

The Individual

The result is that each of us as an individual is earnestly seeking to give our life meaning and purpose by creatively mixing elements from life's "smorgasbord." We are desperately trying to fill our individual plates with the best possible combination of life's entrees in order to be happy. If we don't do it for ourselves, we are told, no one will do it for us. This sets us off on a lonely, individual, errant, and—if the form of existentialism we embrace is secular—godless quest. Such a quest personifies the human-centered perspective for which Jesus rebuked Peter.

However, if you happen to be a religious person, you will notice that "God," "the Bible," "the church," and all other spiritual things are fair game also. These smorgasbord items, like all other items in life, tend to be viewed within the existential worldview *as existing for the purpose of making our individual lives meaningful and fulfilling*. This gives a foundational utilitarian thrust or agenda to the individual's perspective. In other words, we tend to view all other persons and things (including God) as existing to meet our needs! Of course, this is not only utilitarian, it is also narcissistic. We look through a lens that distorts God's and the world's purposes as being *for our fulfillment and satisfaction*. This is pure narcissism, and it leads quite naturally to a relativistic view of values and ethics because all persons and things are evaluated in terms of their utility for our satisfaction. Accompanying this relativism is a loss of the sense of history: increasingly people have no sense of fitting into a broader plan or purpose in history other than their own fulfillment. The result is that many of us have become "ahistorical," or without a sense of history. We think of our lives as floating in space within our little existential bubbles, rather than being part of a plan that God is working out within human history.

Before we turn to how God challenges our worldview through His Word, we need to add a couple more elements to the prevailing pair of glasses in the West. Our individualistic, relativistic, narcissistic, and ahistorical perspective moves the center of authority from the institutions of society that are external (for example, family, government, religious group) to the interior of the individual. In other words, we become self-authorizing in and of ourselves. We become our own authoritative voice. Because we think we are the utmost authorities as to what will satisfy us, we are also the ultimate authority in our lives. Within such a context, it is really not surprising that new age thinking could arise and diabolically twist this perspective by asserting that we are actually gods. Again, this becomes a radical expression of "not setting your mind on God's interests, but man's."

One of the saddest aspects of this existential view of identity and purpose in life is that many of us born since the end of World War II also have what psychologists call "the empty self." This is caused by "a significant absence of community, tradition, and shared meaning."[1] Persons with an empty self experience the loss of group identity in their "interior" as a lack of personal conviction and worth; a chronic, undifferentiated emotional hunger; and a free-floating sense of purposelessness and anxiety.[2] One can easily see how this painful emptiness underscores the individual's frantic, fruitless search for meaning and purpose in life.

Increasingly over the last several decades, especially since World War II, we have viewed the Bible through glasses tinted by this existential worldview. In the church in the West, we have significantly contextualized the gospel for those who have this set of glasses and an empty self. For example, we begin most of our presentations of the gospel with this perspective: "God loves you and offers a wonderful plan for *your* life." The implication is that God loves you as an individual (true) and has an individual plan focused on your personal satisfaction and fulfillment (questionable). However, such a misunderstanding of God's role in our lives makes us vulnerable to the charge from nonChristians, "But I don't need God to make *my life* meaningful and fulfilling. I'm doing quite well on my own, thank you!" Additionally, this perspective seems to picture God as primarily being in the business of creating individual plans for personal fulfillment for every individual who responds to Him. Is this really what God has revealed to us about His concerns? Is this really the emphasis of the Scriptures?

Fortunately, the Bible challenges this rather comprehensive pair of glasses with a very different view of the world. As the following diagram attempts to picture, the believers in both the Old and New Testaments looked out on the world seeking a sense of *historical* rather than existential fulfillment. In other words, they found meaning, purpose, and satisfaction by aligning their lives with God's historical objectives, that is, *with the plan He was working out in history.* Notice how radically different this is from the previous diagram!

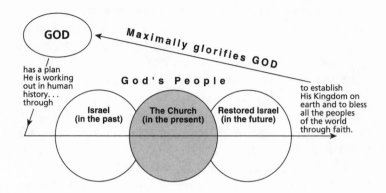

The focus of both the Old and New Testaments is on the fulfillment of *God's plan,* not on our individual plans. God has been working out His plan for thousands of years, first through the nation Israel, now through the church, and finally through restored, ethnic Israel. *The purpose* of God's plan is to establish His kingdom on earth and to bless the people of the world as they respond individually in faith. *The object* of that faith has been clarified progressively in Scripture, and it is Jesus Christ, the crucified and resurrected/ascended Messiah, the Son of God.

As God works out His plan, personal fulfillment for individual Christians is a *byproduct* of fulfilling our role within God's people, the church. As Jesus said, we will find our life (personal meaning and purpose) only when we lose our life (in meaningful and purposeful service for Him among His people). This gives us an historical orientation to the issue of fulfillment, as modeled by believers in the New Testament, that is radically different from the existential view.

This is why the emphasis in the Bible, and especially in the New Testament, is not on individual rights or fulfillment, but on the *unity* of God's people. In fact, our individual rights are frequently subsumed under the cause of unity in the New Testament (see 1 Corinthians 8–10; Romans 14:1–15:6). This unity is essential if God's people are going to work together to accomplish the historical objectives God has given them throughout history. For example, at various times God's people have had different historical objectives, like living in Canaan as pilgrims, being slaves in Egypt, leaving Egypt, traveling back to Canaan, conquering that land and settling in it and so on. Now, under the climactic headship of King Jesus, God's people have been given a very specific mission in history: to make all the peoples of the world disciples of Jesus the Messiah (Matthew 28:16-20). This is the culmination of *God's plan*. And it is also why we must view the world through the right pair of glasses—with lenses that are God-serving, not self-serving, and not overly concerned with our individual plans for happiness and fulfillment. However, for most of us, this demands a radical change in glasses!

Obviously the church in the West collectively, and believers individually, face a massive reeducation process at the most foundational level when it comes to changing the prescription in our worldview glasses. However, this is a nonnegotiable and absolutely must take place for meaningful growth in Christ to occur. In the absence of this transformation, we run the risk of pasting a thin Christian veneer over a radically secular pair of glasses. We run the risk of blandly Christianizing a godless, bankrupt view of the world.

Perhaps by this point, you feel overwhelmed by this task! Changing these glasses seems impossible because most of us don't even realize we are wearing them. However, this is the beauty of God's grace. Not only has He given us His Holy Spirit to transform us to the very core of our beings (see Romans 8:9-11), but He has also given us His Word as our objective standard. We *can* know if we are setting our mind on God's interest, not man's, because of the teaching and examples of the Scriptures. Listen to this wonderfully encouraging passage from Isaiah 55:6-13, where the Lord speaks of the certainty of His restoration of His people under His Servant (the Messiah). Note that central to the restoration of God's people is the restorative Word of God from heaven and its *eternally fruitful nature*. It is this Word that becomes our lifeline in acquiring our new pair of glasses:

> Seek the LORD while He may be found;
> Call upon Him while He is near.
> Let the wicked forsake his way,
> And the unrighteous man his thoughts;
> And let him return to the LORD,
> And He will have compassion on him;

And to our God,
For He will abundantly pardon.
"For My thoughts are not your thoughts,
Neither are your ways My ways," declares the LORD.
"For as the heavens are higher than the earth,
So are My ways higher than your ways,
And My thoughts than your thoughts.
For as the rain and the snow come down from heaven,
And do not return there without watering the earth,
And making it bear and sprout,
And furnishing seed to the sower and bread to the eater;
So shall My word be which goes forth from My mouth;
It shall not return to Me empty,
Without accomplishing what I desire,
And without succeeding in the matter for which I sent it.
For you will go out with joy,
And be led forth with peace;
The mountains and the hills will break forth into shouts of
      joy before you,
And all the trees of the field will clap their hands.
Instead of the thorn bush the cypress will come up;
And instead of the nettle the myrtle will come up;
And it will be a memorial to the LORD,
For an everlasting sign which will not be cut off."
(emphasis mine)

Additionally, the Word of God is potent in changing our glasses through the examples of right and wrong choices it records. If it's true that over 95 percent of what we learn comes from imitating examples, these examples become crucial in our spiritual formation. This is why the Scriptures purposefully target our view of the world via them:

Now these things [in the Old Testament] happened to them
as an example, and *they were written for our instruction,*
upon whom the ends of the ages have come. Therefore let
him who thinks he stands take heed lest he fall.
(1 Corinthians 10:11-12, emphasis mine)

For whatever was written in earlier times *was written for our instruction,* that through perseverance and *the encouragement of the Scriptures* we might have hope.
(Romans 15:4, emphasis mine)

God uses His Word to transform our glasses so that we can see the world increasingly from His perspective.

Penetrating Our Sinful Defenses and Purifying Our Souls

In addition to giving us a new pair of glasses, the fiery nature of the Word of God also burns through the sinful defenses we erect to make ourselves powerful and protected. In igniting these barriers, the Bible reveals to us the core of our being and purifies our inner self. In other words, the Bible has unbelievable penetrating and cleansing power in the lives of those who read it.

No passage speaks more pointedly or vividly of this power than Hebrews 4:11-13:

Let us therefore be diligent to enter that rest, lest anyone
fall through following the same example of disobedience.
For the word of God is living and active and sharper than
any two-edged sword, and piercing as far as the division of
soul and spirit, of both joints and marrow, and able to judge
the thoughts and intentions of the heart. And there is no
creature hidden from His sight, but all things are open and
laid bare to the eyes of Him with whom we have to do.

The context of this passage calls for faithfulness such as Jesus our High Priest expressed (Hebrews 3:1-6); warns about unfaithfulness, like Israel exhibited in the wilderness (3:7-19); and exhorts us to enter into God's rest (4:1-13). Verses 11-13 conclude the exhortation with a challenge to be diligent and not fall into unbelief like the Israelites did in the wilderness (3:16-19;4:6). Of particular interest to us is the explanation in verses 12-13 that God will not miss seeing and judging anyone's choices to believe or disbelieve. His means of confrontation and evaluation is the *Word of God*—including His actual speaking to Israel (3:7,15;4:7); the

Word made flesh, Jesus Christ (John 1:1-5); and the written expression of His words in the Scriptures. It is this word from God that penetrates to the deepest element of our being, both immaterially (soul and spirit) and materially (joints and marrow). This penetrating ability brings comfort to those who live by faith and dread to those who wallow in unbelief. Whatever your response, you must admit that God has imbued His Word with remarkable power.

The significance of Hebrews 4:12-13 for our spiritual formation is great. We don't live in a time when God speaks directly to us, as He did to the Israelites when they left Egypt. Nor does the God-man, Jesus of Nazareth, speak directly to us, as He did during His earthly ministry. Our access to God's words is primarily through the written expression of them in the Bible. It is mainly there that we hear His voice and confront His presence. It is also in the Scriptures that we are most immediately pierced and judged for our good or bad thoughts and intentions (4:12). In the future, when we meet the living Word, Jesus Christ, at His coming, we will be formally evaluated (1 Corinthians 4:5).

However, we are offered this dynamic and compelling feedback *currently* through God's written Word. This seems to be an essential part of the nature of His words. They ultimately reveal our responses to them. Therefore, while there are many reasons for reading and studying the Scriptures, God's immediate, truthful, and convicting evaluation is certainly one of the most important. We can know what pleases or displeases our heavenly Father *today,* rather than remaining uninformed and anxiety-ridden about how He will recompense us in the future. God has expressed this wonderful care for us by giving us His written Word to penetrate in love to the very core of our being. We desperately need this regular feedback for the divine guidelines in our spiritual formation. Faithful are the wounds inflicted by our heavenly Friend!

King David spoke of these "heavenly wounds" through which God purifies His people in Psalm 19:7-14. Listen to his poetic words about the joy of this kind of woundedness:

> The law of the LORD is perfect, *restoring the soul;*
> The testimony of the LORD is sure, *making wise the simple.*
> The precepts of the LORD are right, *rejoicing the heart;*
> The commandment of the LORD is pure, *enlightening the eyes.*

The fear of the LORD is clean, *enduring forever;*
The judgments of the LORD are true; *they are righteous*
    altogether.
They are more desirable than gold, yes, than much fine gold;
Sweeter also than honey and the drippings of the honeycomb.
Moreover, by them Thy servant is warned;
In keeping them there is great reward.
Who can discern his errors? Acquit me of hidden faults.
Also keep back Thy servant from presumptuous sins;
Let them not rule over me;
Then I shall be blameless,
And I shall be acquitted of great transgression.
Let the words of my mouth and the meditation of my heart
Be acceptable in Thy sight,
O LORD, my rock and my Redeemer. (emphasis mine)

Surely the last three lines have been the prayer of God's people for the three millennia since David penned them. However, their context is very instructive to our spiritual formation. Note that the prayer in verse 14 is the thoughtful response to the work of God's Word in the life of a receptive believer. This prayer is the heartfelt follow-up to letting the Scriptures penetrate, evaluate, and purify our innermost thoughts, motives, and meditations. It is the earnest response of a child of God to the heavenly wounds of our heavenly Father through His heavenly Word! Faithful are the wounds of our heavenly Friend who penetrates the deepest recesses of our being with His truth and light. In so doing He becomes the Rock and Redeemer of our life.

My goal in this chapter has been to persuade you of the transforming power of that Word. I have sought to emphasize that reading the Bible is truly playing with fire because of its powerful ability to change us when we respond in faith to its message. In particular, the Word of God challenges our human-centered worldview, it powerfully penetrates to our deepest core, and it purifies us in the central part of being. I can attest to the grace of God in all these dimensions in my life. I invite you to join me in experiencing that same grace. However, in all honesty I must forewarn you, do so only if you want to risk radical transformation. You are playing with fire!

Chapter Two

TRANSFORMATION
THROUGH
INFORMATION

All Scripture is inspired by God and profitable for teaching, for reproof, for correction, for training in righteousness; that the man of God may be adequate, equipped for every good work.

2 TIMOTHY 3:16-17

To know the Bible is not an option for those who want to know true inwardness. No one stays at the table long who does not study Scripture. Mystics without study are only spiritual romantics who want relationship without effort.

CALVIN MILLER[1]

THE SCENE IS THE MOST MEMORABLE ONE OF MY LIFE—ONE that does not dim noticeably with time. My wife Marty and I are walking into a long, narrow room and our son Christopher is at the far end, laying on a table with a pillow under his head. It looks like he is slumbering a typical eighteen-month-old's peaceful sleep. We have not seen him for three days because we have been out of town. We have deeply missed him. We long to hold him, touch him, and kiss him. I especially long to connect with him because this day is Father's Day. However, as we approach Christopher, our anxiety grows. As we reach him and caress him, our anxiety peaks in a heartbreaking crescendo. Christopher is dead. We are stroking his lifeless body in the visitation room of a funeral home. Our son has died unexpectedly in his sleep.

How is it possible that we can withstand such horrifying pain, shock, and grief? How can we deal with such an emotionally excruciating loss? How can we believe that God is good in the midst of a situation where everything seems to be bad—malevolently evil? For my wife and me, God was present with us in our room of heartbreak. In particular, as we held the cold, lifeless body of our toddler, God used *the information* of a beautiful and powerful part of His Word to bring comforting *transformation* to our broken hearts. In fact, as we took turns holding Christopher, Marty and I received deep comfort in our anguished souls as we spoke of God's remarkable perspective of human bodies at death in 2 Corinthians 5:1-8, NIV:

> Now we know that if the earthly tent we live in is destroyed, we have a building from God, an eternal house in heaven, not built by human hands. Meanwhile we groan, longing to be clothed with our heavenly dwelling, because when we are clothed, we will not be found naked. For while we are in this tent, we groan and are burdened, because we do not wish to be unclothed but to be clothed with our heavenly dwelling, so that what is mortal may be swallowed up by life. . . . Therefore we are always confident and know that as long as we are at home in the body we are away from the Lord. We live by faith, not by sight.

We are confident, I say, and would prefer to be away from the body and at home with the Lord. . . .

We have already seen that the Bible is dangerous to hear or read because of its powerful, transforming qualities. My wife and I experienced the reality of this power and transformation when we clung to what the Scriptures reveal about God's own thoughts and values about the death of our bodies. His thoughts are, by their very nature, transforming to us who recognize their supernatural dimension, welcome them as friends, and then apply them to our lives. God uses His Word to change and form us spiritually into what He designed us to be in Christ. The information God graciously reveals about reality is remarkably transforming to us when we painfully intersect the harsh realities of life . . . and death.

READING THE BIBLE FOR SPIRITUAL FORMATION

However, the supernatural dimension of the Bible raises some very interesting questions in the minds of many who read it. Some ask these questions: "If according to 2 Timothy 3:16 the Bible is inspired or 'God-breathed' in its essence, then do we really have to read the Bible with such concern for accurate information about each passage? Because God is God, and His Word is supernatural, can't He transform us no matter how much or how little information we have about His Word?" This is a fancy way of asking, "Because the Bible is the divine *Word of God,* doesn't it limit God's power if we read it like any other book? Can't we just read it however we choose and trust that *God* will transform us according to *His* supernatural power? Do we really need that much information about a passage we are reading?"

Such questions sincerely express the heartfelt convictions of many who read the Bible. To some folks, it is altogether unnecessary to introduce any contextual, historical, or other intellectual information into the reading of the Bible for spiritual formation. There's almost an unspoken rule that it's okay to do these kinds of things when you *study* the Bible, but such knowledge is dispensable when reading the Bible for devotional or spiritual purposes. Experts in the field of spiritual formation express similar ideas about how to read the Bible for the development of our souls:

> Spiritual or *formational* reading is the exact opposite of informational reading. . . . Instead of the text being an object controlled by us, the text becomes the subject; we, in turn, become the "object" addressed by God through the text.[2]

This kind of background reading (doctrinal, exegetical, historical) is to be done, as indicated, at a time other than that set aside for spiritual reading. However, such informational reading can become spiritual to a degree because this kind of study often inspires the reader to learn more about spiritual living. The possibility is great, especially in the beginning, that reading is a mixture of the study approach and the spiritual approach. This mixture is not so bad, provided that slowly on we begin—during spiritual reading time—to center our attention more and more undividedly on *what the text says to us.* True spiritual reading strives to eliminate gently and gradually all utilitarian (in the sense of information gathering) and ulterior motives in order to be solely intent on listening to the word of God as it manifests itself through the reading.[3]

One morning, as the lectionary moved me toward the end of the plagues [of Exodus], I read the portion and then asked the same question I had asked each day, "Lord, what are you seeking to say to me here?" This time the answer came.

"You are Pharaoh!"

"What?" I replied. "Me, Pharaoh? Moses perhaps, even one of the Hebrew people, but *Pharaoh?* Perhaps one of the servants, one of the slaves, perhaps a taskmaster, Lord?"

"You are Pharaoh!"

Then, with that Word, things began to open up—in the text and in me. I began to realize that, as a word spoken forth by God, God had spoken certain qualities into my "word." God had given me certain gifts and abilities and characteristics, certain qualities of personality. God had also shaped my "word" by being an active presence in the various experiences of my life. All of these dynamics of my "word" were God's "children," but I had enslaved them to my own purposes, my own desires, my own intentions, my own plans. Truly I was Pharaoh in my life![4]

The spiritual concerns and goals expressed by these examples are clearly admirable. My concern is certainly not with the sorts of personal insights or spiritual growth that these comments illustrate. I think the primary confusion comes when we move from reading or interpreting a text right into applying the text to our particular place in life—an application that may be absolutely appropriate for our own situation. The problem comes when we call that application or insight for our own life an "interpretation," which would make it a universal, rather than a particular, insight that God may well intend for us to receive. Such applications are more likely either clear personal needs for growth that have been exposed by the Scripture in question or insights from that "still small voice" of the Holy Spirit who indwells all believers. I'm suggesting that we need to be careful not to call such things "interpretations."

Another fear is that this confusion between interpretation and application may lead some toward erroneous views of meaning or even to destructive interpretive models for the Bible. Such confusion is often rooted in part in ancient interpretive errors that have freely allegorized the biblical text since the fourth century. For example, putting oneself in the place of Pharaoh when reading Exodus 7–11 is a widely practiced but very questionable allegorizing or spiritualizing of the biblical text. It may seem very pious—it may even lead to legitimate personal insights or applications of God's truth to our lives—but it does not lead us to the actual meaning of the text. Such practices remove any sense of shared understanding or meaning that other readers could have with the same narrative text. They also obscure the intended meaning of the text, that is, what the Author intended for His universal audience. Again, I'm not quarreling with the idea that while reading we may receive valuable personal applications and insights into our personal situation that God desires for us—I'm simply calling for a clear distinction between the interpretation of the text, which when done accurately leads to spiritual transformation, and the application of certain insights to our personal lives.

It is a mistake to pit informational reading against reading for spiritual formation. Such ideas are to some extent rooted in a recent reaction within Roman Catholic and mainline Protestant circles against the (admittedly, too-often) embalming effect of the historical-critical method in biblical interpretation. There have been many abuses and overemphases on the informational side of interpretation in the history of the church. Such information overemphasis has been distracting and at times counterproductive to growth in Christ. The intellectual aspects of the text have too often triumphed over and silenced the spiritually transforming aspects of the Bible. The result has been spiritual stagnation or even death in many Christian circles for over two hundred years. While there are literally thousands of examples of this, one should suffice. A biblical scholar who uses a recent literary technique called structuralism studied the rich, emotive message of the book of Job, and summarized it in this algebra-like formula:

$$F_x (a) : F_y(b) \cong F_x(b) : F_{a-1(y)} \quad 5$$

Now this is an informational emphasis gone profoundly overboard!

The resulting response has been an emphasis on "spiritual reading" versus the strictly academic reading of the biblical text with its stultifying effects. The goal is to redeem the reading of the Bible from cold, dead, historical-critical methodologies that stripped it of any sense of spiritual life and personal spiritual dynamic. This is a noteworthy and desirable goal, and I heartily commend it. However, the strategy for reaching this goal has to be carefully pursued. Another well-known expert in spiritual formation writes:

> To find self-formation by means of scripture reading I must be open in docility to what its text may eventually tell me about myself; I must abide with formative reading until it

yields to me its treasure. Formative reading implies, more-over, my willingness to change my current self in light of the formative insight scripture may radiate to me. The word as formative has the power to transform me. It can give rise to a new self in Christ, permeating all dimensions of my life. The word as formative can lift me beyond the stirrings of my ego and vital life so that I may discover my graced life form in the Eternal Word.[6]

This author might be accused of asking the reader to purposely create an interpretive keyhole of "insight about myself" and then pull each biblical text through this keyhole. On the other hand, the author does say that this "may" be the case, so he is somewhat off the hook. But you may be saying, "I really like the way this sounds!" It is very appealing because it is very personal and me-centered. Fortunately, the author's goal is, admirably, that the text would help someone find his or her new self in Christ; and further, the elements of grace and the lordship of Christ over all dimensions of life are there. Again, these are goals we can respect, and the author can be commended.

What we want to avoid, however, is taking such language too far and creating that interpretive keyhole I mentioned. As we discovered in the previous chapter, such a move would belie one of the funda-mental weaknesses in our view of the world. Many of us view the world in narcissistically wounded categories that assume every pas-sage in the Bible is about us. Fortunately, God has a grand plan that He is revealing in the Bible that encompasses insights into ourselves, but that plan doesn't rotate around that knowledge. Indeed, *most pas-sages in the Bible are about things other than us!* To assume otherwise can lead to a systematic distortion of every biblical text that does not happen to have such a purpose or meaning. This, then, requires some effort on our part, even in reading for spiritual growth purposes, that helps us get at the textual meaning or interpretation, before we go about seeing how it might be applicable to ourselves. Without this real-istic approach, we could fall prey to reading something into the text that simply was never intended by the Lord Himself. Realism helps us avoid such errors as romanticism and irrationality.

Nevertheless, these kinds of thinking are too often the norm in any kind of "devotional reading" of the Scriptures. This is why a new work and a new paradigm for the use of the Bible in spiritual formation from an evangelical perspective is clearly needed. We must avoid both the pitfalls of the historical-critical method—no one wants to be embalmed—*and* the sometimes romantic or irrational overreaction it has engendered—none of us wants to read something into the Bible that God never intended. This chapter (and book) attempts to strike a balance between these two poles and to bring remedies to these weaknesses. So, how can this be done?

ENRICHING FORMATIONAL READING OF THE BIBLE

First, we must reject the idea that there is a chasm between informational reading and formational reading. No such false dichotomy should exist in our reading of the Bible. Rather, we should first be reading to understand the intention of the biblical author within the biblical book we are reading. This involves *some* "informational" emphasis, but it is not an end in and of itself, nor is it as intensive as an academic study of a passage. Rather, it is a means to the end of being spiritually formed according to the meaning of the biblical passage. There can be no true spiritual transforming apart from the true meaning of the biblical text! Although this demands some initial informational emphasis in the reading of the Bible, it should be balanced. It is both author- and text-centered (for the *meaning* of the passage) and reader-responsive (for the *significance* of that meaning to us).

Studying the Bible

Informational Emphasis	Transformational Concern

Devotionally Reading the Bible

Informational Emphasis	Transformational Concern

What we are advocating is a *both/and* approach to studying and devotionally reading the Bible. In other words, *in the study of the*

Bible, we should not lose sight of the transforming impact of the truths we discover. This means that we should periodically pause along the way to ponder deeply the truths before us. We should then ask, "What is the significance of these truths to my life?" This pause adds a rich and necessary devotional emphasis to any study of the Bible. To delete this step is to distort the nature of God's Word.

Conversely, when we *read the Bible devotionally for spiritual formation,* we must be mindful that a certain amount of information about the passage we are reading is absolutely necessary. Again, we are not trafficking in as much information as we would if we were studying the passage in a more formal manner. But we are also not eliminating such foundational information. Formation reading also involves a *both/and.* However, as the diagram on page 43 illustrates, the dials are turned to different percentages of informational emphasis and transformational concern in that task.

Perhaps an illustration from a familiar passage would be helpful at this juncture. The passage is from the Gospel of Matthew 16:24-25:

> Then Jesus said to His disciples, "If anyone wishes to come after Me, let him deny himself, and take up his cross, and follow Me. For whoever wishes to save his life shall lose it; but whoever loses his life for My sake shall find it."

This is a well-known description of the attitude that followers of Jesus Christ should have toward themselves. These are potent words. If we were reading them devotionally for transformational purposes, they might stimulate us to evaluate our commitment as Jesus' disciples. We might focus on the psychological aspect of denying what we want to do and choosing, instead, to do what Jesus wants us to do. We realize that real fulfillment and the discovery of what life is all about are found in Jesus Christ. Such truths are foundational to our spiritual formation.

However, might that stimulation be heightened if we had a little more information about the context to ponder and meditate on? Humor me and let's see if it helps. For example, we might note that the broader context is a pivotal one in Jesus' life. He has spent the first three years of His ministry teaching and performing miracles. He has been seeking to persuade His disciples that He is the Messiah and He has been teaching them to follow His way. Matthew 16:13-20 is crucial because Peter confesses on their behalf the disciples' official, definitive belief that Jesus is the Messiah: "Thou art the Christ, the Son of the living God" (verse 16). Jesus responds to this confession by giving Peter (and the eleven others) significant spiritual authority within His church (verses 17-20).

Moreover, it is extremely important that Jesus' words about denying ourselves follow immediately His *first* declaration of His suffering and death (verses 21-23). His disciples had it right when they confessed that He was the Messiah. However, there was one thing they needed to add to their understanding: "From that time Jesus Christ began to show His disciples that He must go to Jerusalem, and suffer many things from the elders and chief priests and scribes, and be killed, and be raised up on the third day" (verse 21).

The response of the disciples, led by Peter, was to rebuke Jesus for such a perverse understanding of Messiah's role (verse 22). Jesus' retort is a corresponding rebuke for Peter's wrong focus. This interchange highlights that Jesus' words were confusing to the disciples because He linked rejection and suffering at the hand of Israel's religious establishment with His messianic identity and glory. This was incomprehensible and reprehensible to them, as Peter's rebuke in verse 22 reveals.

It is at this point that Jesus utters the words in verses 24-25. Strategically, Jesus describes what anyone following Him will look like. He will spend the last six months of His ministry trying to explain this to His followers. To them, it was unthinkable that the long-awaited Messiah would be a rejected religious outcast and a king with an immediate kingdom of suffering, not glory. Jesus' words about self-denial and the losing of our lives strike at the heart of these dashed expectations. Being Jesus' followers will look quite different from what they expected!

Now ponder again Jesus' words about self-denying, cross carrying, and life losing in light of this additional information.

Doesn't it add depth and resonance to verses 24-25? Don't we have richer resources for growing in Christ with this modest addition of information? Can't we honestly say that understanding the pivotal nature and intensity of the context adds far greater significance to our meditation about being Jesus' disciples? If Jesus' words about following Him are unsettling to us, then we are in good company. This seems to be their thrust within their context. If we are to be transformed by God's use of them in our lives, then this type of information seems an undeniable element in that process.

Second, a very important byproduct accompanies this emphasis on both information and transformation in the enriching of our formational reading. With this emphasis, we can meaningfully avoid any relativistic interpretive approaches that ask questions like, "Now, what does this verse *mean to me?*" Again, you may be saying, "But I thought everyone used this as the main interpretive question for reading the Bible devotionally! I often use it in my quiet times. Many of the Bible study and Sunday school classes that I have been a part of use it to interpret the Bible. How can you say that this question introduces a relativistic interpretation of the Bible?" Before we go on, remember, the question is legitimate when seeking to apply some truth—if appropriate—to our lives. But to use it as an interpretive question is to skip right over the interpretive process and proceed directly to asking questions of application or significance! Perhaps a bit of historical perspective would help explain why this can be such a disastrous question to ask in the interpretive process.

As the diagram on page 47 shows, there has been a significant shift in the locus of meaning over the last one hundred years. Essentially, we have moved from viewing texts as objective things created by authors to express their intentions to a very radical understanding that is rooted in relativistic philosophical thought and in a disturbing view of reality.

For thousands of years, the classical emphasis for discovering meaning was on authors and their intentions and their historical setting.

Early in the twentieth century, the author was banished and the focus moved to a "close reading" of the text, which supposedly had a life of its own as an artifact.

Since the 1960s, the emphasis has shifted even more radically to the astonishing belief that not only is meaning now created by readers, but also the text itself!

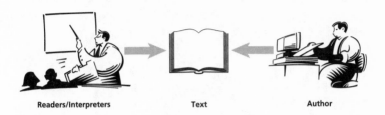

Readers/Interpreters   Text   Author

Some well-meaning Christians have unintentionally adopted this radical relativism and subjectivism by assuming that the locus of meaning is not in authors or texts, but *within them* as readers and interpreters. All of this is expressed through the seemingly innocuous question, "What does this verse mean to you?" But in reading a text for interpretation, this is nonsensical, because "meaning" is not an affair of private consciousness but a public thing comprised of words, phrases, and ideas that are given their content by group consensus. For example, we call canines "dogs" and felines "cats" because we all agree to make those designations. We can communicate with one another about dogs and cats because we choose to abide by those group decisions. Should we choose to make up our own words, phrases, or ideas apart from our group consensus, no one would understand us! From the perspective of the group (society), we are speaking nonsense. We have ignored the first fundamental of communication: its public creation. At any level we may choose, communication is using public things like words, phrases, genres, and ideas to express our intentions. If this were not so, then none of us could communicate with anybody else. The pond that we all must fish in when it comes to communication is a shared pond, as the diagram on page 48 reflects.

Communication is dipping into the common pool of words, genres, and ideas and using these shared, reproducible, public instruments to express our personal, individual intentions.

Society's shared language, genres, ideas, words, and so on

Additionally, by thinking that we can somehow privatize interpretation, we undercut the appeal of the general, "public" authority of the Bible. We must avoid the widespread tendency of much of our devotional and spiritual formation literature to reduce the meaning of the Bible to insights and statements about ourselves; almost every passage is reduced to some "truth" about myself or other human beings. Thus the Bible becomes an anthropology textbook with remarkable "insights" into ourselves. Without such a lens in place, how else could we leap from the ten plagues on Egypt, which demonstrate that our God is superior to the ten things the Egyptians considered most sacred, to insights into our own selfishness? My fear is that we too often simply baptize this kind of narcissistic perspective with a thin spiritual veneer. In the process, both the meaning and the transforming power of the Bible may be lost.

An interesting example of the absurdity of this "what it means to me" approach circulated recently on the Internet. Because I teach hermeneutics, or how to interpret the Bible, at least five of my friends sent me this little piece. It wonderfully illustrates that meaning is a corporate, public thing, not primarily a construction of our own making. I have included the first seven of the thirteen vignettes:

HERMENEUTICS IN EVERYDAY LIFE

Suppose you're traveling to work [on an east-west street] and you see a stop sign. What do you do? That depends on how you exegete [interpret] the stop sign:

1. A postmodernist deconstructs the sign (that is, knocks it over with his car) ending forever the tyranny of the north-south traffic over the east-west traffic.
2. Similarly, a Marxist sees a stop sign as an instrument of class conflict. He concludes that the bourgeoisie use the north-south road and obstruct the progress of the workers on the east-west road.
3. A serious and educated Catholic believes that he cannot understand the stop sign apart from its interpretive community and their tradition. Observing that the interpretive community doesn't take it too seriously, he doesn't feel obligated to take it too seriously either.
4. An average Catholic (or Orthodox or Anglican or Methodist or Presbyterian or Coptic or whoever) doesn't bother to read the sign, but he'll stop if the car in front of him does.
5. A fundamentalist, taking the text very literally, stops at the stop sign and waits for it to tell him to go.
6. A preacher might look up "STOP" in his lexicon and discover that it can mean: (1) something which prevents motion, such as a plug for a drain, or a block of wood that prevents a door from closing; or, (2) a location where a train or bus lets off passengers. The big idea of his sermon the next Sunday on this text is: "When you see a stop sign, it is a place where traffic is naturally clogged, so it is a good place to let off passengers from your car."
7. An orthodox Jew takes another route to work that doesn't have a stop sign so that he doesn't risk disobeying the Law.

This bit of tomfoolery shows us that if meaning is something each of us creates as individuals, then anything, including a simple stop sign, can easily be reduced to an absurdity. Any word or text then loses its essential public quality and becomes captive to the subjective whims of each person's understanding. This is especially true of the Bible. But as Christians, I'm confident we're all after the same thing: God's message, not one we construct for ourselves. When we read a biblical passage primarily in terms of "what it means to me," we ignore the public, corporate meaning of the words and ideas, as well as God's original intentions in His inspiration of the text. In place of these shared, public things, we too often substitute our individualistic, private interpretations. Without much information about the meaning of text, we are then free to read it subjectively and thereby privatize interpretation. Perhaps you are asking at this point, "Why is this so?" Please let me illustrate again from the words of Jesus in Matthew 16:24-25:

> Then Jesus said to His disciples, "If anyone wishes to come after Me, let him deny himself, and take up his cross, and follow me. For whoever wishes to save his life shall lose it; but whoever loses his life for My sake shall find it."

Given our propensity to interpret in terms of "what it means to me," we may tend to follow our culture's strong psychological tendency and "psychologize" Jesus' words. We might translate the denying of ourselves into psychological terms like the putting to death of our selfish desires on a cross. We might even ponder the "crosses" we have to bear in life, including relationships, restraints, and circumstances. We might also set about to deny ourselves and our desires and focus on cultivating Jesus' desires.

Again, these are not bad or terribly errant meditations about this biblical passage. The weakness of this kind of interpretation, though, is that it focuses primarily on our view of the world and would be hardly recognizable to Jesus and His disciples, *from whom and for whom the words were initially crafted!* Therefore, again, we need a bit of information about the passage to give some tracks for our interpretation and some boundaries for our musings.

Apart from the broader context, one of the best pieces of information we can get about a passage is an understanding of the immediate context. Let's develop this a bit more:

Matthew 16:13-20 — the disciples' confession that Jesus is the Messiah and their resulting spiritual authority from Him

↓

Matthew 16:21-23 — Jesus' first declaration of His suffering, Peter's rebuke of Him, and Jesus' corresponding rebuke of Peter for his man-centered perspective

↓

Matthew 16:24-28 — Jesus' correction of the disciples' understanding of what a follower of Him will look like during this age in contrast to the coming age

Thus we can see that the focus of the passage is a right understanding of Jesus and His messianic authority and a resulting right understanding of what it means to be a follower of Jesus in this present age. The emphasis in the passage is on the ironic fact that Jesus' identity as Messiah will bring great glory *in the coming age* to His disciples, but perhaps suffering and the loss of life (a cross) to them *in the present age:*

"For whoever wishes to save his life shall lose it; but whoever loses his life for My sake shall find it. For what will a man be profited, if he gains the whole world, and forfeits his soul? Or what will a man give in exchange for his soul? For the Son of Man is going to come in the glory of His Father with His angels; and will then recompense every man according to his deeds." (Matthew 16:25-27)

Given this ironic, present lack of status and "the good life" of being Jesus' followers, we can see why Jesus fully discloses the kind of life one should have in choosing to be His disciple. Such a choice demands giving up present fulfilling expectations (verse 24) in light of the promise of future reward (verse 27). It is a choice to live for the Messiah's sake and not just our own.

It is a choice to join Jesus in suffering in the present and postpone glory and status until the coming age.

This additional bit of information changes the context of our interpretation and formational application from "How can I be fulfilled as a Christian?" to "What hard choices do I need to make to follow Jesus in this age?" Of course, personal fulfillment is one of the byproducts of choosing to follow Jesus ("whoever loses his life for My sake shall find it," verse 25). But personal fulfillment is not what Jesus focused on, nor is it what we should establish as our interpretive lens. Introducing some information about the biblical passage into the mix is one of the safeguards that will help keep us from such errors.

Lastly, in order to enrich the devotional or formational reading of the Bible, we need to recognize that God has spoken "in many portions and in many ways" (Hebrews 1:1). He has expressed the things He wanted us to know through a wide variety of *genres,* or types of literature, in both the Old and New Testaments. As we saw earlier, genres, like words, phrases, and ideas, are public things floating around in the societal pool of communicable items. In fact, a *genre* can be defined as "a public, sharable form of communication."[7]

Any kind of meaningful reading of the Bible for spiritual formation must begin by recognizing the generic guidelines of the biblical passage being examined. We need to identify the biblical genre we are reading and then form appropriate expectations of how to read and interpret this particular genre. This is a preliminary part of the informational side of our reading. Recognizing and appropriately weighting the biblical genre gives us very specific interpretive rules within which we must read and interpret.[8]

I am not making some kind of special plea here. Rather, this is the way communication works for everybody everywhere all the time. For example, when I approach my wife, Marty, and wrap my arms around her (as I have frequently for over twenty-six years of married life), she may say to me, "Oh, get out of here!" Now, I understand what the words mean, but I must know the genre or type of communication she is using in order to understand her intentions. Option 1: the genre is an angry response and she wants me to start packing and vacate the premises immediately. Option 2: the type of communication is a playful genre in which she is using "Oh, get out of here!" in an idiomatic, ironic manner that means the *opposite* of what the words mean. In other words, she wants me to keep doing what I'm doing. The only solution is to determine correctly (and quickly!) the genre of her statement and then interpret the words "Oh, get out of here!" in light of their appropriate genre. I'd better be correct in my genre identification because the options and consequences are radically different. You see, genre does matter!

Genre matters as much in reading the Bible as it does in relating to other human beings in everyday life. For example, understanding how the genre of Old Testament narrative should be interpreted would prohibit us from interpreting a given story as though it were about us. That would be a profound violation of how to read narrative literature, and it would lead us to distort almost any biblical narrative we read, including the New Testament narratives of the Gospels and Acts. Or, understanding a proverb as a promise could be a significant distortion of the proverbial genre, and totally unthinkable in light of the characteristics of that type of literature. Or, assuming that the Old Testament laws about the purity of the Levitical priesthood applied to Christians would be a basic misunderstanding of the genre, Law.

Information about genre is some of the most important and foundational information for understanding the Bible as God intended. We can say that definitively because God in His infinite wisdom communicated *every word of the Bible* in the genres of human beings! Not one word is of a heavenly, unintelligible genre. All of it is communicated within the confines of human genres— which still exist today. If this were not so, we could not read the Bible with any sense of understanding. This is why we must not ignore the genre of a biblical passage. To do so is to ignore the most obvious, public, sharable form of communication that God used to communicate His intentions. To do so may lead unobservant Christians to pack up immediately and leave town, or continue in inappropriate behaviors because they ignored the genre of the biblical passage, rather than draw closer to God! This is the sort of mishap created by refusing to attend to genres.

However, this sensitivity to genres should not be seen as overly restrictive. Rather, it should give us a wonderful sense of expectation of how God may want to use a particular passage in light of its generic qualities. This is a part of God's intention in choosing these genres. In other words, He has chosen to work within the genre-confines that He has used. If this were not the case, all interpretation and application would be reduced to the private realm and any sense of public meaning or appropriate applications would be lost. This would be far too great a price to pay for the sloppy reading of God's Word. Rather than individualizing and privatizing the meaning of the Bible, we should be appealing expectantly to the specific meaning of the biblical passage in light of its particular genre. With this appeal should come a profound expectation of how God may want to use this meaning and this type of literature to transform our souls. However, before we can be *spiritually formed* through this meaning, we have to be *informed* of its content. Realistic understanding must precede transformation.

To illustrate this one last time, let's return to the passage about Jesus and His disciples in Matthew 16:13-28, this time focusing on the fact that this passage is a part of the genre, Gospel. As a preview of our full discussion of this genre in chapter 10, one point is appropriate here: the focus of this genre is on the person of Jesus. That seems to be a statement of the obvious, but it bears underscoring. Again, the recent tendency has been to interpret the Gospels as narratives that give us insight into ourselves. There is certainly some of this in the Gospels, but it remains secondary to the focus on Jesus. Almost every passage in the Gospels should be queried with, "What does this passage tell us about Jesus or His kingdom?" We could hardly go wrong as interpreters of this genre if we followed this advice. Absorbing this point will do as much as anything to help develop proper expectations about reading the Gospels for our spiritual formation. If we wish to go further and consider application of the truths we discover through such interpretation to our own lives, we need to ask much different questions, such as: "How does the focus on Jesus affect my own transformation?"

To take our own advice, "What does Matthew 16:13-28 tell us about Jesus or His kingdom?" And also, what insight does this give us into our formation into the likeness of Jesus Christ? True to the genre Gospel, this passage is primarily about Jesus' identity as the

Messiah. The passage begins with Peter's confession of Jesus' messianic identity (16:13-20) and ends with Jesus' own words about His messianic future in verses 27-28:

> "For the Son of Man is going to come in the glory of His Father with His angels; and will then recompense every man according to his deeds. Truly I say to you, there are some of those who are standing here who shall not taste death until they see the Son of Man coming in His kingdom."

While there are wonderful challenges to us who want to follow Messiah Jesus as disciples (see 16:24-26), these challenges are really derived from the emphasis on Jesus' messianic identity. In particular, Jesus' point in this passage is that He is the Messiah of Israel who will manifest His kingdom glory, but He first must suffer and be rejected at the hands of the religious leaders of the nation. To encourage His befuddled disciples, Jesus next promises (16:28), then gives them a glimpse of, His future kingdom glory when He transfigures before three of them (17:1-8). The disciples are awed at His appearance—"His face shone like the sun, and His garments became as white as light" (17:2). The point of His transfiguration is that glory is surely coming! However, before the glory comes, the suffering of the cross must be endured. This is the way of Messiah Jesus.

This marvelous passage relates to our choices in spiritual formation in that Jesus' suffering-first/glory-later timetable is *the same* for those of us who will follow Him in this age. The people rejected Him; they will reject us. He suffered; we will suffer. He did not try and save His life, but lost it for the sake of God's kingdom; we should not try and save our lives (for our own fulfillment), but should lose them for His sake (verse 25). If we don't, we could gain the whole world in our search for fulfillment but would forfeit our souls (verse 26). But Jesus is debtor to no one; when He returns in His fully revealed messianic Glory, He will reward those of us who choose to follow Him in losing our lives (verse 27).

Attending to the genre of this Gospel passage with its emphasis on Jesus gives us the boundaries for the most edifying reading for our spiritual formation. Such a reading demands a bit of information about what we are reading. However, this is not information just for the sake of information. It is information harnessed to the end of spiritual growth as God uses His rightly interpreted Word to transform His children. This is absolutely necessary because before we can be *transformed,* we have to be *informed.*

A SUMMARY: ENHANCING OUR SPIRITUAL FORMATION THROUGH THE BIBLE'S INFORMATION

Our discussion in this chapter has been about some foundational and important issues. Therefore, it may serve us well to summarize the specific steps we can take to enrich our reading of the Bible for the transformation of our souls and bodies.

Realize That Spiritual Formation Includes Biblical Interpretation

Our desire in this book is to bring a bit more interpretive sanity to the task of "spiritual reading" without embalming or destroying the spiritual dynamic and fervor so desperately needed in such reading. To do this we must first discover *the meaning* of a biblical passage before we can determine *its significance* to our spiritual formation.

Underscore the Bible's Centrality in Spiritual Formation

If we assume that every biblical passage is primarily about our spiritual development, this "assumed idea" becomes a mental winnowing fork in our hands that sifts out any elements of biblical chaff that do not fit into our spiritual formation bin. This leads to an unintended reduction of the real thought of the passage and to *the loss of the transforming idea that was Spirit-breathed into the passage.* We thereby replace the centrality of the Bible with our own conceptions. Instead, we need to mobilize accurate information about the biblical text for potent spiritual growth through the text.

Avoid Peering Through the Keyhole Darkly!

The solution is to let the Scriptures speak for themselves according to their own genres and their own ideas. This demands some sensitivity to genre distinctives not normally found in spiritual formation books, but rather in books on interpretation. We start with appropriate genre sensitivity and build corresponding expectations as to how the biblical ideas within the various scriptural genres could be used in our spiritual development. This implies a two-step process of first understanding the passage within its genre and then determining its significance for our spiritual formation. This is the goal and distinctive of this book.

Recapture the Role of the Gifts of the Body of Christ

Foundational to our perspective is the belief that the Bible is really designed and intended by God and its human authors to be heard or read and then interpreted *within the community of God's people and their spiritual gifts.* When we overly individualize this process, we perform a great disservice to Christians and set ourselves up either to be frustrated because we don't really understand a passage or, more likely, to distort it out of ignorance. The way out of this swamp is not to ignore or even minimize the informational aspect of the Bible. Rather, the proper solution is to bring our reading of God's Word into continuity with the exercise of the informational gifts of the body of Christ such as teaching, pastoring-teaching, wisdom, and knowledge. This book is an expression of my role within the body to help equip fellow body members in their reading of the Bible for spiritual formation. We are in this thing together!

Chapter Three

ILLUMINATION: TRUTH FROM THE TOP DOWN

Now we have received, not the spirit of the world, but the Spirit who is from God, that we might know the things freely given to us by God, which things we also speak, not in words taught by human wisdom, but in those taught by the Spirit, combining spiritual thoughts with spiritual words.

1 CORINTHIANS 2:12-13

All Holy Scripture should be read in the spirit in which it was written.

THOMAS À. KEMPIS[1]

THE BIBLE AND THE VOICE OF GOD

I RECENTLY MET A DELIGHTFUL CHRISTIAN WOMAN—WE'LL call her Sylvia—while teaching a seminar at a solid, evangelical church. My role was to stimulate a particular group of believers in this church to read and interpret the Bible more accurately and passionately for their growth in Christ. It is something I delight in doing. Early in the seminar, Sylvia began to seriously question some of the things I was teaching the group. She had a very different approach to reading and meditating on the Bible than I was espousing. Because of her personality and passionate nature, she was not hesitant about showing her disagreement with her words and whole body! In other words, this situation had the potential to be a teacher's nightmare.

During one of the seminar breaks I sought Sylvia out and asked her some questions about her views. I was trying to understand where she was coming from and see if we had some common ground on which to build. The bottom line was that Sylvia believed that the nature of the Bible, being a supernatural book, was such that God would use it to transform us whether we understood it accurately or not! In fact, the effort to understand and interpret the Bible was of really limited value to her. She asserted that dealing with the words, paragraphs, genres, and ideas would only take us to a certain point of understanding, after which God took over and communicated whatever He desired to tell us personally. Of course, the content of that communication could be very different for each of us.

In Sylvia's system, the words of Scripture were like a launching pad. The real action occurred mystically as God launched off from the meaning of the words of the Bible and spoke whatever words He desired to His child. This happens because of the Bible's supernatural nature and the illuminating work of the Holy Spirit. In other words, in Sylvia's approach, both the speaking of God and the enlightening of the Holy Spirit were only loosely attached to the words and thoughts of the Scriptures. God's Word is just the beginning of His real "words" to us. The real action is over, above, and beyond the words of the Bible. The real action is *strictly* a relational, and never a cognitive or intellectual, process. At its core this perspective is actually *irrational!* It is an approach to the Bible that is not grounded in the very words, thoughts, or logic of the Scriptures. Rather, reading the Bible simply gives Christians the occasion to hear the voice of God in, through, or more likely, *apart from or even contrary to the very words of the Bible!* This is supposed to be possible because the Bible is a supernatural book (true) and God will speak however He desires (false). This view is far more widespread than most of us would care to admit. It is reinforced weekly with devotional reading guides, Sunday school lessons, sermons, Bible studies, and so on that assume this irrational, existential, individualistic view of the Word of God. Such a view makes the whole spiritual formation process an irrational venture, in that it does not meaningfully engage our minds. The assumption seems to be that God skips over our reasoning faculties and directly communicates to us "Spirit-to-spirit." This is wrongly believed to be more spiritual and godly than seeking to understand the words, thoughts, and teachings of the Bible.

To counter this perspective, may I suggest looking up the words *mind, heart* (the center of reasoning and thoughts, not just emotions), and *renew* in a concordance. Simply reading the vast number of verses in the Old and New Testaments that emphasize the centrality of thinking and reasoning will destroy the irrational assumptions that many Christians now have. Let me highlight one passage. Note the emphasis on how Christians are to be formed spiritually in Ephesians 4:20-24 in contrast to the Gentiles (pagans) in verses 17-19, who walk "in the futility of their mind":

> But you did not *learn* Christ in this way, if indeed you have heard Him and *have been taught* in Him, just as *truth* is in Jesus, that, in reference to your former manner of life, you lay aside the old self, which is being corrupted in accordance with the lusts of deceit, and *that you be renewed in the spirit of your mind,* and put on the new self, which in the likeness of God has been created in righteousness and holiness *of the truth.* (emphasis mine)

At the very center of the process of spiritual transformation from futile-thinking unbelievers to Christlike believers is the renewing of the Godward side of our mind to the truth that God has revealed to us. This is both a spiritual *and a rational* process! No understanding of truth, then no experiencing of renewal! This is an expression of God dignifying our capacity as believers to think rightly about Him.

But that brings up a number of questions: How are our souls transformed by the truth of the Bible? Is it a mystical process or is it a purely rational, cognitive one? We might also ask whether reading is enough, or do we need to memorize God's Word? How much must we understand the actual content to be transformed by it? Can we be spiritually formed by passages that we misunderstand or misinterpret? Is our transformation contingent on our reading and interpretive abilities? Can one verse transform us just as significantly as a paragraph or an entire biblical book? Such questions are central to understanding the relationship of the Scriptures to the spiritual formation process. We will attempt to answer some of them as we investigate the interaction of our souls with the Bible.

ILLUMINATION AND SPIRIT SUBMISSION

A major premise of this chapter is that we must read the Bible with as much humility and submission to the Holy Spirit as we can muster. This commitment expresses itself in two ways.

Relating in Spirit Submission
First, we should pray and invite the Spirit's help as we read and interpret. This involves the doctrine of the "illumination" of the Scriptures (1 Corinthians 2:6-16). Much of Sylvia's misunderstanding stems from an incorrect comprehension of illumination.

While sometimes debated, the basic thrust of the Holy Spirit's illumining or enlightening work relates primarily to our *welcoming of the truths of Scripture* rather than to our *understanding* of them.[2] In other words, the Holy Spirit will not demean our God-given responsibility as interpreters by doing the interpretive work for us! To pray for such comprehension apart from the necessary process is to duck our responsibility in understanding God's revelation. Rather, the Holy Spirit aids us in appraising or assessing the significance of the passages we are reading. He spiritually helps us to accept them as truth and apply their messages in our lives. He helps us focus the blaze of the truth on the woodpile of our souls, but He doesn't do the work of interpretation for us:

> If illumination had to do with conveying esoteric information about the original meaning of the Bible, there would be cause for anxiety. But it does not. It has to do with drawing readers deeper into the world of the text, deeper into the kingdom of God, closer to God's heart. Illumination is what happens to readers who dialogue with the text, in which the Spirit is helping them know what to do with it in Christian existence.[3]

Reading in Spirit Submission

Second, we should submit ourselves to the Holy Spirit by aligning our reading of the Bible *to the contours of the biblical text that the Holy Spirit intended.* The Holy Spirit worked with the human authors in the writing of Scripture, a process the apostle Peter described as "men moved by the Holy Spirit spoke from God" (2 Peter 1:21), and we also submit to the Holy Spirit's authority in our lives when we humbly seek to read and interpret a passage according to the meaning that the Holy Spirit (and human author) intended to convey. In cooperation with the human authors, the Holy Spirit intended to communicate certain ideas through the choice of certain genres and through the development of specific arguments and themes in the books of the Bible. One of the great ironies of reading the Bible is that ignoring things like genre and context is not an act of humble piety. On the contrary, it is an act of pride and self-reliance! In essence, we are saying, "Holy Spirit, I don't care what *You* wanted to say to God's people through this passage. I'm going to read it as *I* desire!" Like too many religious practices, this is pride cloaked as humility.

Therefore, submitting to the Holy Spirit in understanding and applying the Word of God to our lives is both a relational and an intellectual act. In other words, we must both *relate* and *think and read* in submission to the Holy Spirit. Our present focus will be on how to submit to the Holy Spirit as we read the Book He coauthored with fifty-plus humans.

PRETEXT OR CONTEXT?

There is a lot of wisdom in the little saying about interpreting the Bible, "A text without a context is a pretext." My immediate goal here is to add some depth of understanding to this saying and argue for a greater sensitivity to context. In particular, I'd like to offer an alternative to another widespread and rather deadly reading habit among God's people, even among mature believers: the habit of ignoring the broader context of biblical passages and interpreting them in an "atomistic," or tiny-piece, manner. That is, we tend to interpret verses or biblical stories primarily as free-standing units of truth (which they are in some sense) rather than as parts of the broader whole of a specific biblical book. This ignoring of both genre and context greatly hampers the transforming work of God's Word in our souls! Let's explore how this is so.

We can summarize this thought in a sentence: *meaning comes from the top down, not from the bottom up, from the larger units of Scripture to the smaller units.* As the diagram on the next page illustrates, when we communicate and read or listen to communication, we structure it from the top down, from the larger units to the smaller.

As listeners we identify the genre or type of communication automatically. For instance, when you turn on the television, you listen and interpret differently if Tom Brokaw is reading the evening news than if Jerry Seinfeld is telling a joke. This is based on your immediate identification of the genre of communication and the difference between the news and a situation comedy.

As speakers we do this as well. If we want to communicate to someone about how hot it has been lately, the first thing we automatically do is determine the genre or type of communication we want to use. If we want to be funny, we choose humor as the appropriate genre. This is the top-level or largest unit of thought. Our goal is to use the genre of humor to communicate how hot it has been lately. So our big idea is, "It has really been hot lately!" Next we determine how we will develop our main idea and how long or short our communication will be. Let's say we intend to tell three funny, short stories to develop our idea. This means we will have three paragraphs with three different big ideas, each relating to and developing the main idea of the unit of thought about how hot it has been lately. Thus each sentence within each paragraph will develop that paragraph's big idea and also meaningfully relate to the big idea of the whole unit of thought. Ultimately, each sentence will also fit into the genre of humor and thereby contribute to being funny. Indeed, each word will fit with the genre and will contribute to making sense of the idea of the sentence and the entire paragraph, which develops the unit of thought, which exemplifies the genre of humor.

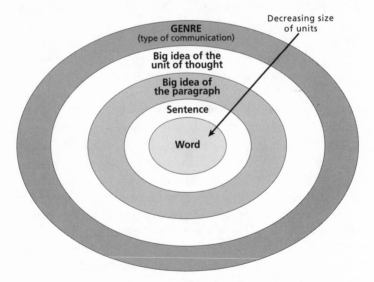

You get the idea of the multiple levels of communication going on simultaneously. However, the key to understanding one another's communication is that we work our way from the top down. That is, we start with the largest unit (identifying the genre as humor) and then develop a sense of the whole unit (this is humor about the hot weather). We then develop a sense of each paragraph's meaning as a unit (each funny story's point), but only in light of how each paragraph fits into the whole unit of thought. This is always the way communication works when we write or speak to one another. We don't start with one single word in one single sentence of one single paragraph and work our way upward from that word. A word is only meaningful because it is a part of larger units of thought that make that word purposeful within its context.

The amazing thing is that we often assume the opposite perspective when we read the Bible! We turn normal communication on its head and wrongly think that we should start interpreting a biblical passage at the smallest unit of thought, the word. We then falsely assume that as we string together a few words and come up with a verse or sentence, we will understand what God is communicating through the biblical passage. We frequently ignore the fact that meaning comes from the top down, and we start from the wrong end! The result is that we end up misreading many parts of the Bible.

Perhaps the most vivid way to address this problem is to contrast the typical noncontextual interpretation of familiar passages with more contextually sensitive readings. The goal is to reveal more clearly God's transforming power within our souls when we read biblical passages within their context. Grasping this basic principle should be life-changing for our reading of God's Word. It should also encourage us by revealing a richer dimension to God's transforming power through His Book, and give a more suggestive context for meditation and discovering the significance of the meaning for our own lives. If the goal is reading the Bible more meaningfully for spiritual formation, then seeing how the broader context profoundly affects our souls should also encourage us to embrace better reading practices. Let's develop this concept as we visit a familiar passage.

Where Two or Three Are Gathered: Matthew 18:19-20
A widely used and greatly loved passage is Jesus' statement about gathering for prayer in Matthew 18:19-20:

"Again I say to you, that if two of you agree on earth about anything that they may ask, it shall be done for them by My Father who is in heaven. For where two or three have gathered together in My name, there I am in their midst."

The promises in this passage are claimed by Christians in a broad variety of settings. Some focus on Jesus' words in verse 19 that promise answered prayer through agreement in prayer requests. Others claim verse 20 and the promise of Jesus' presence when two or more of God's children gather for group prayer, worship, decision making, or just about anything in His name. Jesus' promises about prayer are understood to be broad and open-ended because He speaks of believers agreeing on earth "about anything that they may ask" (verse 19). The expansive nature of Jesus' promise about His presence is also underscored because believers have simply "gathered together in My name" (verse 20)—a very broad purpose for meeting. Therefore, within these verses themselves, there seems to be ample support for their widespread use as either very general prayer or "presence" promises.

However, a very different sense of meaning emerges when we put these verses within the context of their unit of thought. Generally speaking, the basic unit of thought in the Bible is the *paragraph*. The chapter and verse notations were added in the sixteenth century by a Parisian publisher/printer named Robert Estienne (also known as Stephanus). Given the unfortunate chapter divisions in certain places (for example, Philippians 4:1, not 4:2), we are tempted to believe the perhaps legendary story that Estienne made some of these divisions while journeying on horseback and fighting the jumping pen! Nevertheless, we know that the Bible's chapters and verses are not necessarily the basic units of thought intended by their authors and should therefore be used primarily for Scripture reference and location, not necessarily as interpretive guides.

If the paragraph is the basic unit of thought, especially in the New Testament, we would be wise to put these verses within their unit and look at the meaning from the top down, from the paragraph to the sentences. In doing this, it is wise to consult a literal translation of the

Bible like the KJV, NKJV, ASV, NASB, RSV, or NRSV (but not the NIV and other "dynamic equivalent" translations—see appendix 1) because they follow more faithfully the paragraphing of the original language versions (that is, Hebrew Bible and Greek New Testament). Because all paragraphing in original or translated versions is a judgment call and wasn't in the original manuscripts, it is best to defer to the original language experts, who are the best judges of the units of thought in the biblical text, in this matter. In other words, there was certainly paragraphing in the structure of the writers' thought, but not in the written expression of it.

What is the basic unit of thought that contains Matthew 18:19-20? A literal translation reveals that these two verses are the climax of a paragraph that begins in verse 15. Therefore, the paragraph (unit of thought) is Matthew 18:15-20:

> "And if your brother sins, go and reprove him in private; if he listens to you, you have won your brother. But if he does not listen to you, take one or two more with you, so that by the mouth of two or three witnesses every fact may be confirmed. And if he refuses to listen to them, tell it to the church; and if he refuses to listen even to the church, let him be to you as a Gentile and a tax-gatherer. Truly I say to you, whatever you shall bind on earth shall be bound in heaven; and whatever you loose on earth shall be loosed in heaven. Again I say to you, that if two of you agree on earth about anything that they may ask, it shall be done for them by My Father who is in heaven. For where two or three have gathered together in My name, there I am in their midst."

If the part (verse 19-20) derives its meaning from the whole (the larger unit), then verses 19-20 must be understood in light of verses 15-20. We should then ask, "What is this paragraph about? What is its big idea or main theme?" As you read verses 15-20, you will recognize that this paragraph, this unit of thought, is about how we are to discipline those within the church when they sin. In other words, this paragraph is about church discipline.

If this is true, then how do verses 19-20, the last two sentences in the paragraph, fit into this unit of thought about "church discipline"? Let's show the structure of the paragraph before we answer this question:

> **Verses 15-17** = the four stages of confrontation of a sinning Christian: (1) go alone; (2) go with one or two other believers; (3) bring it before the whole (local) church; and (as a last resort) (4) excommunicate the person.
>
> **Verse 18** = a summary statement of the fact that God honors in heaven what believers decide on earth in matters of church discipline!
>
> **Verses 19-20** = a repeat ("Again I say") of the heavenly authorization that the two or three witnesses have in church discipline matters, including some special sense of Jesus Christ's presence with them when they testify.

Notice how verses 19-20 bring to finality earlier points that Jesus stated in the paragraph. Jesus is repeating Himself at the beginning of verse 19 ("Again I say to you") to underscore its connection to the rest of the paragraph. He also repeats in verses 19-20 the numbers "two or three" mentioned in verse 16. Having at least two or three witnesses to establish the facts of a case was standard legal procedure under the Mosaic Law (Jesus quotes Deuteronomy 19:15 in verse 16 to establish the point). Therefore, the "two" in verse 19 and the "two or three" in verse 20 are not new numbers of believers being introduced, but are repeated references to those who testify as witnesses in church discipline matters. Given the scary nature of such thankless responsibilities, *Jesus wanted those of us who might be witnesses to know that God will honor our testimony in heaven when we ask for discipline on earth* (verse 19). Not only is this true, but Jesus so values such testimony that He also wants us to know His authorizing presence will be with us when we gather to testify in church discipline matters in His name (verse 20).

Perhaps you're reading this and saying, "But it says 'agree on earth about *anything*' in verse 19!" Also you may assert, "But verse

20 is about those who simply *'have gathered together in My name.'"* Both statements seem to point to broad applications of Jesus' words to *any* prayer request and *all* gatherings in His name. Because both issues deal with the same principle of language and context, permit me to discuss them at the same time—with a personal illustration of this principle.

Picture me sitting at my computer in my home office trying to write this book. Late in the afternoon, my lovely wife, Marty, comes into the room and says, "Walt, we're having leftovers for dinner tonight. I have chicken, beef, or pork. Which do you want?" Now, my wife is a fabulous cook, and I know that she has prepared each of these three meats equally wonderfully. Additionally, I am distracted with writing chapter 3 and don't really care which of these dishes I eat. So I say somewhat vacantly, "Honey, I don't really care. I'll eat anything."

With my statement, "I'll eat anything," am I making an absolute declaration that I will eat anything in the world that is set before me? Am I declaring that I'll eat wood, concrete, nails, carpet, and so on? Of course not. Within the context of the unit of thought, the paragraph, it is overwhelmingly obvious that my use of *anything* is limited to the kinds of foods we are discussing. My statement is not an all-encompassing statement in terms of *anything*. Rather, it is a use of *anything* that is tempered and limited by the immediate context. This is not unusual or odd, but rather a perfectly normal use of language. This is the way language works. Words are contoured, shaped, limited, or expanded by the immediate context (by the unit of thought) in which they are embedded. It should be obvious by now that this is because meaning comes from the top down, from the larger units like paragraphs to the smaller units like sentences.

Back to my illustration. If you take my statement out of its context, you can freely absolutize it and say that the author of this book will eat anything in the world. But doing this would distort my intentions and meaning by wrenching my statement out of the context of its unit of thought. None of us would think of doing this in everyday dialogue, yet it is often done without flinching in our Bible reading when we take Matthew 18:19-20 out of its context! We absolutize certain statements that are of interest to us and make them say something that the divine and human authors never intended. This is not thinking submissively to the Holy Spirit, but thinking independently and proudly. We re-create the meaning of the biblical passage in our own image and, in this act, express great arrogance.

Perhaps you're reeling with "interpretation shock" at this point! How could these verses mean this when we use them so frequently and widely in a very different way? The answer is, of course, because we haven't corrected our bad habit of reading from the bottom up and, therefore, don't read these verses within their context! The result of not looking at meaning from the top down, of not reading from the larger units of the text to the smaller, is that we sometimes misinterpret and misapply a part of God's Word. In terms of spiritual formation, too many of us wrongly claim these verses in contexts that Jesus never intended. His words are for an extremely important and extremely narrow context: church discipline. By not looking at the part in light of the whole unit of thought in which it is embedded, we distort the part and ignore the whole. But let's not beat ourselves up here. Rather, let's focus on the wonderful significance that Matthew 18:19-20 *should have* for our spiritual development.

One of the most challenging truths of this passage relating to spiritual formation is that my sin or your sin affects all who are in the church of Jesus Christ. Therefore, like it or not, we have a serious accountability to one another! Our accountability is not only to deal with our sin individually, but also to deal with our brother's or sister's sin, especially when it affects the testimony of the whole body of believers. In terms of our spiritual formation, such a concept challenges our very individualistic concepts of seeking to grow in isolation from other believers. The Bible knows of no such formation! Rather, the emphasis of both the Old and New Testaments is that we are in this thing together. While there is plenty of room for focus on our own individual growth in Christ, the overwhelming emphasis is on the growth of all of us together in community with Christ and with one another. This passage on church discipline jerks us rather abruptly into this view of reality.

Note also that this concept of church discipline is bookended by Jesus' teaching about not causing the children ("little ones") among us to stumble spiritually (Matthew 18:1-14) on one side, and exhortation for doling out forgiveness to our brothers and sisters with the same generous measure that God forgives us (18:21-35) on the other. Thus, even the broader context is about our relationships with one another in the people of God. Again, this underscores the corporate or group dimension to our spiritual formation. From one perspective we are formed individually, but from the transcendent perspective we are formed together with one another in the body of Christ. Therefore, our individual growth should always be subsumed under the desire to see the whole body grow to maturity. The apostle Paul elegantly expresses this goal in Ephesians 4:13, using the language of striving for a destination while on a journey— "until *we all attain* to the unity of the faith, and of the knowledge of the Son of God, to a mature man, to the measure of the stature which belongs to the fulness of Christ" (emphasis mine). Note that the destination of unity, knowledge, maturity, and full stature is expressed in group rather than individual terms. This is because all of us Christians are on this journey together! Both our destinies and growth are inextricably bound together.

Bringing all these contexts together, as we meditate on Matthew 18:15-20 and see its emphasis on church discipline, we should not conclude that this is abstract "church business" and has nothing to do with the growth of our souls in Christ. Rather, just the opposite conclusion is warranted. This passage gives us practical advice about how to confront one another when we fall into sin. This is not merely a peripheral truth for spiritual formation, but a central one that is probably regularly needed. It is also central because our heavenly Father takes special note of our earthly decisions in this area and records corresponding heavenly decisions to bind or loose the sinning believers from their sin *according to our decisions* (18:18-19)! Moreover, the risen, ascended Jesus Christ manifests His presence with those of us involved in testifying in these matters as a statement of His interest and our authority (18:20). Therefore, to miss reading Matthew 18:19-20 within its important context is to miss some rich formational truths. In their place we substitute general, out-of-context moralizing contrary to Jesus' intentions. Also, we miss the joy of *thinking in submission* to the Holy Spirit, who superintended the writing of this passage by Matthew.

Reading the Bible with sensitivity to meaning coming from the top down, not the bottom up, will revolutionize our application of the Word of God to our life. We will begin to apply it according to the contours that *God* intended. We will be thinking in submission to the Holy Spirit, who contoured the passage in and through the human author. We will be on the solid ground of sensitivity to genre and broader context. We will avoid pretext, and glory in context.

CONCLUSION

In this chapter we've looked at how the voice of God is heard through the Scriptures as well as how the Holy Spirit both enables us to understand the message of the text and convicts us to apply the truths of God's Word to our own lives. We have learned the primary lesson that God is not interested in irrationality, but by the sheer abundance of emphasis in the Scriptures on things being done decently and in order, on the mind and heart as receptacles for His truth, and on His use of a broad variety of genres to communicate His truth, we must be prepared to do our part of the work in understanding His message. Understanding the genre, and the specific context of each passage, will lead us not toward an embalmed faith, but toward a living and active transformation into the likeness of Jesus.

Chapter Four

INGESTING
THE FIRE

How blessed is the man who does not walk in the counsel
    of the wicked,
Nor stand in the path of sinners,
Nor sit in the seat of scoffers!
But his delight is in the law of the LORD,
And in His law he meditates day and night.
And he will be like a tree firmly planted by streams of water,
Which yields its fruit in its season,
And its leaf does not wither;
And in whatever he does, he prospers.

PSALM 1:1-3

O how I love Thy law!
It is my meditation all the day.

PSALM 119:97

There is a great market for religious experience in our world;
there is little enthusiasm for the patient acquisition of virtue, little
inclination to sign up for the long apprenticeship in what earlier
generations of Christians called holiness.

EUGENE PETERSON[1]

PLEASE REJOIN ME IN THE PROCESS THAT I WENT THROUGH AS I sought to deal with the death of our son, Christopher. The setting now is the cemetery of our family's hometown in Bolivar, Missouri. We have completed the graveside service and I am standing beside our son's open grave. It is an unspeakably painful moment in my life. If I could muster any more tears, I would be uncontrollably weeping as I watch four men struggle to lower a steel vault lid to cover the grave vault holding Christopher's little casket. I will see his little smiling face no more. I won't run my fingers through his beautiful blond hair again. We'll never snuggle together or touch one another. This is the end. And as I stand there looking into what feels like the abyss, I realize that this could be the most despairing, skeptical, and faithless moment of my life. I feel like I could curse God for emotionally gutting me for the rest of my days. It is as if I am standing beside the deep, dark, bottomless abyss.

However, it is at this moment that God in His remarkable grace and kindness brings to mind a passage of Scripture that I have been pondering for the last month. It was exactly thirty-five days ago that I stood a short distance away in this same cemetery and buried my 91-year-old maternal grandmother. I had been very close to her and her death had been painful, although different in texture. However, losing her had moved me to revisit a very comforting passage in God's Word about the death of loved ones. I had been meditating on and off for the last month on Paul's words-for-standing-beside-a-grave in 1 Thessalonians 4:13-18, NIV:

> Brothers, we do not want you to be ignorant about those who fall asleep, or to grieve like the rest of men, who have no hope. We believe that Jesus died and rose again and so we believe that God will bring with Jesus those who have fallen asleep in him. According to the Lord's own word, we tell you that we who are still alive, who are left till the coming of the Lord, will certainly not precede those who have fallen asleep. For the Lord himself will come down from heaven, with a loud command, with the voice of the archangel and with the trumpet call of God, and the dead in Christ will rise first. After that, we who are still alive and

are left will be caught up together with them in the clouds to meet the Lord in the air. And so we will be with the Lord forever. Therefore encourage each other with these words.

The Spirit of God brought these remarkable graveside words to me as I stood by this painful grave. Not only did God bring them to mind, but I was overwhelmingly comforted and encouraged about seeing our little son again when Jesus comes to raise His people. My self pity and abiding loneliness began to be absorbed in this glorious hope in Christ. I began to experience profound, soulish comfort in the deepest recesses of my being as God used His Word to renew hope and courage in me. My humble attempts at planting the seed of God's revelation in my soul over the past month were suddenly flowering in my moment of need into comforting transformation. I was so overcome with this hope and comfort that I bubbled over about it with my grieving paternal grandparents as we drove away from the cemetery. I had ingested the fire and God was now warming my soul with its power.

I hunger for you to experience this same transformation as you ingest the Word of God into your soul. It is to this task we now turn. After absorbing some principles of good reading and interpretation, we now move to applying them in the reading of the Word of God for the transformation of our souls. After focusing on getting more dynamically into the Word, we now turn to getting the Word more dynamically into us, to implanting an accurate and trustworthy understanding of a biblical passage into the deepest recesses of our souls. The goal we seek is fourfold: to mobilize the information we glean from study and embrace it with every fiber of our being; to be transformed by the truth as we *meditate* on the Word of God; to ingest the fiery Word of God in order to inflame our souls; and to embrace the *transforming* intention of Scripture along with its informing intention.

FOLLOWING A SAVIOR WHO MEDITATES

A good place to start an investigation of spiritual formation is to observe the life of Jesus the Messiah, the Son of God. It appears that

Jesus probably meditated regularly during the times He withdrew to a lonely place (literally, "wilderness place"). The Gospel writers record some of these withdrawals during Jesus' ministry (see Matthew 4:1-11; 14:13,23; 17:1-9; 26:36-46; Mark 1:35; 6:31; Luke 5:16; and 6:12).

However, we will focus on the one time of solitude when the biblical text gives the best evidence that Jesus was meditating on the Word of God—at the beginning of His official ministry as Messiah, immediately after His baptism by John the Baptist. While Mark briefly records this time of temptation in the wilderness (1:12-13) along with Luke (4:1-13), we will concentrate on the account in Matthew 4:1-11. Of these three "synoptic" Gospels, Matthew underscores most emphatically the nature and content of Jesus' meditation in the wilderness.

Jesus' Meditation in the Wilderness: Matthew 4:1-11

> Then Jesus was led up by the Spirit into the wilderness to be tempted by the devil. And after He had fasted forty days and forty nights, He then became hungry. (4:1-2, NASB)

While the crowds were still buzzing about Jesus' heavenly anointing with the Holy Spirit (3:16-17), the same Spirit leads Jesus into the wilderness for *the specific purpose of temptation by the Devil* (4:1). Jesus' first task as the newly anointed Messiah is to prove that He is morally capable of reigning as Messiah by withstanding all that the Devil can throw at Him! He must validate His virtuous character as Messiah so that His people will know that He is trustworthy and worthy of being followed. He must prove Himself in the wilderness.

Why *the wilderness?* Apparently, this was an abandoned or uncultivated place, and not necessarily a desert. To the Jews, the wilderness was the place where demons roamed and evil prevailed (Matthew 12:43-45; Luke 8:29; 11:24-26). All of this fits with their belief "that the wilderness, being beyond the bounds of society, is the haunt of evil spirits."[2]

The Jews' trepidation about the wilderness is justified given Israel's history of unbelief, especially after she left Egypt. Particularly onerous was the great unbelief at Kadesh Barnea when the Israelites decided they were too weak to enter Canaan and possess the land (Numbers 13–14). This lack of faith cost the lives of the entire adult generation that had left Egypt (except for Caleb and Joshua), all of whom died and were buried in the wilderness. Thus the wilderness was viewed as a disastrous place of failure and misery in the history of Israel.

Into this godless, demon-haunted wasteland the Holy Spirit leads the newly anointed Messiah. What a testing ground! What a place to begin His ministry in hand-to-hand combat with the Devil. What a place to prove His sinless character. To do so, Jesus chose to heighten His spiritual sensitivities and vulnerabilities by going without food for forty days and nights. It is amazing how such bodily deprivation clears one's mind and sharpens one's spiritual sensitivity. However, as those who have fasted for long periods have discovered, waves of hunger sweep over the fasting saint at various times. One of the most brutal of times apparently comes at the forty-day mark, when the fasting person is most vulnerable to the demands of hunger pangs. So it was with Jesus the Messiah. When Matthew tells us, "He then became hungry," it is a heavily laden statement. Messiah Jesus was at a very vulnerable and fragile place in this spiritual wilderness:

> And the tempter came and said to Him, "If You are the Son of God, command that these stones become bread." But He answered and said, "It is written, 'Man shall not live on bread alone, but on every word that proceeds out of the mouth of God.'" (Matthew 4:3-4)

Because of his diabolical brilliance, the Devil tempted Messiah Jesus when He was in His most vulnerable state. Apparently, the Devil knew that Jesus, as Messiah, could have easily turned the stones into bread and quickly satisfied His hunger. Therefore, he first struck at the point of physical need. Note that Jesus' response is exactly on-point. Human beings do not survive in this world solely by eating food; indeed, they can do without food for lengthy periods of time. Humans also need to digest every word that God has spoken that is recorded in His Book, the Bible, and will die rather quickly in the face of satanic temptation without it. In order for human beings, including the Messiah, to survive, feasting on God's Word is even more essential than feasting on bread. Jesus' rebuff of Satan's temptation in the wilderness proves that:

> Then the devil took Him into the holy city; and he had Him stand on the pinnacle of the temple, and said to Him, "If You are the Son of God throw Yourself down; for it is written, 'He will give His angels charge concerning You'; and 'On their hands they will bear You up, lest You strike Your foot against a stone.'" Jesus said to him, "On the other hand, it is written, 'You shall not put the Lord your God to the test.'" (4:5-7)

Having failed with his hunger temptation, the Devil transports Jesus to the pinnacle of the temple in Jerusalem for a second temptation. The temple pinnacle is probably the southeast corner of the temple mount in the Holy City, overlooking the deeply carved Kidron Valley. Having recently stood on this spot, I can attest that it is well over two hundred feet from the pinnacle down to the jagged, rocky floor of the valley. This is why the Devil drew a biblical passage from his vast knowledge of Scripture that promised safety from the threat of striking a stone. How appropriate! Additionally, the verses the Devil quotes, Psalm 91:11-12, lie in the midst of one of the most beloved and powerful psalms speaking of God's deliverance from a vast array of threats for the one who trusts in the Lord. At the immediate level, the Devil is correct in appealing to these encouraging verses.

However, at the broader level, Jesus points out the Devil's inappropriate and faulty usage of the passage. The right understanding of these verses was being mobilized in a wrong cause: the presumptuous testing of the Lord God. Therefore, their truthfulness was being distorted to a diabolical end that negated their teaching. In other words, Jesus rebuked Satan for claiming a promise of God's protection in a scheme to test God's character. Right scripture; wrong purpose:

> Again, the devil took Him to a very high mountain, and showed Him all the kingdoms of the world, and their glory; and he said to Him, "All these things will I give You, if You fall down and worship me." Then Jesus said to him, "Begone, Satan! For it is written, 'You shall worship the Lord your God, and serve Him only.'" (Matthew 4:8-10)

For his third and climactic temptation, the Devil acknowledges what is at stake in Messiah's ministry: rulership over all the kingdoms of the world. The Devil knew that Jesus Christ's ultimate goal of lordship over the world's kingdoms was in direct conflict with his similar goal! In a delegated and secondary sense, the Devil has some present authority over these kingdoms (Luke 4:6); he is the ruler of this world (John 12:31; 14:30; 16:11). Otherwise, his offer to hand these kingdoms over to Jesus would have been nonsensical.

Because Satan knew that Jesus Christ was going to destroy his authority when He established God's kingdom, his intention was to derail Jesus at the very beginning of His messianic ministry. The Devil tempted Jesus with an evil and twisted shortcut. If Jesus would only worship him at this moment, Jesus would allegedly achieve His goal of establishing God's kingdom on earth. Jesus knew that worshiping Satan would destroy everything that He was and represented. Therefore, Messiah's response to the Devil is again right on target. He once more quotes the very words of God: "You shall worship the Lord your God, and serve Him only." With these words Messiah summarily dismisses the Devil from His presence:

> Then the devil left Him; and behold, angels came and began to minister to Him. (Matthew 4:11)

What could the Devil do? The Lord of life and King of kings had commanded him to scurry away defeated, and that is exactly what he did. Matthew focuses on the presence of the angels ministering to the physically depleted Savior. It is instructive that they should come now and meet Jesus' needs when it does not appear that He demanded their presence, or even invited it. In other words, God is not hesitant about sending His angels to minister to Messiah (or to us), but we should never be demanding or presumptuous about their aid. Jesus refused to put Himself in a situation—that is, by leaping frivolously—that assumed that God would rescue Him with angels (4:6). Such behavior would be self-serving, not God-honoring. Moreover, such choices did not mesh with Messiah's sacrificial choice to seek His Father's will, not His own.

WHAT WE LEARN FROM JESUS' MEDITATION

Three months ago I spent half a day in the wilderness about four miles west of Jericho in eastern Israel, believed to be the site of Jesus' temptation in the wilderness. This area is one of the most Godforsaken, lonely, hot, dry, and unfriendly places I have ever been in, and I can easily appreciate the Jews' view of the wilderness after spending several hours there. For one of those hours I curled up in a shady cleft in a canyon wall trying to avoid the searing sun and focused on Jesus' wilderness temptation. To help me identify with Jesus, I meditated on the same passages He seemed to be pondering in the wilderness. I also read about His temptation in Matthew 4:1-11, Mark 1:12-13, and Luke 4:1-13. The following are some of my insights into His meditation gleaned from previous study and as I sought to walk rather feebly in our Master's steps.

First, it appears that Jesus meditated on larger chunks of the Word of God, rather than on isolated verses. We know this by looking at Messiah's three responses to the Devil's temptations:

- Matthew 4:4—But He answered and said, "It is written, 'Man shall not live on bread alone, but on every word that proceeds out of the mouth of God'" (quoting Deuteronomy 8:3).
- Matthew 4:7—Jesus said to him, "On the other hand, it is written, 'You shall not put the Lord your God to the test'" (quoting Deuteronomy 6:16).

- Matthew 4:10—Then Jesus said to him, "Begone, Satan! For it is written, 'You shall worship the Lord your God, and serve Him only'" (quoting Deuteronomy 6:13).

During His time in the wilderness Jesus was probably meditating on the whole book of Deuteronomy—at a minimum, on Deuteronomy 6–8. The verses He uses with the Devil seem to be very fresh and alive to Him, and He readily appropriated them. This is perfectly understandable because Deuteronomy is Moses' exhortation to the new generation of adults in Israel, fresh from forty years of burying their parents in the wilderness. What we learn from observing His model of meditation is the value of knowing and pondering larger chunks of Scripture. As already mentioned, this is swimming against the present current in evangelical circles. We seem to be enamored with sound bites of God's Word, rather than larger chunks. This is to our detriment and theological impoverishment! Our Lord's example is in the opposite direction. Do we think that we are wiser than He in our choices of meditative material?

There are three advantages to meditating on larger chunks of the Word of God rather than just focusing on an isolated verse here and there. First, *a larger portion of Scripture gives us a full thought and not a fragment of an idea;* we read, study, and then ponder a unit of thought and not just a sliver of one. This ensures the context of the Word and prevents us from supplying our own, which may distort the part we isolated from its whole. Jesus obviously knew that meaning comes from the top down, from the larger units to the smaller, and He meditated in accordance with this truth.

Additionally, *we see the connection between the parts of a unit of thought* when we meditate on a larger portion of Scripture. This second advantage is crucial because, in some sense, much of the meaning flows out of the connection between the parts. For example, the significance of Jesus' temptation in Matthew 4 builds on His baptism in Matthew 3 (which officially began His messianic ministry). Much of the meaning of this narrative lies in the connection and flow of thought from one section to the next. We lose this if we isolate each section or lift one or two sound bites out of it. As a result, we literally miss most of the meaning of a passage because we refuse to read and think about it humbly in accordance with its nature and structure. Again, it is no mark of great piety to argue for the great power of an isolated fragment of the Word of God. Rather, it is an act of uninformed self-reliance that denies the very essence of the Scriptures! While these words may sound harsh, they are absolutely essential because of the high cost of misreading the very words of God.

A third value of meditating on larger portions of Scripture is that *we give the Holy Spirit more to work with in renewing our minds to the truth.* This may strike you as odd, but it is a very important point. It relates again to the dynamic interface between our responsibilities and God's. God the Holy Spirit's delight is in transforming us into the image of God the Son in our mental and moral choices (see Galatians 4:19). Although this is a supernatural transformation that only God can do, God, as part of His dignifying of us, will not do those things for us that He has deemed us capable of doing for ourselves. And one of our responsibilities is to hear or read the Word of God regularly and to hide it in our hearts (see Psalm 119:11). God will not violate our sanctity by force-feeding His Word to us. We must choose to feed on it ourselves in response to the wonderful wooing and enabling of the Holy Spirit in our lives. Does the Holy Spirit enable us to read and meditate on God's Word? Absolutely! Will the Holy Spirit do the reading and meditating for us? Absolutely not! This is our choice and our responsibility in response to the loving prompting of the Spirit. Within this dynamic interaction, the more we respond to the Holy Spirit and choose to digest God's Word, the more the Holy Spirit has to use to transform us. He brings these truths to mind; He prompts us to implement them in our lives; He convicts us when we violate them; He leads us more precisely because we have greater knowledge of God's ways; and on and on. The more we know and ponder of the Word of God, the more we give the Holy Spirit to use in the transformation of our souls. Out-of-context verses are just not adequate to accomplish this task!

Second, Jesus appeared to allow the previous experience of

God's people to inform how He should respond in a similar situation. This is exactly how we should read the Bible! The apostle Paul says this very thing to two different churches:

> For whatever was written in earlier times was written for our instruction, that through perseverance and the encouragement of the Scriptures we might have hope. (Romans 15:4)

> Now these things happened to them as an example, and they were written for our instruction, upon whom the ends of the ages have come. (1 Corinthians 10:11)

However, the parallels between Jesus' experience and Israel's are more staggering than we could imagine. They both occur in the wilderness after a significant water experience; they both last for a forty-unit period of time; they both happen at the beginning of a "conquest" in the land of Israel. And the purpose of both experiences was testing:

> [Moses speaking to Israel] "And you shall remember all the way which the LORD your God has led you in the wilderness these forty years, *that He might humble you, testing you, to know what was in your heart, whether you would keep His commandments or not."* (Deuteronomy 8:2, emphasis mine)

> Then Jesus was led up by the Spirit into the wilderness to be tempted by the devil. (Matthew 4:1)

By allowing the Devil *to tempt* Jesus to sin, God accomplishes His purpose of testing Messiah and revealing Messiah's perfect heart and infallible commitment to keep His Father's commandments. Unfortunately, Israel failed miserably, terminally in this same test.

In short, Jesus the Messiah gives us a positive model of how to respond to testing in the wilderness and thereby fulfills what was previously lacking in Israel. Israel the son (Exodus 4:22) gives us an example of wilderness tragedy; Jesus the Son gives us an example of wilderness triumph. And it appears that much of the Son's triumph is grounded on His meditation on the previous son's experience. By meditating on this part of God's Word, Jesus' heart was freshly shaped and strengthened to make the right choices in His time of testing and suffering. The author of Hebrews refers to this general process in the God-man's life when he says, "For it was fitting for Him, for whom are all things, and through whom are all things, in bringing many sons to glory, *to perfect the author of their salvation through sufferings"* (2:10, emphasis added). Because of this, Messiah can now accomplish what Israel failed to do: be a light to the peoples of the world.

Third, Jesus' experience shows us that meditation gives us specific, God-centered responses to the Devil's temptations. Satan's three solicitations were appeals to real physical need and presumption and pride. Jesus' three responses were specific antidotes to these temptations. And they came from the larger chunk of God's Word that appears to have been His meditative focus. All three responses were centered in preserving and magnifying God's honor. Jesus emphasized that God preserves through His words, that He should not be tested, and that He alone should be worshiped and served. All three responses appeared to flow out of Messiah's recent meditation on His Father's Word. What a model for us!

As I sat huddled in the little niche in the rock in the wilderness of Israel, overlooking a rugged canyon below me, I recalled our Savior's wilderness testing. I sat stunned at His choice to suffer for an extended period of time in such a rugged, bleak, and physically demanding place. He must have been a very strong, disciplined, and physically fit man. I pondered His loneliness in wandering by Himself each day for forty days through such a harsh, barren land. I meditated on the fear of sleeping on the ground in deep darkness in the midst of creepy crawly things and wild beasts (Mark 1:13). I focused on the bravery of our Lord for going by Himself into what appeared to be a stronghold of the Devil and facing Satan's best shot in His weakened physical state. I meditated on His meditative passages and derived strength as He must have done some twenty centuries before. I also marveled afresh at how Jesus' temptations in the wilderness must have given Him insight into our weaknesses and vulnerabilities to temptation. The author of Hebrews, in 2:18, reflects on this great truth: "For since He Himself was tempted in that which He has suffered, He is able to come to the aid of those who are tempted." Again, in 4:15, he revels in Jesus' sympathetic understanding of our frailties: "For we do not have a high priest who cannot sympathize with our weaknesses, but one who has been tempted in all things as we are, yet without sin."

By meditating on Jesus' contemplative time, I also gained new appreciation and insight into the centrality and power of the Word of God in His life. He must have devoted massive amounts of time to reading, studying, and meditating on the Scriptures. Certainly the Word of God was absolutely essential to His survival and success in His testing from the Devil. I was struck afresh at my arrogance and foolishness in thinking that I could believe in Jesus Christ and follow in His steps as His disciple and not intentionally ingest the fiery words of God as meaningfully as He did! If He who was without sin regularly meditated on the Scriptures, who am I to think that I do not need to do the same in my battle with sin? We follow a Savior who meditates on God's Word. Should we not follow Him in this practice? Should we not also regularly ingest the fire of God's words to purify and reshape our souls?

WHAT IS BIBLICAL "MEDITATION"?

The biblical concept of meditation involves both a thought emphasis and a speech emphasis. The Hebrew term *śiah* brings out the mental aspect in most contexts and essentially means "to muse about or consider deeply and at length." It is, if you will, a "talking in the mind" and therefore nonverbal. For example, the author of Psalm 119 instructs us to muse about or consider deeply God's precepts (verses 15, 78), statutes (23, 48), word or promise (148), law (97), and testimonies (99). Elsewhere in the Psalms we are encouraged to muse or meditate about God Himself (77:3), His deeds (77:12), and our song to Him (77:6). We should also ponder the work of God's hands in history (143:5) and His wonderful works in general (145:5). All of this demonstrates that an aspect of meditation is mental and nonverbal. It is a musing on or contemplating about God, His deeds, and His Word.

There is also a speech aspect to meditation that the other primary Hebrew word, hāgâ, emphasizes. This word means to "mutter or speak or read in an undertone." Interestingly enough, hāgâ is used in other Old Testament passages of the coo or moan of a dove (Isaiah 38:14; 59:11) and the growl of a lion (Isaiah 31:4). In other words, this is a low, indistinct tone emanating largely from the throat, without much movement of the lips—what parents in the throes of raising teenagers do: mutter to themselves!

This verbal aspect of meditation is what God commanded Joshua to do with the Book of the Law so that he muttered it day and night (Joshua 1:8). It is the same Law of God that the psalmist delightfully murmurs day and night (Psalm 1:2). David remembers God on his bed and mutters about Him in the night watches (Psalm 63:6). All this is part of meditation on God and His Word. It is talking to yourself as you think about the wonders of God and His Book.

The thought and speech emphasis—the nonverbal and verbal—are probably two sides of the same coin. We *cannot* mutter about something we haven't thought about, and conversely, we most surely *would* mutter about those things that are gripping our souls. Therefore, it does not seem to be the intention of the biblical writers to dig a ditch between the thought and speech aspects of meditation. Rather, both concepts work together in the marvelous process of deeply pondering God and His majesties.

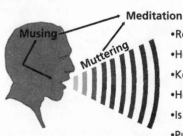

Meditation

•Restructures our thinking

•Helps us learn God's thoughts/ways

•Keeps us from "wandering"

•Helps us fight temptation

•Is a basis for growing holiness

•Puts God's Word on our lips

Please bear with me for a biological illustration. One of the best word pictures of meditation is the digestive system of a cow, goat, buffalo, deer, or any other animal considered a "ruminant." These animals have three- or four-chamber stomachs and handle unchewed food in a unique manner: It is swallowed by the ruminant and passes into either of the first two stomach chambers where it is mixed with fluid to form a soft mass called "cud" or "bolus." This soft mass is then regurgitated and chewed very slowly and swallowed again, this time passing through the rest of the stomach's chambers. While such a system probably doesn't make for great breath, it works incredibly well in digesting food!

Similarly, in meditation we initially digest God's Word and briefly chew it and swallow it. However, choosing to meditate on it—musing and muttering—causes us to bring it up again in our thoughts and "rechew" it, perhaps several times. In this manner our digestion of the Word of God continues over a period of time, rather than just during the few minutes we specifically set aside for the study and application of the Scriptures. Perhaps we continue to muse and mutter throughout the day while performing dozens of other tasks like showering, eating, driving, walking, or the repetitive jobs of work or home. In other words, we are intentionally letting the Word of God *abide in us,* as Jesus directed us to do in John 15:7-10.

When we make such choices, we are making the meditation on the fiery words of God a meaningful part of our day. This adds much more depth and soul-shaping to our interaction with the Scriptures. It forces us beyond superficially glossing over a passage of Scripture and gently leads us into profound interaction with the truth. God uses such choices to contour our minds and hearts to respond much more readily in tender obedience to the promptings of the Holy Spirit. Our abiding in His Word leads very wonderfully to our abiding in His love and in His commandments (John 15:7-10). Meditation should readily result in hearing God's voice and obeying His Word.

Eastern religions have long emphasized meditation as a practice that inhibits and allegedly transcends rational thought and carries the meditator into a state of ecstasy. Some of the Christian mystics after the biblical period share in this emphasis. Biblical meditation emphasizes *both the relational and rational interchange* between the believer and God. This is the highest, noblest, and most desirable experience for the worshiper! Biblical meditation is a personal, fully rational experience dependent on active contemplation, not on wandering reverie.

While the Old Testament (especially the Psalms) speaks of this purposeful concentration of the mind and mouth, there are no specific terms in the New Testament for meditation. However, the *concept of meditation* is clearly present. Perhaps the best example of this is Philippians 4:8-9, where Paul exhorts the church to ponder certain things with great intentionality and practice:

> Finally, brethren, whatever is true, whatever is honorable, whatever is right, whatever is pure, whatever is lovely, whatever is of good repute, if there is any excellence and if anything worthy of praise, *let your mind dwell on these things.* The things you have learned and received and heard and seen in me, *practice these things;* and the God of peace shall be with you. (NASB, emphasis mine)

Most certainly, Paul's emphasis includes the practice of meditation. In particular, his emphasis aligns with the Old Testament focus on the mental aspect of meditation. Such a focus aims at restructuring our thinking and contouring our minds to think more like our heavenly Father.

Lectio Divina, or Spiritual Reading

Lectio divina is the Latin phrase for the discipline of "spiritual reading"; it is the ancient and classical expression within the Christian church for what the Old Testament calls "meditation." Essentially, *lectio divina,* or spiritual reading, is defined as "a posture of approach and a means of encounter with a text that enables the text to become a place of transforming encounter with God."[3] This starts with the reading of the Bible, but has traditionally included other spiritual formation literature like the journals and writings of great believers. Generally, a balance between Scripture reading and the reading of classical formation writings is central to spiritual reading.[4] Because our focus is on the role of the Bible in the spiritual formation process, we will leave the important interaction with extrabiblical texts to others.

The classical practice of spiritual reading has traditionally included four elements:

- **Lectio** (reading)—We receive the information of the text before us and "taste" it.
- **Meditatio** (meditation)—We next begin processing the text's information by "chewing" it as we think about it and study it more deeply.
- **Oratio** (dialoguing)—Flowing out of our meditation is our personal dialogue with God about the text's meaning and our emotional response to it. Essentially, we are praying to God in a heartfelt dialogue about the text.
- **Contemplatio** (contemplation)—Lastly, we release our will to God by choosing to wait on His direction and will for us in light of the emphasis of the text.[5]

It should be immediately obvious from our prior discussion that the biblical concept of "meditation" essentially encompasses all four steps. After reading or hearing the Word of God (step 1), the believer then muses (step 2) and mutters (step 3) about the text. In all likelihood, the process of musing and muttering also includes contemplation (step 4)—musing encompasses it and muttering facilitates it. In other words, the biblical concept of meditation that we see modeled in the Psalms (for example, Psalm 143) is perfectly compatible with spiritual reading according to good interpretive principles.

My concerns about *lectio divina* are not about its theory. This is biblically solid and interpretively sound. Rather, my main concerns are in its practice. In particular, some use *lectio divina* to *pit the informational aspect of the text against the formational aspect.* I have strongly suggested that it is a both/and, not an either/or, proposition. We must have some informational basis even when we are primarily reading for formational purposes. We do not leave the informational aspects of the Bible behind and move into some higher, more spiritual plane when we seek formation, as many piously assume. Rather, we simply move from the informational intention of the Bible to the formational intention of the Bible. The Word of God has both intentions, and they are inextricably intertwined![6] God wants first to inform us and then transform us through the renewing of our mind. Neither purpose exists without attachment to the other. Otherwise, the information exists for its own, unspiritual end, or our spiritual formation becomes a mindless enterprise under the guise of mystical spirituality. Neither extreme could be further from the biblical emphasis![7]

A second major concern about the traditional practice of spiritual reading is the widespread tendency to pull every passage of the Bible through the interpretive keyhole of our spiritual formation. In other words, the premise is that every biblical passage exists *primarily* to tell me something helpful about myself that will foster *my* spiritual development. Now, this is true at one level, but it is false at another. At the micro level, every passage is not about us. In fact, most of the Bible is about God and His purposes in the world!

While at the macro level the Bible does tell us amazing things about ourselves, we must not run roughshod over the Book's great diversity of genres or types of literature with their dazzling variety of emphases and perspectives on God and us. We do the Bible a great disservice if we simply reduce its various genres to "insights about myself." The information about the Bible and within the Bible holds us accountable to read each genre as it was intended to be read. The result will not be less emphasis on spiritual formation, but rather a dizzying variety of emphases that have been previously misshaped by a wrongheaded interpretive keyhole. This is why it is worth improving our interpretive habits in the traditional practice of spiritual reading. The rest of this book is dedicated to this improvement.

In short, practicing *lectio divina* is an important spiritual discipline if it is appropriately tempered with good interpretive principles. In its historical practice, such has not always been the case. Therefore, one must tread carefully and wisely through the spiritual formation literature that espouses this discipline. Like eating fish, there is a lot of good meat in this literature, but there are some very large bones that wise believers will leave on their plates!

HOW DO I START MEDITATING?

In order to begin to meditate meaningfully on the Word of God, we must first work through the hindrances that tend to keep us from this discipline. The four major roadblocks that stop most of us from ever getting started are busyness, noise, other people, and general distraction. These hamper our specific focus on God and His Word.

Busyness. The need to be busy is so deeply ingrained in modern life that we hardly recognize it anymore. The tragic catch phrase, "Time is money," has robbed millions of the joy of not having to be doing something all the time. With all of our modern conveniences and "time savers," we are not less busy, but more so. This is why most Christians' immediate response is, "I don't have time to meditate!"[8]

Noise. This is a constant modern phenomenon. Even driving in your car is no haven from noise due to car radios, stereo systems, cell phones, pagers, and fax machines. What is the first thing you do when you get into your car? Turn on the radio or sound system? Like many of us, you may be noise-addicted. Meditation generally thrives in an environment of quietness.

Other people. While it is possible to meditate on God and His Word in the presence of other people, their presence makes meditation more difficult for those just getting started. However, like the little boy who was scared in his room at night, most of us prefer "someone with skin on"! Thus we let our need to be around others keep us from being with the One Other we meet in meditation and prayer. We settle for the skin-encased beings and sacrifice the Sacred One.

General distraction. Another characteristic of modern life, due to the busyness, noise, and constant interaction with other people, is general distraction. No wonder so many of us have trouble quieting our racing hearts and minds—we're overstimulated by our environment. This is why most Christians need to retreat to some kind of solitude and silent setting in order to calm their frenzied pulse and thoughts. Ability to concentrate in meditation will grow with practice. However, it demands that we begin to resist some of the frantic impulses of modern life that act as anesthesia to many of life's pains.

Anyone who has done much meditating knows it is impossible to separate this discipline from the study of the Word of God. This is why Dallas Willard discusses meditation within his explanation of the spiritual discipline of *study*.[9] Meditating on the Scriptures really does begin during the process of studying a passage and seeking first to understand its meaning and then to appreciate its relevance or significance to us. Interwoven with the study of the biblical text is the persistent question, "What is God saying in this passage and how does this relate to my life?" The discipline of meditation has already begun! We are on our way.

Additionally, I have found the following principles and practices helpful in fostering fruitful and meaningful meditation on the Scriptures.

1. Schedule a block of time for study and meditation. Fifteen minutes will not suffice! Better to have a two-hour block for study one day a week and then spend the next six days meditating on your insights than to have a superficial fifteen minutes seven days a week. Don't let the form of your "quiet time" negate the function of meditation!

2. After studying a passage and pondering it for a bit at your place of study (your desk or table), take a walk. I find that walking helps me deal with the hindrances of busyness, noise, other people, and general distraction. I can focus more clearly. I can begin to talk to God about the passage. I ask Him things like: "What does this mean?" "How are these points related?" "How can this be true in light of this or that?" "If this is what it says, what should I be doing in response to it?" I also talk to the Lord about the idea of the passage and praise Him, or express my love for Him in light of the truth, or confess

my sin due to being convicted by the passage, or even whine if I don't like how the truth pinches me!

3. While walking, I may stop and ponder the great truths before me or mutter about them or just walk in silence. All these responses are part of the discipline of meditation. Meditation is ruminating or digesting a part of God's revelation to us. It is getting the Word of God into the deepest recesses of our being. It is letting the fiery Word of God form the character of Christ in us.

PART TWO

Igniting
Changes in
Your Soul

Chapter Five

GOD'S PLAN: OLD TESTAMENT NARRATIVES

Now the LORD said to Abram,
"Go forth from your country,
And from your relatives
And from your father's house,
To the land I will show you;
And I will make you a great nation,
And I will bless you,
And make your name great;
And so you shall be a blessing;
And I will bless those who bless you,
And the one who curses you I will curse.
And in you all the families of the earth shall be blessed."

GENESIS 12:1-3

And as for you, you meant evil against me, but God meant it for
good in order to bring about this present result, to preserve many
people alive.

GENESIS 50:20

The aim of spiritual maturity is to magnify God's glory for people
to see and admire.

JOHN PIPER[1]

FOLLOW WITH ME AS I RECOUNT THE LEAD STORIES FROM THIS morning's newspaper. A large passenger jet crashed off the coast of Nova Scotia and killed all 229 people on board. The final sixteen minutes, from the time smoke began to fill the cabin until the plane fragmented with terrifying impact in the Atlantic, must have been horrifying. Mixed with this tragic loss of life is the news of hurricanes and tropical storms in various parts of the United States that also killed several people.

In another front-page story, a leader in the U.S. Senate rebuked the president for "immoral behavior" and for the tragic moral modeling that his actions have been for all Americans, especially children. Added to this are the ongoing economic crises in Asia and Latin America and another economic meltdown in Russia. Consequently, the American stock market has dropped like a rock over the last week and the usual fears about a possible economic recession have arisen. Investors are running scared, and the evening news is headlining how much money people are losing as the stock market plummets.

I could go on, but you get the idea. We face unexpected tragedies due to mechanical failures or weather eruptions. Recurring moral and management failures of leaders around the world fuel political and economic disasters. People's lives are shattered as their countries are destabilized and their money becomes worthless. The question for many of us quickly becomes: "Is God really in control or does chaos reign?" Can we have confidence that God is sovereign and trustworthy, even in the midst of immediate tragedy, incomprehensible suffering, the moral dysfunction of our leaders, and accelerating economic and political crises? Who is in control?

OUR PLAN OR GOD'S?

These kinds of questions flow from the lips of a people that has focused almost exclusively on personal fulfillment and happiness. Many of us relate to suffering and tragedy by asking, "How is this going to affect me and my quest for happiness?" Not only do we relate to the events of life in this manner, but this is also how we view our spiritual formation: We see our formation in Christ as simply a means to be a self-fulfilled, individual Christian. We subsume it under our grander plan for achieving happiness. And we then approach the Bible seeking reinforcement and encouragement that God will help us fulfill *our plan* for our lives.

We addressed this very Western, existential "pair of glasses" in chapter 1. The Word of God really does confront and challenge this distorted view of life. Even though existential thinking remains widespread and may contain truthful aspects, it is still essentially a wrong view of the world, morally and spiritually defective. In its place the Scriptures advocate a pair of glasses that looks like the following:

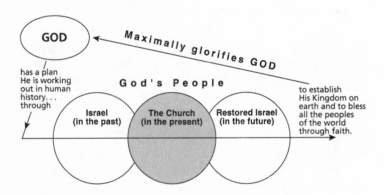

At the very heart of this pair of worldview glasses is the fact that God is sovereign and in control of history. Not only is He all-powerful and all-knowing about the events of history, He is also initiating and working out *His plan* for human history. How do we know this? And how can we know that He is intimately involved in the events we humans experience?

Here the narratives and histories of the Old Testament shed valuable light. These biblical books declare in story after story and event after event that God is the shaper of history. He is not removed, nor uninvolved, nor silent. He is not surprised by human choices or mortal actions. He is ultimately in control of this world and the next. Additionally, God does have both a sense and a scenario as to where history is going and where it will end. He ordained it; He planned it; He will bring it to the completion and fruition that He desires. How do we know this? Because the narratives of the Old Testament are brimming with such truths. The biblical books of Genesis, most of Exodus, most of Numbers, Joshua, Judges, Ruth, 1 and 2 Samuel, 1 and 2 Kings, 1 and 2 Chronicles, Ezra, and Nehemiah establish God's heroic involvement in history. Additionally, the prophetic books Daniel, Jonah, and Haggai are primarily narratives, along with large portions of Isaiah, Jeremiah, and Ezekiel, and the poetic book Job. All or parts of these twenty-one Old Testament books underscore the intentional and purposeful involvement of God in human history for over two thousand years.[2]

Moreover, in the narratives and histories of the Old Testament, God co-labors with His people through events far worse than those in the morning paper. For example, consider the catastrophic loss of life, moral crises, political turmoil, and consequent economic collapse connected with the fall of Jerusalem in 2 Kings 25 (or Jeremiah 34–39). How bad did it get? Listen to Jeremiah's grievous account of the moral and economic depths to which God's people had fallen in Lamentations 4:10-12:

> The hands of compassionate women
> Boiled their own children;
> They became food for them
> Because of the destruction of the daughter of my people.
> The LORD has accomplished His wrath,
> He has poured out His fierce anger;
> And He has kindled a fire in Zion
> Which has consumed its foundations.
> The kings of the earth did not believe,
> Nor did any of the inhabitants of the world,
> That the adversary and the enemy
> Could enter the gates of Jerusalem.

We can be confident that God is working out a plan in human history because only a divine plan could survive the catastrophic collapse and exile of God's people! Only a supernatural plan could rebuild a people devastated by such horrific events. Only a God-ordained plan in history could give meaning to such malevolent and terrifying evils as Jeremiah recounts in Lamentations. It is this plan of God that the Old Testament narratives and histories record.

Finally, God's plan for history is, at its core, a plan to bless, not curse, the people of planet earth. It is obvious from the very beginning of His plan, in Genesis 1–2, that His primary purpose in creating humans as co-rulers of the earth with Him is so He can bless our lives rather than blight them. God makes this a definitive part of the account of creation in Genesis 1:27-31, which asserts that we are created in God's image and blessed to subdue and have dominion over all the earth's plants and creatures.

One wonders whether God could have possibly graced our existence any more than by creating us in His own image to rule over the earth *with Him.* What honored and privileged creatures we are! However, sin entered the idyllic setting of the Garden of Eden, and history took a painful and distorted turn. Although God's ultimate purpose of blessing and not cursing was still intact, such blessing would now have to be mediated through the seed of woman (Genesis 3:15). More specifically, after the Flood, the One who would bring the blessing and negate the cursing would also have to come from the seed of Noah through his son Shem (9:26). Even more specifically, within the line of Shem and several hundred years later, God would focus the line of blessing through the descendant of Shem named Abram (11:10-32).

This leads us to one of the most important passages in the Bible for spiritual formation. In Genesis 12:1-3 God promises blessing to Abram (later Abraham) in the form of a covenant He makes with him. Note the three very significant, far-reaching aspects of God's covenantal promise to Abram involving *land, seed,* and *blessing:*

Now the LORD said to Abram,
"Go forth from your country,
And from your relatives
And from your father's house,

■ To the land which I will show you;

■ And I will make you a great nation, and I will bless you,
and make your name great;

■ And so you shall be a blessing; and I will bless those
who bless you, and the one who curses you I will curse.
And in you all the families of the earth shall be blessed."[3]

The passage is significant because it reveals the specific means
and the specific focus of God's blessing now that sin has entered
the world. Through the seed of Abram/Abraham, God will mediate
His blessing to the peoples of the world. This blessing will be universal in focus in that it is intended to reach down to the level of
"families" (literally *tribes* or *ethnic groups*). That is, through the
seed of Abraham God will pass on His blessing to every different
ethnic group in the world. All are in God's focus for His blessing.

In our lives we must realize that our spiritual formation should
relate *directly* to the plan God is working out in history through the
seed of Abraham. Regarding our time on earth, we can say that this
blessing of all peoples is in some meaningful way God's plan for
our lives. We must connect purposefully to His agenda for human
beings if we are to be obedient to Him. While the New Testament
greatly clarifies this connection, the Old Testament narratives and
histories record its beginning in history and God's structuring of the
agenda. As the spiritual seed of Abraham (Galatians 3), we new
covenant believers are privileged to co-labor with God in His
ancient plan of blessing all the peoples of the world when they exercise faith in Him through Jesus Christ. We have been blessed in
order to be a blessing to the world.

SPIRITUALLY FORMED BY NARRATIVES AND HISTORIES

Almost everyone loves a good story. Is this why about half of the
Bible is narrative literature? Quite simply, to understand at least half
of the Bible we must grasp the nature of this genre and how God

wants to use these remarkable stories in our lives. If the Bible is a critical catalyst of our formation into the likeness of Jesus Christ, then the sheer volume of the narratives and histories indicates they are pivotal to this function. Our spiritual formation, remember, occurs within the boundaries of God's plan for the world, which the narratives and histories declare. But our formation in Christ could easily become self-serving or narcissistic without the parameters of God's concerns and emphases in human history. That is, if our spiritual formation is to please God, then it must be according to the historical emphases that *God* has chosen!

Therefore, we need to read and interpret well the genre of narratives and histories in order to enjoy the formational intentions that God has given them. This entails understanding three crucial aspects of this genre of biblical literature.

The Three Levels of Narratives and Histories

As numerous literary experts have noted, there are three levels to the narratives of the Bible. At the lowest level are *stories of particular individuals* who create the history of Israel in the Old Testament and of the church in the New Testament. Most Western readers never get past this level of understanding. This is unfortunate because in a very real sense this is the least important level of the narratives. It certainly has been the least interesting to most readers/hearers throughout history because of their cultures' group orientation and the emphasis in most societies on group identity.

This is why the middle level is more important, in that it focuses on *the story of God's people,* Israel and the church. This level tells us who we really are as God's people and what our history and heritage are as the children of God.

However, it is at the top level that we experience the greatest insight into our identity and God's purposes. At this level the stories of the Bible express *the eternal plan God is working out universally.* Understanding biblical narratives at this level means comprehending what God is doing in human history and the plan He is working out through the lives of His people. This level underscores that God, not the individual, is the decisive focus of the narratives and that, ultimately, these stories reveal *His plan* for our lives.

If we read the Old Testament narratives and histories concentrating primarily on the stories of individuals as models for us, then we glean a *secondary emphasis* from this immense part of the Bible. This emphasis is not bad, but it is still secondary! Why not fix our attention on the *primary thrust* of this exciting genre, the level of *God's* strategy for His people and His universal plan for history? Such a focus gives us a more accurate and balanced setting that *encompasses* our focus on individuals. However, to read the Old Testament histories and narratives only as stories about individuals distorts them at a substantive level.

The Three Narrative Levels

■ **Top Level** = *The eternal, universal plan of God* (most important for understanding life)

■ **Middle Level** = *The story of God's people* (most important for identity and heritage)

■ **Lowest Level** = *The stories of individuals* (important in offering models)

While this may not satisfy Western readers, it is absolutely essential to developing a biblical worldview and a Christian perspective of history. Therefore, we should not lament what we lose with a focus on God and His people, but glory in what we gain! Without such an understanding of God's plan and our identity and role within it, we default to secular perceptions of the world and human-centered conceptions of historical events. While we may spread a thin Christian veneer over these secular interpretations, they remain, at their core, human-centered and ultimately self-serving.

How does this change in focus help us read this part of God's Word better? Grasping two more aspects of this genre will help answer this question.

GOD IS THE HERO!

We all need heroes. The rigors of life often demand that we draw strength and encouragement from the men and women of life and literature who have exceptional qualities and have made exceptional choices. Who can estimate the remarkable inspiration provided by contemporary heroes like Mother Teresa or missionary martyr Jim Elliot? Or how many millions have been strengthened by the lives of Francis of Assisi or Teresa of Ávila or Martin Luther? It is no wonder that we gravitate to the accounts of individual heroes in the Old and New Testaments—they play an important role in our lives. I am not attempting to diminish that role, but rather, like so many things, I simply want to place the role of human heroes within an accurate biblical framework.

Our Western cultural worldview causes us to see primarily individuals in the biblical narratives. When we do this, we make two mistakes. *First, we look at them as models of how a believer should behave, and we imitate their choices.* The scary thing about this is that God and the human author of the narrative may not have intended to commend them to us as sterling examples! Rather, their story may simply have been included to make a broader point about God or His people.

We have long followed the example of Gideon laying out an animal's fleece to determine what God's will is in a certain situation (Judges 6:36-40). We call it "putting out a fleece." This means that if God does something special in whatever area we are testing Him, that must reveal His will for us in that situation, just as it did for Gideon. However, if we use this method of determining God's will for our life, then we ourselves may have been fleeced! Why? Because Gideon's example of laying out a fleece two different times in response to God's call to him to lead Israel against her enemies was actually an expression of the weakness and frailty of his faith! It was a statement of Gideon's *unbelief*, not his faith in God. It is probably included in the narrative of Judges to show that *God* is really the hero of the story, not Gideon. The details of the story corroborate this: the number of soldiers was whittled down from thirty-two thousand to three hundred; the battle was effectively won with trumpets and empty jars, not swords. Both emphasize it was God's victory, not Gideon's. God accomplished the victory *despite* the leadership of Gideon, who had only a tentative, wavering faith in the Lord. At one level, Gideon's frailties encourage us that God can use weaklings to accomplish His purposes. However, the fleece accounts are likely included to help document God's greatness in light of Israel's weakness in dealing with her enemies during the unbelief of the judges' period. Therefore, when we overindividualize the narrative, we ironically miss the main point (God's character and actions) and actually end up applying the opposite point (using fleeces) in our spiritual formation!

A second mistake we regularly make is overpersonalizing Old Testament narratives and histories. Again, this takes us away from recognizing the emphasis on God being the Hero of the narrative. In His place we put ourselves—it seems so natural to think the thrust of the history or narrative is to give us some insight about ourselves. For example, when Gideon puts out the fleece, we usually think the purpose of this story is to tell us how we can determine God's will for *our* lives. We leap without blinking from God, Gideon, and Israel's deadly struggle with the unbelieving Midianites and Amalekites to our lives and how we can know God's leading! We take a nonhistorical approach to an historical passage. While this story, and every other one in the Bible, has significant relevance to our lives, none of them is directly about us! Rather, the narratives and histories of the Old Testament are about how God dealt with His old covenant people, Israel. From these dealings we can learn about who God is and how He may want to deal with us, His new covenant people. *But before we can leap to the significance of the story for us, we must understand the meaning of the story for them!* Personalizing the biblical account too quickly destroys this progression from meaning to significance. Also, we lose the biblical text's emphasis on God as the Hero of the narrative.

IT'S BEST TO TAKE BIG BITES!

One last point about spiritual formation when reading Old Testament histories and narratives: *we should emphasize the*

broader sweep, the larger chunks, of the narrative, rather than looking primarily at individual units. But this is common sense, isn't it?
Is there any other way to understand a story than to read the whole
story? Why should a narrative in the Bible be any different in nature
from any other narrative?

By reading all of a narrative we can identify the repeated
emphases and the recurring theme. Authors of histories and narratives use repetition to communicate the central message and main
points of the whole story. It's simply logical that the things that are
most important to the author will keep surfacing in various forms
throughout the whole account. These recurrences should therefore
be our main focus. It is these points in a biblical narrative like the
book of Judges that should be emphasized and highlighted.

The author of Judges has structured a very clear pattern of
recurring cycles within Israel's history at this time:

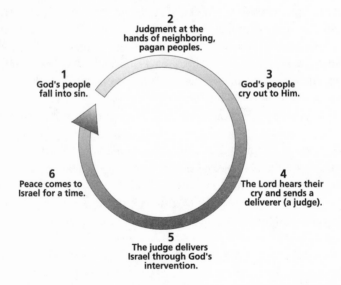

By the time we get to Judges 6–8 and the deliverance by
Gideon, this pattern has occurred five times already, and we are well
prepared to note what is important in the individual story about
Gideon. But we had to read Judges 1–5 to develop the vision to see

what was most important to God and the human author. Such is the nature of a narrative.

Concentrating on the larger units also delivers us from a couple common application errors of this genre. One of the most common, with a long and checkered past, is the allegorizing of narrative passages. Allegorizing is an interpretive approach that finds another meaning beyond the literal, historical meaning of the passage. When we hear an interpreter say something like, "Now, the ten plagues represent problems in our lives" or "The storms on the Sea of Galilee represent the storms of life," we can know that the biblical text has been allegorized or spiritualized. The interpreter is looking for meaning and applications that are over, above, and beyond the literal, historical meaning of the text. When the meaning of a text is taken out of its community-oriented pond that we discussed in chapter 3, then the meaning has been privatized and individualized. It is no longer equally accessible to all of us, but primarily controlled by the interpreter.

An error similar to allegorizing is the moralizing or principlizing of a narrative or history. This is the attempt by the interpreter to find "the moral of the story" or "some biblical principles" that God is allegedly teaching in the narrative passage. Both moralizing and principlizing do great harm to the very nature of narratives and histories. Fee and Stuart speak insightfully to such harm: "The fallacy of this approach is that it ignores the fact that the narratives were written to show the progress of God's history of redemption, not to illustrate principles. They are historical narratives, not illustrative narratives."[4]

Therefore, we should look for how an individual narrative functions within the broader narrative or history to advance the recurring points or main themes of the story, rather than seeking to find morals or embedded principles within the passage before us. This means that we shouldn't be searching for principles for success in our personal lives or business dealings that God has allegedly placed within Old Testament narratives or histories! Rather, these "principles" or "morals" may simply be incidental historical aspects of the narrative. They do not represent the things God wants us to glean from the narrative, but instead are a step removed from discovering His true intentions. Taking such a step may certainly be counterproductive to our spiritual formation.

Let's summarize the main concerns of this chapter. Old Testament narratives and histories are prominent in the Word of God, covering all or part of twenty-one books of this Testament. Simply by volume, this part of the Bible is weighty and crucial. But the foundational contribution of this genre of Scripture makes it doubly important.

THE SPECIFIC CONTRIBUTION OF OLD TESTAMENT NARRATIVES AND HISTORIES TO OUR SPIRITUAL FORMATION

■ **The Biblical Books:** Genesis, most of Exodus, most of Numbers, Joshua, Judges, Ruth, 1 and 2 Samuel, 1 and 2 Kings, 1 and 2 Chronicles, Ezra, and Nehemiah. Additionally, the prophetic books Daniel, Jonah, and Haggai are primarily narratives, along with large portions of Isaiah, Jeremiah, and Ezekiel, and the poetic book Job.

■ **Primary Contribution:** To inform and shape our worldveiw about the eternal plan that God is working out universally in human history and also to underscore our continuity with the children of Israel as the people of God.

> **Therefore, ask,** "What does this passage tell us about God (the Hero), His plan, or the role that His people should be playing in His plan?

■ **Secondary Contribution:** To give us positive and negative models of old covenant believers making choices to trust God.

> **Therefore, ask,** "What positive or negative model might this passage be setting before us to teach us about trusting God in the midst of His plan?"

Spiritually Formed by a Narrative: David Versus Goliath

Few Old Testament narratives are as well known and well loved as slingshot-bearing David confronting heavily armed Goliath in 1 Samuel 17. I think of the young underdog toppling the giant opponent as I stare at the glass bowl on my desk containing five small stones from the actual *wadi* (riverbed) where David defeated Goliath. Rumor has it that the Israeli Department of Tourism regularly replenishes the rocks in this little creek bed for visitors like me! However, in spite of this, those rocks and this story are incredibly inspiring.

In addition to stirring the imaginations of the young, how did *God* and the human author Samuel *intend this account to be used* to help form the spiritual identity and confidence of the people of God? Perhaps a bit of the context of 1 Samuel may help us answer this question:

- Chapters 1–8 — The focus is on the early life and prophetic ministry of Samuel.
- Chapter 9 — God reluctantly gives Israel the king they "asked for" (this is what "Saul" means in Hebrew).
- Chapters 9–31 — Saul is officially king but is rejected by God in chapter 15.
- Chapters 16–31 — Young David is anointed Israel's king (chapter 16), yet serves Saul until his death (chapter 31).

This sets the table for 1 Samuel 17 and the confrontation between the army of the Philistines (coming from the Mediterranean coast) and the army of Israel, coming from Gibeah, the capital of Israel (three miles north of Jerusalem). These armies meet in the foothills of western Israel, about eighteen miles southwest of Jerusalem. First Samuel 17:1-3 tells us that the Philistines arrayed for battle on the south side of the valley and the Israelites gathered on the north side. From here the story is a familiar, well-told drama.

The Philistine champion, a giant of a man named Goliath of Gath, came out every morning and evening for forty days and taunted the army of Israel with the challenge to send out a man to fight him. The rules of the challenge were painfully simple and straightforward. Whichever man came out the loser, that man's people would be servants to the winner's people. This was truly a winner-take-all contest! However, Goliath got no takers from Israel because "when Saul and all Israel heard these words of the Philistine, they were dismayed and greatly afraid" (verse 11).

Into this forty-day, fear-filled standoff steps young David. He hears Goliath's evening taunt and sees the men of Israel flee with great fear (verse 24). After hearing about King Saul's great reward for the Israelite who kills Goliath, David asks, "What will be done for the man who kills this Philistine, *and takes away the reproach from Israel? For who is this uncircumcised Philistine, that he should taunt the armies of the living God?*" (verse 26, emphasis mine).

David then quickly volunteers to fight Goliath, even though his status among these warriors and in Saul's eyes is that of "a youth" (verse 33; note Goliath's same assessment of him in verse 42). In order to get the job, David then recounts his history of trusting God when he herded his family's sheep and was able to kill a lion and a bear (verses 34-35). Note his application to Goliath:

> "Your servant has killed both the lion and the bear; *and this uncircumcised Philistine will be like one of them, since he has taunted the armies of the living God.*" And David said, *"The LORD who delivered me from the paw of the lion and from the paw of the bear, He will deliver me from the hand of this Philistine."* (verses 36-37, emphasis mine)

Of course, this incident has a happy ending (for David!), as he kills Goliath and Israel routs the Philistines, chasing and killing them as far as Gath (ten miles due west) and Ekron (fourteen miles northwest) (verse 52). Goliath's severed head ends up in Jerusalem with David (verse 54), and his heroic status in Israel is established forever (18:6-7). However, the question we now need to ask is the one we asked earlier: *What does this passage tell us about God (the Hero), His plan, or the role His people should be playing in His plan?* This question will take us to the heart of God's and Samuel's intentions in this narrative for our formation as God's people.

First Samuel 17 displays once again that God has a plan that

He is working out in history to bless His people. God wanted Israel to possess all the land that He gave them, but Israel had to trust Him in order to accomplish this task. Some four hundred years after they entered the land under Joshua's leadership (Joshua 3), they were still struggling in their obedience to God's plan and missing out on His heroic enabling of them to accomplish the plan. However, in this regard, David stands in stark contrast to his own brothers, the army of Israel, and certainly Saul. This narrative underscores David's faith in facing Goliath, and he is certainly admirable and a wonderful model for us to imitate (the secondary contribution of narratives and histories). However, as David himself realizes, his faith and his accomplishment point to *God as the Hero* of the narrative. Note his words just before he killed Goliath:

> Then David said to the Philistine, "You come to me with a sword, a spear, and a javelin, *but I come to you in the name of the LORD of hosts, the God of the armies of Israel, whom you have taunted. This day the LORD will deliver you up into my hands,* and I will strike you down and remove your head from you. And I will give the dead bodies of the army of the Philistines this day to the birds of the sky and the wild beasts of the earth, *that all the earth may know that there is a God in Israel, and that all this assembly may know that the LORD does not deliver by sword or by spear; for the battle is the LORD's and He will give you into our hands."* (17:45-47, emphasis mine)

David's marvelous defeat of Goliath gives us a remarkable model of a faith-filled old covenant believer and what he could accomplish through great trust in the God of Israel. But by now you should recognize that this is only looking at the narrative at the level of the individual, the lowest level. At the middle level, the story of God's people, it shows us how rare such faith is among God's people. Not only was God's army paralyzed by fear, but Saul, its leader, was trying to buy a victory by promising financial incentives to anyone who would fight the enemy! What a contrast to this young, faith-filled man who cared passionately about the honor and name of God. No wonder God had recently rejected Saul (1 Samuel 15) and anointed David (1 Samuel 16). David was enraged that a pagan would taunt God and His people without being punished! His passion for God's honor drove him to defend that honor in word and deed. This is what God expects His people to do. And it is a task that He deems *us* capable of doing and a task that He will greatly honor!

However, it is at the top level of the narrative that we get the glimpse into the eternal, universal plan of God. At stake in David's confrontation with Goliath is not just a battle between two champions. Nor is it just a battle between Israel and a pagan neighbor, whom she must oust from the land. Rather, raging in and through and over and above David and Goliath and Israel and the Philistines was the battle with the objective "that all the earth may know that there is a God in Israel" (17:46). This is the ultimate battle that was raging, and David had spiritually discerning eyes to see this warfare that Saul and his armies did not.

How did David understand so clearly what God was doing in the world and what God expected His people to do? We cannot say for sure, but David had likely saturated his heart and mind with the narratives and histories of Genesis to Joshua.

Chapter Six

GOOD BOUNDARIES, GOOD NEIGHBORS: THE LAW

"Now then, if you will indeed obey My voice and keep My covenant, then you shall be My own possession among all the peoples, for all the earth is Mine; and you shall be to Me a kingdom of priests and a holy nation."

EXODUS 19:5-6

A COUPLE YEARS AGO MY WIFE AND I ATTENDED THE WEDDING of a friend. It was a lovely, Christ-centered ceremony. It was obvious throughout the service that the couple was trying to make a meaningful statement about the centrality of their relationship with Jesus Christ. This rather long ceremony reached a lively climax when the pastor read a "Blessing of the Marriage" from Deuteronomy 28:2-14. He selected a series of verses in this passage that promised many diverse, juicy blessings "if you will obey the LORD your God" (verse 2). For example, they would be blessed in the city and in the country (verse 3); blessed would be the offspring of their body, the produce of the ground, the offspring of their beasts, the increase of their herd, and the young of their flock (verse 4); blessed would be their basket and kneading bowl (verse 5); blessed would they be when they come in and when they go out (verse 6); and so on. This well-meaning and good-hearted pastor promised that all the blessings enumerated in this passage would be given to this young couple if they would but obey the Lord.

I was so fascinated by this use of the Deuteronomy passage that I just had to take out a pew Bible and read it for myself. As I sat there and grappled with the theological implications of applying this passage in this manner, I could not resist turning to my wife, Marty, and whispering in her ear, "Don't you think it seems only fair to announce the curses, including exile, that the Lord promised if they *don't obey Him* in the rest of this chapter?" As my wife turned and gave me one of her don't-be-such-a-bore smiles, it struck me that ending a wedding ceremony with a "Cursing of the Marriage" would not be a thoughtful thing to do!

However, this does raise an important point about how we apply the Mosaic Law in our lives as new covenant believers. Is it appropriate, even desirable, to use a passage from the Old Testament Law that promises blessings (and curses!) to God's people Israel? Are these blessings and curses still in effect with believers in Christ? Is this the way we should read the Law of the Old Testament? How *do* we apply this part of God's Word to our lives?

But this raises another issue that many of us also have to grapple with in our lives. The mere mention of the word *law* strikes an emotional cord, even terror, in the hearts of some of us. Or we think:

How can there possibly be any value in a part of the Bible that is restrictive by its very nature? How can reading a legal code, some laws, be interesting or helpful to us as Christians—especially if the laws were given to govern someone else? Anyway, wouldn't reading "Law" feed my weakness toward legalism? If I already have a bad attitude toward authority, won't reading a bunch of laws just pour gasoline on the fire? These are some of our more honest responses to the part of the Bible called *Law.*

THE PURPOSE OF THE LAW

It will take meaningful understanding to get past these negative responses to the four Old Testament books that fit the genre of Law: Exodus, Leviticus, Numbers, and Deuteronomy.[1] First, we have to understand that the Law is really *the covenant or relational agreement* that God made with Israel at Mount Sinai after He delivered her from four hundred years of bondage in Egypt. Therefore, the laws are not to be viewed as a comprehensive legal code.

Instead, they present a select sample of illustrative cases or topics whose legal principles were to serve as a guide to Israel. Their purpose was to teach the Israelites fundamental values, not to provide them with a handy legal reference tool. In short, their aim was instructional rather than judicial.[2]

In addition to this relational and instructional purpose, the Law provided the internal structure for the nation of Israel and functioned as her constitution. From this perspective, the Law was to give the Israelites objective standards as both worshipers and citizens so that they would have good personal boundaries with one another. However, even more importantly, it was to empower Israel to have good national boundaries in order to be good neighbors to the peoples of the world. God tells them as much in Exodus 19:5-6:

"Now then, if you will indeed obey My voice and keep My covenant, then you shall be My own possession among all the peoples, for all the earth is Mine; and you shall be to Me a kingdom of priests and a holy nation."

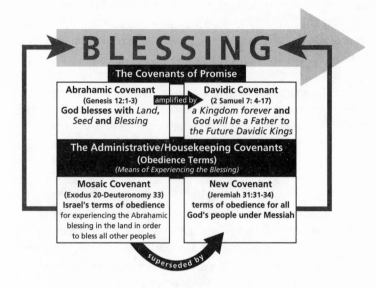

By obeying the covenant or Law, Israel would live out her calling as the descendants of Abraham who were to be the means of God's blessing of all the peoples of the world (Genesis 12:1-3; 13:14-17; 15:1-6,7-21; 17:1-21; 22:15-19). The Law was to be the *administrative* or *housekeeping covenant* that structured Israel's daily walk with God and her behavior in the world.[3] While all Israelites were saved by grace through faith in God alone (just as we are under the new covenant; see Romans 4:13), they were to express their life of faith in faithfulness to the Law and in obedient living according to the Law's objective standards. In a very real sense, the Law was Israel's guide to spiritual formation. It provided instruction for the formation of Israelites in almost every area of life. Some divide this formational guidance into five distinct areas: criminal law, civil law, family law, cultic or religious law, and charitable law.[4] In each of these areas, the Mosaic Law guided Israelites each day by giving the covenantal terms of their obedience by which they could enjoy the blessings of the Abrahamic covenant.

While there are at least five distinct *categories* of law or terms of covenantal obedience in the Mosaic Law, most scholars recognize only two *kinds* of law here. This distinction should help us read the

Law for spiritual formation. First, there is *apodictic law.* This is "absolute law," or law that states a command or prohibition in a categorical or unconditional manner. This type of law tends to fit most people's stereotype of law in the Bible. For example, all of the Ten Commandments are apodictic law in that they state absolute commands about right and wrong with no exceptions: "You shall have no other gods before Me." "Remember the sabbath day, to keep it holy." "Honor your father and mother. . . ." This kind of law also includes the absolute statements about certain crimes that deserve absolute penalties. For example, there are laws that prohibit disrespect or abuse of parents: "And he who strikes his father or his mother shall surely be put to death" (Exodus 21:15); "And he who curses his father or his mother shall surely be put to death" (Exodus 21:17). Apodictic laws give us the most direct understanding of God's heart and His standards of holiness. They are straightforward, blunt, and definitive in their focus. God reveals His righteousness in unblinking fashion in this kind of law.

The second type of law found here is *casuistic law,* or case law. This law is easily recognizable by its "If A, then B" grammatical structure. In these laws God gives His people representative and illustrative examples of case law in which they could see righteous and just principles at work and thus make just judgments not only in cases like the examples, but also in similar instances. For example, the following casuistic law is instructive about the protection of a baby in the womb:

> And if men struggle with each other and strike a woman with child so that she has a miscarriage, yet there is no further injury [that is, she delivers a live baby], he shall surely be fined as the woman's husband may demand of him; and he shall pay as the judges decide. But if there is any further injury [that is, she delivers a dead baby], then you shall appoint as a penalty life for life, eye for eye, tooth for tooth, hand for hand, foot for foot, burn for burn, wound for wound, bruise for bruise. (Exodus 21:22-25)

This example appeals to the *lex talionis,* or law of retaliation, which refers to the broad legal principle of equal penalty or injury.

In this case, injury to the child demands that equivalent injury be wrought on the person who caused it. Such an example is representative of a broad legal principle to apply in cases involving injury to children before their birth. While not as categorical or unconditional as apodictic law, casuistic law still gives us a remarkable insight into heaven's view of justice and righteousness. At a principle level, this expression of God's heart and concern for the protection of the pre-born is a primary factor undergirding the modern struggle against abortion.

For mature Old Testament believers, the Mosaic Law was the greatest thing God ever gave Israel. It was God's particular gift of grace that made them special and set them apart from other peoples. It was the written proof that Israel was unique to God and had a distinctive function among all the peoples of the world (see Exodus 19:5-6). The Law was considered such a wonderful expression of the grace of God that a whole psalm (song), Psalm 119, was written about it—176 verses that praise the wonders of God's Law and reveal the heart of a people who love the Law given them by a gracious God.

Such a positive view of the Mosaic Law may strike you as contradictory to the negative assessment given it in the New Testament. For example, the apostle Paul pictures the Mosaic Law primarily as Israel's "jailer" and "tutor" (or "baby-sitter") in Galatians 3:22-24. Add to this Paul's statements about the Mosaic Law having primarily a *sin-revealing purpose* in Romans 3:19-20, 5:20, and 7:12-13, and we quickly arrive at a negative valuation of the Law in the New Testament.

How do we reconcile the Old Testament's praise of the Mosaic Law with the New Testament's emphasis on its limitations? Two points of clarification should help resolve this tension. First, when God's people only had the Mosaic Law during the old covenant era, they thought it was wonderful because, at the time, there was no better covenant with God. For example, if the only car I know and have ever seen or driven is a thirty-year-old, beat-up Chevrolet, I will consider it the most wonderful car in the world. But if you give me a new Mercedes sports car, I will realize there are nicer vehicles to drive than my old Chevy. You have expanded my horizons and my categories of what a car is.

The same is true of Israel. From the time of Moses, all that the children of Israel knew was life under the old covenant, which they entered into at Mount Sinai (see Exodus 19:7-8). Therefore, they cherished it and praised it, even in their songs. It was their old Chevy. However, when the Mercedes arrived and the new covenant era began at the Messiah's death, then a new standard was set (see Galatians 4:1-7). The main argument of the epistle to the Hebrews is that Jesus brought a new covenant that was better than all elements of the old covenant (Mosaic Law). Therefore, why would anyone want to revert to a surpassed covenant that is wanting by comparison?

A second reason for the negative statements about the Mosaic Law in the New Testament is due to the threats from Judaism to the early believers in Jesus as Messiah. Certain Jewish believers tried to foist the practices of the Jewish sect of the Pharisees onto the Gentile believers in the church, and this created the dynamic theological problems that Paul addresses in Galatians and Romans. Paul launches polemical (argumentative) attacks on those who overstate the role of the Law in the life of Jesus' followers. He makes primarily strong, negative statements about the Law in order to undercut the Pharisaic (Judaistic) overemphasis on the Law. In fairness to Paul and the Law itself, these strong statements in Galatians and Romans are not his full "Law theology." For slightly different reasons, we should also balance the similar negative statements in Hebrews. While the Mosaic Law is clearly superseded, it is not negative and bad. Rather, it has been fulfilled and accomplished in Jesus the Messiah (see Matthew 5:17-18).

CHRISTIANS' RELATIONSHIP TO THE LAW

We need to understand that the Mosaic Law is God's relational covenant with the ethnic nation of Israel. However, in part, because God now has a multiethnic church transcending a one-ethnicity nation, He has replaced this covenant with His new covenant (see

Jeremiah 31:31-34; Ezekiel 36:24-27). Therefore, is the Law binding for us new covenant believers today? If so, how is it binding? And if not, is it still the Word of God for us and of any edifying value to us as Christians?

To the first question, "Is the Mosaic Law binding for us today?" we can say, "No, it is not, *as a whole law.*" Numerous statements in the New Testament make this very clear. Granted, a few parts of the Law have been repeated or renewed in the new covenant, and these parts are clearly binding (for example, "Honor your mother and father" in Ephesians 6:2-3). But as an historical entity expressing God's will for ethnic Israel, the covenantal authority of the Mosaic Law has ended.[5] The following New Testament passages bluntly state that those who are in Christ are "not under the Law": Galatians 3:17-25; 5:18; Romans 6:14; 7:4-6. Moreover, 2 Corinthians 3, Acts 15:1-29, and Hebrews 7:11-12 emphasize the change from the covenant of the Law to the new covenant.

Additionally, the New Testament is very clear that the Mosaic Law has been *personalized in Jesus Christ:* "Christ is *the end* of the law for righteousness to everyone who believes" (Romans 10:4, emphasis mine). Also, the Mosaic Law has been replaced with something more appropriate for the *end-of-the-age* "fulness of the time" under the Messiah (Galatians 4:4-5). Moreover, now that the people of God have been *internationalized* beyond ethnic Israel and her proselytes, we need a covenant that encompasses *Gentile* sons and daughters of Abraham (Galatians 3:7-9,13-14,26-29). In all three perspectives, Paul makes the same point: *the Mosaic Law has ended and the new covenant has superseded it.* This is why the Mosaic Law is not binding on Christians today.[6]

HOW THE MOSAIC LAW HELPS FORM US SPIRITUALLY

This leads to our second question: "If the Law is not binding, is it still the Word of God for us and will it edify us as Christians?" In a word we can say, "Yes, it is very clearly still the Word of God (see

Matthew 5:17-19), and it is of definite spiritual value." But if the Law was the guide for the spiritual formation of Israel in a previous, preparatory, and less mature era of God's economy (Galatians 4:1-7), how can it be valuable to the spiritual formation of we who live in the surpassing era of the new covenant? The answer is this: While the Law is not *regulatory* for us as a binding covenant with God, it is still *revelatory* for us in a bonding relationship with God.

In other words, the Law is of unspeakable value in revealing to us who God is and what sin is like. It is primarily in the Law that God gives us objective statements of what He considers "holy" and "righteous" standards and behaviors for His people. In the process we can see how pervasive and far-reaching the holiness of God is and how different He is from us. While this may be overwhelming from the perspective of how far short we fall, it is encouraging in that the Law enabled God's people to be holy so that God could dwell in their midst (Deuteronomy 23:14).

The Law is still remarkably instructive as to how God views sin and how that sin affects *our relationship* with Him when Jesus walks in the midst of us, His new covenant people (see Revelation 2–3). In this sense, the Law still functions as a pedagogue or teacher of righteousness for us in certain, irreplaceable ways:

> What does this law reveal about God and his ways? A law, as mentioned, reveals a great deal about the lawgiver. What does this law reflect about God's mind, his personality, his qualities, attitudes, priorities, values, concerns, likes and dislikes, his teaching methodologies, the kinds of attitudes and moral and ethical standards he wants to see in those who love him?[7]

As we read the Law and gain insights into who God is and what He expected from Israel, we also need to evaluate the significance of these insights to our situation as new covenant believers. On the one hand, we are *in continuity* with the old covenant believers because we are people of God and the offspring of Abraham, although our lineage is spiritual, not physical (Galatians 3:7-14). On the other hand, we are *in discontinuity* with old covenant believers because we live on this side of the empty tomb and experience the indwelling Holy Spirit. We experience as new covenant believers what the old covenant saints saw from a distance and longed to experience: "It was revealed to them that they were not serving themselves, but you, in these things which now have been announced to you through those who preached the gospel to you by the Holy Spirit sent from heaven—things into which angels long to look" (1 Peter 1:12).

Moreover, we have been blessed with far richer spiritual resources and far greater freedom and covenantal privilege than they. But we cannot draw a straight line from the Old Testament Law and its circumstances to our circumstances under the new covenant. The line must pass through the empty tomb of Jesus the Messiah, which changes its trajectory because the history of the world pivoted when Jesus died and rose again (Galatians 6:14-15). Therefore, as new covenant believers, much of the time we must delight in theological insights rather than in specific steps of action, as old covenant believers would have from reading the Law. So, for us, the Law is yet *revelatory* even if it is not still regulatory in our lives.

Exactly how should we read the Mosaic Law for our spiritual formation? The following summary seeks to capsulize the emphasis we have been advocating:

THE SPECIFIC CONTRIBUTION OF THE LAW TO OUR SPIRITUAL FORMATION: *REVELATORY, NOT REGULATORY*

- **The Biblical Books:** Exodus, Numbers, Leviticus, and Deuteronomy (Exodus 20 through Deuteronomy 33).

- **Primary Contribution:** To explain how God relates to us within a covenantal relationship and how His holiness and Israel's sin could be reconciled through Israel's obedience to the covenant (Law). Within this covenantal relationship, the law also demonstrates the concrete, practical, and multi-faceted areas in which God's people should obey and be transformed.

continued on next page . . .

> **Therefore, ask,** "What does this passage tell us about God and His holiness, about Israel and her sin, and about how Israel needed to obey in order to maintain her covenant relationship with God?" Also ask, "What specific areas of life does God expect holiness and transformation within His people?"
>
> ■ **Secondary Contribution:** To give us ethical and moral illustrations of godly responses to a wide variety of life's situations.
>
> **Therefore, ask,** "Are these areas still relevant under the new covenant as areas I should be concerned about and areas in which I should be seeking to obey God?"

SPIRITUALLY FORMED BY A PART OF THE LAW

Deuteronomy 30:11-20 is a fascinating passage that illumines how much God expected Israel to respond to the demands of the Mosaic Law. This passage answers the question, "Did God really expect Israel to keep the Law?" This is an important issue for our spiritual formation (and certainly for Israel's). There is a lot of confusion about whether Israel could really obey the Law or not. Many argue that it was *impossible* to keep the Law during the old covenant era (or *any* era). To these advocates the primary purpose of the Mosaic Law was to demonstrate continually to Israel that Law obedience was an impossible task. Through their constant failure to keep the Law, Israel and all humanity would be taught that the only viable option is to throw oneself on the mercy of God, at the foot of the cross. Verses like Leviticus 18:5, for example, offer an impossible solution for achieving eternal life due to our sin: "So you shall keep My statutes and My judgments, *by which a man may live if he does them;* I am the LORD" (emphasis mine). Because it is impossible to live eternally by keeping the Law, our only hope is in God's mercy expressed in Jesus the Messiah.

While there is some truth in this perspective, it also has some fundamental flaws. If it is true, then we should read the Law to see our sin, acknowledge our failure, confess our sin, ask for forgiveness, and then press on. However, if God really did expect Israel to obey the Law, and if doing so was *not* an impossible task, then we read the Law with a different set of expectations as new covenant believers. We realize that it sketches out the general contours of God's *realistic expectations* for His people under the old covenant. Because God did not expect nor demand perfect obedience to the Law, He included the sacrificial system as a part of its provisions. Therefore, if Israel failed to obey the Law, it was not a designed failure but rather was due to her unbelief—God did not expect and design such failure for His people.

This brings us back to Deuteronomy 30:11-20. Listen to Moses' words of exhortation to the new generation of Israelites standing on the plains of Moab at the door of the Promised Land. They have been burying their parents' generation for almost forty years due to their great unbelief in the wilderness. It is now the children's turn. We pick up the account after Moses has reexplained the Law to them and clearly delineated its blessings and curses:

> "For this commandment which I command you today is not too difficult for you, nor is it out of reach. It is not in heaven, that you should say, 'Who will go up to heaven for us to get it for us and make us hear it, that we may observe it?' Nor is it beyond the sea, that you should say, 'Who will cross the sea for us to get it for us and make us hear it, that we may observe it?' But the word is very near you, in your mouth and in your heart, that you may observe it.
>
> "See, I have set before you today life and prosperity, and death and adversity; in that I command you today to love the LORD your God, to walk in His ways and to keep His commandments and His statutes and His judgments, that you live and multiply, and that the LORD your God may bless you in the land where you are entering to possess it. But if your heart turns away and you will not obey, but are drawn away and worship other gods and serve them, I declare to you today that you shall surely perish.

You shall not prolong your days in the land where you are
crossing the Jordan to enter and possess it. I call heaven
and earth to witness against you today, that I have set
before you life and death, the blessing and the curse. So
choose life in order that you may live, you and your
descendants, by loving the LORD your God, by obeying His
voice, and by holding fast to Him; for this is your life and
the length of your days, that you may live in the land
which the LORD swore to your fathers, to Abraham, Isaac,
and Jacob, to give them."

It appears that both God and Moses expected Israel to know the
Mosaic Law and to obey it. Again, the expectation was not for perfect obedience, but rather for informed and consistent obedience
according to the provisions of the Law. This concept included failing to keep the Law and thereby *sinning at times and then availing
oneself of the appropriate sacrifices prescribed in the Law.*
However, it is extremely clear from this passage (and also from
Leviticus 18:5) that what the Law promised was not eternal life, but
rather *physical life within the land of Canaan* (see Deuteronomy
30:16,18-20).

Eternal life came as a free gift of God's grace through faith in
God like Abraham had (see Genesis 15:6). Such was the blessing
of the Abrahamic covenant. However, the Mosaic covenant
promised that the Abrahamic blessing would be lived out *with a
long physical life in the land* if the Mosaic Law were obeyed. It is
an administrative or housekeeping covenant, and therefore supple-
mentary to the Abrahamic covenant. Obedience of the Law
promised no eternal life, only the blessings of earthly life within the
Promised Land. This is the blessing of the Mosaic Law. Notice that
the cursing that God promised is exactly the opposite: shortened life
outside the land (see Deuteronomy 30:15,17-19). Both the blessing and the cursing center in the Israelites' physical life on earth.
God expected them to obey their covenantal responsibilities or else
experience a miserable earthly existence!

What is the significance of this clarification and the exhortation
of Deuteronomy 30:11-20? What insight into spiritual formation

does this passage give us? Let's revisit the primary questions we suggested earlier when studying a Law passage:

"What does this passage tell us about God and His holiness, about Israel and her sin, and about how Israel needed to obey in order to maintain her covenant relationship with God?" Also ask, "In what specific areas of life does God expect holiness and transformation within His people?"

The Deuteronomy passage gives foundational answers to these questions. We learn that God did not give Israel an unattainable standard for her spiritual formation. Knowing and keeping the relational terms of her covenantal relationship with God was something Israel could and should do. Faithfulness in the covenantal relationship with God was expressed in terms of obedience to the provisions of that covenantal relationship, delineated in the Mosaic Law. Basically, God was saying to Israel, "If you love Me, you will obey My commandments!" Does this sound familiar? Sure it does. Jesus the Messiah says the same thing to those of us who have a new covenant relationship with God through Him:

"If you love Me, you will keep My commandments. And I will ask the Father, and He will give you another Helper, that He may be with you forever; that is the Spirit of truth, whom the world cannot receive, because it does not behold Him or know Him, but you know Him because He abides with you, and will be in you. I will not leave you as orphans; I will come to you." (John 14:15-18)

Notice that life under the new covenant is similar to life under the old covenant in that we still need to obey the specific terms of our covenantal relationship with God. Living the Christian life is not just filling in the blank with whatever we feel at the time—"led by the Spirit"! Rather, we can *definitively know* that we are led by the Holy Spirit when we are obeying those specific things that God has delineated for us in the New Testament. While there is greater freedom in doing this under the new covenant than there was under the Old, there is also greater responsibility.

But our life is dissimilar to life under the old covenant in that the Holy Spirit dwells within each new covenant believer and enables each of us to obey God much more than He did the old covenant believers. This is what the world waited six hundred to seven hundred years to see when the Old Testament prophets promised a new covenant (see Jeremiah 31:31-34 and Ezekiel 36:24-27). However, the wonderful joy of the Spirit of God abiding within His people individually and collectively does not negate our need to believe God's Word and obey it. Like Israel of old, our spiritual formation will be wonderfully enhanced by such a response. Reading the books of the Law gives us a vivid reminder of how we can simultaneously be spiritually formed and express our love for God *in His language of love:* by obeying His commandments.

Chapter Seven

SOULS THAT SING:
THE PSALMS

*May God be gracious to us and bless us
and make his face shine upon us,
that your ways may be known on earth,
your salvation among all nations.
May the peoples praise you, O God;
may all the peoples praise you.
May the nations be glad and sing for joy,
for you rule the peoples justly
and guide the nations of the earth.
May the peoples praise you, O God;
may all the peoples praise you.
Then the land will yield its harvest,
and God, our God, will bless us.
God will bless us,
and all the ends of the earth will fear him.*

PSALM 67, NIV

*The Psalms are poetry and the Psalms are prayer. These two
features, the poetry and prayer, need to be kept in mind always.
If either is forgotten, the Psalms will not only be misunderstood
but misused.*

EUGENE PETERSON [1]

IF THE LAW REPRESENTS THE AGONY PART OF THE OLD Testament for Bible readers, then the Psalms surely represent the ecstasy part. Clearly, the 150 psalms continue to be loved by God's people generation after generation, probably due in large part to their nature. While other Scriptures speak about God, the Psalms capture the people of God *speaking to Him* about a wide variety of subjects. Psalm writers express themselves in an amazing array of individual and group laments, songs of trust, individual and corporate thanksgiving, various kinds of praises describing God's character and acts, and lessons about wisdom and Torah and other aspects of life. The Psalms seem to cover the gamut of life's anguishing and ecstatic moments in their lyrics. Because of this heartfelt range and expression, no other part of the Bible engenders such powerful emotional connections between the reader and our God. Why do the Psalms make such a potent connection with us? While our love of the Psalms is probably intuitive, understanding a little about their nature may help us appreciate why we love them so much and why they move us so deeply.

THE NATURE OF THE PSALMS

Prayers and Poems

At their core, the Psalms are prayers and poems by Old Testament believers that have been set to music and sung individually or corporately in Israel. Many of the psalms were likely used as part of worship services in the tabernacle or temple in Jerusalem. The phrase "for the choir director," which is a part of the title of fifty-five psalms, seems to emphasize their use in public worship.[2]

In public worship, most likely the psalms would be performed by the Levitical singers and instrumentalists assigned to the tabernacle, and later to the temple (see 1 Chronicles 16:4-6,41-42; 23:5; 25:1-8; 2 Chronicles 5:11-14). During David's and Solomon's time, there were apparently 288 skilled or senior musicians (see 1 Chronicles 25:6-7) and an additional four thousand singers, many with instruments, praising God at the tabernacle or in the temple (see 1 Chronicles 23:5). The heartfelt prayers and poems that were put to music and became the

Psalms were given a wonderful and majestic musical accompaniment when sung in the assembly!

The Old Testament believers who collected these songs divided them into five "books" or groupings, with each "book" ending in a doxology: Psalms 1–41, 42–72, 73–89, 90–106, and 107–150.

While many contemporary songwriters gain great fame and wealth from writing widely loved songs, can we say the same for the writers of the Psalms? Certainly David is well known for his contribution to the Psalter. However, we do not know the authors of about one-third of these heartfelt poems or prayers. Additionally, other than David, most of the authors we do know are not exactly household names! Note the authors' names mentioned in the titles of 101 psalms (about two-thirds):

- 73 by David (Psalms 3–9, 11–32, 34–41, 51–65, 68–70, 86, 101, 103, 108–110, 122, 124, 131, 133, and 138–145)
- 12 by Asaph (Psalms 50, 73–83)
- 12 by the sons of Korah (Psalms 42–49, 84–85, 87, and 88)
- 2 by Solomon (Psalms 72 and 127)
- 1 by Heman the Ezrahite (Psalm 88, also under the sons of Korah)
- 1 by Ethan the Ezrahite (Psalm 89)
- 1 by Moses (Psalm 90)
- 49 by unnamed authors (Psalms 1–2, 10, 33, 66–67, 71, 91–100, 102, 104–107, 111–121, 123, 125–126, 128–130, 132, 134–137, 146–150)

We love the psalms whether we know the authors' names or not because these songs deal with universal issues that strike at the very core of our being. Who hasn't cried out to the Lord with hearts weighed down with concerns about death, or defeat, or impending disaster, or sin in their lives, or sin in the life of their community or nation, or the triumph of their enemies, or the triumph of the wicked, or the confusion of unanswered prayer, or loneliness, and on and on? By contrast, whose hearts haven't at some time in their lives been so full of gratitude that they wanted to dance before the Lord; or thank Him for His mercy, or kindness, or faithfulness, or deliverance; or recount His answer to crucial prayers; or praise His character or deeds before the gathered saints; or delight in His steadfast love that never fails? Even when unnamed authors convey these universal issues, God's people can identify deeply with their anguish or delight.

Emotion and Theology United

The very essence of the Psalms dynamically unites human experience and emotion with a vibrant theology about God. This balanced emphasis is sorely needed in the contemporary church, especially with the recent movement toward experience-centered theology. Increasingly we moderns are primarily persuaded by emotional appeals. We base our decisions on sound bites of information or small fragments of truth, rather than on well-developed arguments and meaningful persuasion. If something moves us emotionally, we deem it true or legitimate. If something does not stir our emotions rather quickly or vibrantly, we hardly give it consideration, especially if it demands a bit of reasoning.

To some degree, this helps explain the appeal of the Psalms — they are, after all, vibrant expressions of human emotion and real experience. We are drawn especially to their experience-centered orientation. However, a fair reading of the book reveals that this emphasis is coupled with a rich theology that centers on God and His revelation in His Word. In other words, *the writers of the Psalms strike a balance between experience and theology that is generally unknown in the modern church!*[3]

Allow me to prove this with an experiment. I am right now picking up my Bible and selecting a psalm. I am so confident of the balance between human emotion/experience and God-centered theology that I will randomly choose a psalm to demonstrate this balance.

I single out the book of Psalms and close my eyes. Then I let my Bible fall open and place my finger on the page. I open my eyes — I've chosen Psalm 32. (Don't try this at home — it's a lousy way to pick something to read from God's Word!) Most consider Psalm 32 David's praise to God after he confessed his sin of adultery with Bathsheba and his murder of her husband Uriah. Perhaps it chronologically follows David's sorrowful lament in Psalm 51. In the table on the next page, I have placed individual verses from the psalm, taken from the NIV and set in italics but not in poetic style, on whichever side they seem to fall.

Psalm 32 typifies the remarkable combination of human emotion/experience and rich theology about God and His ways. But don't just take my word for this. Test this claim as you read the Psalms for yourself! Simply ask, "Is the psalmist just emoting about life and his feelings, or is he also integrating his emotions with truths about God?" I'm confident you will discover that the latter is wonderfully the case. No other part of God's Word is so full of this dynamic combination. We see human experience in all of its pain and glory here, but through the eyes of psalmists who have founded their world on God and His revelation. These songs intricately weave these two strands of truth into the beautiful tapestry that is the book of Psalms.

Poetic Parallelism

The Psalms are written in poetic parallelism, a form that differs from our modern expectations about rhyming words. Essentially, in parallelism the author states an idea in the first line, then repeats it in a different way in the second line, or in additional lines (perhaps a whole stanza). In most Old Testament genres, when the speakers or authors express themselves poetically, they use the dynamic of parallelism. It has many forms in Hebrew poetry, but the main types are the following:[4]

■ *Synonymous parallelism*—the second line basically
repeats the idea in the first line. Example: Psalm 32:1, NIV:

Blessed is he whose transgressions are forgiven,
whose sins are covered. (transgression forgiven =
sin covered)

Focusing on Human Emotion/Experience

■ *Blessed is he whose transgressions are forgiven, whose sins are covered. Blessed is the man whose sin the LORD does not count against him and in whose spirit there is no deceit.*

■ *When I kept silent, my bones wasted away through my groaning all day long. For day and night your hand was heavy upon me; my strength was sapped as in the heat of summer. (Selah)*

■ *Then I acknowledged my sin to you and did not cover up my iniquity. I said, "I will confess my transgressions to the LORD" —and you forgave the guilt of my sin. (Selah)*

■ *Therefore let everyone who is godly pray to you while you may be found; surely when the mighty waters rise, they will not reach him. You are my hiding place; you will protect me from trouble and surround me with songs of deliverance. (Selah)*

■ Notice how the focus has shifted to David instructing others with truths about God based on what he has experienced in God's instruction of him. After his instruction about walking uprightly before the Lord (verses 8-10), David also exhorts those who hear his song to praise the Lord if they are righteous in heart (verse 11).

Focusing on God and Truths About Him

■ Notice how this emotion of joy is in response to a wonderful theological truth: God forgives and covers sin! This is especially gracious when the Mosaic Law had no provision for a sin, as in David's case.

■ Observe that this is a classical description of the convicting work of the Spirit of God in a believer's life. This is not a ministry of the Spirit that you want to get extremely familiar with and experience regularly!

■ This is David's report of deliverance based on admitting his sin, confessing to the Lord, and then experiencing God's forgiveness, in spite of no sacrifice.

■ David's renewed vow of praise expresses great confidence in God's ability to deliver him from the guilt of his sin, based on God's specific forgiveness of his sin regarding Bathsheba and Uriah.

■ *I will instruct you and teach you in the way you should go; I will counsel you and watch over you. Do not be like the horse or the mule, which have no understanding but must be controlled by bit and bridle or they will not come to you. Many are the woes of the wicked, but the LORD's unfailing love surrounds the man who trusts in him. Rejoice in the LORD and be glad, you righteous; sing, all you who are upright in heart!*

- *Antithetical parallelism*—the second line is the opposite or antithesis of the first line. Example: Psalm 32:10, NIV:

Many are the woes of the wicked,
but the LORD's unfailing love surrounds the man who
    trusts in him. (The woes of the wicked offer stark
    contrast to the protection of the saints.)

- *Synthetic parallelism*—the second line enriches or develops the idea of the first line. Example: Psalm 32:6:

Therefore let everyone who is godly pray to you while
    you may be found;
surely when the mighty waters rise, they will not reach
    him. (Protection from calamities may result when the
    godly pray.)

- *Specifying parallelism*—the second line makes the idea of the first line more specific. Example: Psalm 32:2:

Blessed is the man whose sin the LORD does not count
    against him,
and in whose spirit is no deceit. (Having no deceit in your
    spirit specifies not having your sin count against you.)

- *Intensifying parallelism*—the second line restates the idea of the first line in a potent way. Example: Psalm 32:4:

For day and night your hand was heavy upon me;
my strength was sapped as in the heat of summer. (God's
    convicting of David was like the most intense
    summer heat.)

While we may be delighted by the great variety of parallelism in the Psalms (and there are many more), we cannot lose sight of one very important point: *each psalm must be read as a literary whole, as a unit of thought.* We would not jump into the middle of a contemporary song and seek to interpret the second or third verse as a freestanding thought. And we should not do that with these ancient, God-ordained songs. Rather, we should interpret each set of parallelism within the sense of the whole literary unit of the psalm. Again, with the advent of verse numbering, we tend to see the sets of parallel lines as freestanding units. Such is not the case. They are integral parts of the larger thought of the whole psalm. Let the idea of the whole song dictate the understanding of a particularly meaningful line within it.

THE CATEGORIES OF THE PSALMS

We have looked at psalms as prayers or poems written in poetic parallelism that dynamically unite theology about God with human emotion and experience. We now need to add one more tool to our bag of interpretive skills so we can read the book of Psalms for maximal spiritual formation. Let's unpack the distinctive categories of the Psalms and the respective structures that each category manifests.

May I anticipate a concern and a growing sense of angst that may be developing in you? Perhaps as you read this book you're thinking something like this: *No, please don't embalm the Psalms for me! This is the one last bastion of carefree, devotional reading in the Bible and the biblical book I flee to when I need to connect emotionally with God. Please don't drain it of its lifeblood and turn it to dust!*

I deeply appreciate this sort of concern and I share it. However, I have one request: Please see if the following information about the different types of psalms enhances your reading, understanding, and spiritual formation as you read them. If knowing the categories and structures of the various types of psalms does not enrich your understanding of them, then don't use this information. But I think you'll find it both fascinating and helpful.

Being genre-sensitive to the Psalms demands that we be sensitive to the type of song that each represents. In contemporary culture, we distinguish between love songs, parodies, patriotic songs, protest songs, hero songs, rap, jazz, heavy metal, and so on. One would never interpret a love song like a school fight song! Or mistake soft jazz for heavy metal! We have the same need to distinguish between the types of songs in the Psalms. Noting which type of psalm we are reading will pay enormous dividends in our understanding of that psalm. The categories of psalms are listed in the first chart (pp. 144–145). Simply locate the number of the psalm under the proper category in that chart, then note the structure that psalms of this type usually have on the second chart (pp. 146–147). We now have some wonderful information to mobilize for our spiritual transformation as we read a specific psalm. The value of this information will become clear as we interpret Psalm 8 in the next section.

To help us with these two involved charts, it may be useful first to define some of the categories that may be culturally distant from us.

- A *lament* is a song that expresses sadness to the Lord by an individual or group and asks His help to remedy the situation (this is the largest category; more than sixty psalms are laments).
- *Declarative praise* is a song that praises God for His specific deliverance in a situation.
- *Descriptive praise,* by contrast, praises God for His great attributes and His mighty deeds in general (these include royal psalms about kingship, enthronement psalms, Songs of Zion, and covenant renewal psalms).
- *Didactic psalms* teach about wisdom (for example, Psalm 1), Torah, or other key topics.
- *Songs of trust* emphasize that God is trustworthy and can be trusted, even when the circumstances are bleak and despairing.

BEING SPIRITUALLY FORMED BY THE PSALMS: PSALM 8

In addition to emotionally warming us and connecting us to Him, how might God want to use our reading of these songs to form us spiritually? Perhaps we should first learn what a God-centered life looks and feels like in the midst of crushing concerns and problems, deeply perplexing questions, and overwhelming joys. Through all the travails and triumphs of life, the psalmists consistently reflect a God-centered view of the world. While profoundly connected to their own issues and emotions, they are not bound to a context or a world shaped by their humanness! Rather, they consistently transcend their circumstances to see a God who cares and stays involved with them, yet remains bigger than they. In this transcendent condition, they, and we, can derive great comfort and meaning in the midst of life's ebb and flow.

THE SPECIFIC CONTRIBUTION OF THE PSALMS TO OUR SPIRITUAL FORMATION

- **The Biblical Book:** Psalms

- **Primary Contribution:** To model what a God-centered view of life is like, through expressions of worship and prayer, and the way believers may express their deepest needs, pains, and concerns to God in passionate prayer and worship.

  Therefore, ask, "What does this psalm tell us about how God's presence and work connects with our deepest concerns and emotions in the midst of difficult or joyous circumstances?"

- **Secondary Contribution:** To give us models for worshiping God.

  Therefore, ask, "What does this psalm tell us about how we should pray, praise, and generally express our hearts' desires to God in individual and corporate worship?"

The Psalms also model how God's old covenant people were able to connect profound, complex ideas with stunning emotional range and freedom. They neither slide into a sterile intellectual

THE PSALMS ARRANGED BY CATEGORIES[5]
By F. Duane Lindsey

	Lament				Declarative Praise			Descriptive Praise			Didactic Psalms		
	Lament Psalms		Songs of Trust		Thanksgiving Psalms								
	Individual	Communal	Individual	Communal	Individual	Communal	Hymns	Songs of God's Kingship	Songs of Zion	Royal Psalms	Wisdom Psalms	Torah Psalms	Others
Ps 1											1	(1)	
Ps 2										2			
Ps 3	3												
Ps 4			4										
Ps 5	5												
Ps 6	6												
Ps 7	7												
Ps 8							8						
Ps 9–10	9-10												
Ps 11			11										
Ps 12	12												
Ps 13	13												
Ps 14	14												
Ps 15												15?	
Ps 16			16										
Ps 17	17												
Ps 18					18					18			
Ps 19							19:1-6					19:7-14	
Ps 20										20			
Ps 21					21					21			
Ps 22	22				(22)								
Ps 23			23										
Ps 24							24						
Ps 25	25												
Ps 26	26												
Ps 27	27		(27:1-6)										
Ps 28	28												
Ps 29							29						
Ps 30					30								
Ps 31	31		(31:3-8)										
Ps 32					32								
Ps 33							33						
Ps 34					34								
Ps 35	35												
Ps 36	36?						36?				36?		
Ps 37											37		
Ps 38	38												
Ps 39	39												
Ps 40	40:11-17		(40:1-10)		(40:1-10)								
Ps 41	(41)				(41)								
Ps 42–43	42-43												
Ps 44		44											
Ps 45										45			
Ps 46				46?		46?			46?				
Ps 47								47					
Ps 48									48				
Ps 49											49		
Ps 50													50
Ps 51	51												
Ps 52					52?						52?		52?
Ps 53	53												
Ps 54	54												
Ps 55	55												
Ps 56	56												
Ps 57	57												
Ps 58		58?											
Ps 59	59												
Ps 60		60											
Ps 61	61												
Ps 62			62								(62)		
Ps 63			63										
Ps 64	64												
Ps 65						65							
Ps 66					66:13-20	66:1-12	(66)						
Ps 67						67							
Ps 68						68?			68?				68?
Ps 69	69												
Ps 70	70												
Ps 71	71												
Ps 72										72			
Ps 73											73		
Ps 74		74											
Ps 75						75?							
Ps 76									76				
Ps 77	77												
Ps 78							78?						78?
Ps 79		79											
Ps 80		80											
Ps 81													81
Ps 82		(82?)									82?		
Ps 83		83											
Ps 84									84				
Ps 85		85											
Ps 86	86												
Ps 87									87				
Ps 88	88												
Ps 89		(89)								89			

The Psalms Arranged By Categories[5], continued
By F. Duane Lindsey

	Lament				Declarative Praise			Descriptive Praise			Didactic Psalms		
	Lament Psalms		Songs of Trust		Thanksgiving Psalms		Hymns	Songs of God's Kingship	Songs of Zion	Royal Psalms	Wisdom Psalms	Torah Psalms	Others
Individual	Individual	Communal	Individual	Communal	Individual	Communal							
		90		(90)									
			91								(91)		
					92								
								93					
		94									(94)		
							95						
								96					
								97					
								98					
								99					
							100						
										101			
102													
							103						
							104						
							105						
	108	106				(107)	107						(106)
	109						111						
										110	112		
							113						
							114						
		115?		115?									
					116		117						
					118								
											(119)	119	121?
120		123	121	(123)		124			122				
				125									
		126				(126?)					127		
											128		
		(129)				129							
130			131							132			
											133		(134)
							(134)						
							135						
							136						
(139?)		137	139		138								
140													
141													
142													
143 144							145			144			
							146						
							147						
							148						
							149						
							150						

Special Categories or Topics:

Alphabetical psalms: 9/10,25,34,111,112,119,145
Exodus psalms: 44,66,68,74,77,78,80,83,95,105,106,114,135,136
Imprecations on national/religious foes: 14,52,59,79,83
Israel's election psalms: 66,100,111,114,149
Messianic psalms: 2,8,16,22,40,45,69,72,89,96,97,98,102,109,110,132
Pilgrim psalms: 15?,24?,42-43,50?,78?,81?,84,87?,91?,95?,100?,120-134

Creation psalms: 8,19,29,33,104,148
Imprecatory psalms: 5,7,35,40,41,55,58,59,69,79,109,137,139,140,141
Innocence psalms: 7,15,17,26
Lord of history psalms: 33,103,113,117,145,146,149
Penitential (Confession) psalms: 6,32,38,51,102,130,143
Torah psalms: 1,15?,19?,7-14,24?,119,134?

PRIMARY CATEGORIES OF THE PSALMS[5]
by F. Duane Lindsey

Lament of the People	Declarative Praise of the People	Lament of the Individual (Open)	Lament of the Individual (Heard)	Declarative Praise of the Individual	Descriptive Praise
Introductory Petition Address Cry for help Report of "God's deeds of old"		**Introduction** Address and/or immediate turning to God Cry for help (introductory petition and/or lament)	**Introduction** Address and/or immediate turning to God Cry for help		
Lament We Thou Foes		**Lament** I Thou Foes	**Lament** I Thou Foes		
Confession of Trust		**Confession of Trust**	**Confession of Trust**		
Petition Hear! Save! Punish! Because . . .		**Petition** Hear! Save! Punish! Because . . .	**Petition** Hear! Save! Punish! Because . . .		
		(Confidence of being heard)	(Confidence of being heard)		
Vow of Praise		**Vow of Praise** (or renewed trust) (or blessing) (or instruction)	**Vow of Praise**	**Proclamation** (or intention to praise God)	

Primary Categories of the Psalms⁵, continued
by F. Duane Lindsey

Lament of the People	Declarative Praise of the People	Lament of the Individual (Open)	Lament of the Individual (Heard)	Declarative Praise of the Individual	Descriptive Praise
	Introduction Exhortation Praise			**Introductory Summary of Praise** (often one sentence)	
	Reflection on past need			**Reflection on past need** (= previous lament)	
	Report of Deliverance (i.e., declarative praise)		**Faith Statement of Deliverance** (Advance, declarative praise)	**Report of Deliverance** (i.e., declarative praise) I cried (= previous petition) He heard He delivered	
				Renewed vow of praise	**Call to praise** Prologue: Hallelujah! Proclamation/invitation
				Praise (descriptive) **and/or Instruction**	**Cause for praise** Summary statement God's greatness (Lord of creation) God's grace (Lord of history) Specific Illustrations
					Renewed Call to Praise or Restatement of Cause for Praise or Blessing or Instruction Epilogue: Hallelujah!

wrestling match with difficult concepts and issues nor default to a frenzy-filled emotional purging in an attempt to escape from such issues. Instead, they combine in psalm after psalm the remarkably insightful expression of heart-wrenching issues with opulent, heartfelt emotion. Seldom in modern culture is such a combination encountered, even in Christian circles. We have much to learn from the Psalms in this area, both individually and corporately. Studying Psalm 8 will give us a taste of how these remarkable songs/prayers can be used in the spiritual re-forming of our souls as we learn to sing to God.

Before we ask these questions of Psalm 8, let's note what type of psalm it is and what its structure may look like. First, by checking the chart "The Psalms Arranged by Categories," we observe that Psalm 8 is a "descriptive praise" psalm of the "hymns proper" category. "Descriptive praise" extols God for His great attributes and His mighty deeds in general, as compared to praising Him for a specific deliverance ("declarative praise"). By correlating this category of psalm with the various psalm structures on the second chart, we see that a descriptive praise psalm generally has the structure shown in the outline on the next page.

It begins with a "Call to Praise" (either a prologue with "Hallelujah!" or a proclamation or invitation), followed by a "Cause for Praise" divided into two parts: a summary statement (of God's greatness in creation or His grace in history) and specific illustrations (of His greatness or grace). A conclusion rounds out the psalm (either a renewed call to praise or a restatement of the cause for praise or a blessing or instruction or an epilogue with "Hallelujah!").

The good news is that Psalm 8 fits this structure perfectly. Notice how the parts of the song are skillfully put together. The quotations are from the NIV. (See outline on next page.)

If it were up to me, I would entitle this psalm, "How Majestic Is Your Name . . . in Unexpected Ways!" David's two illustrations of how God manifests His glory above the heavens drip with the surprise of the unexpected and the shock of the out-of-the-ordinary. In part, this is because when David praises God in verse 1, Israel was no doubt prepared for some obvious examples of God's majesty and splendor to follow (for example, creation or the Exodus). However,

I. **Call to Praise** (verse 1) = *Proclamation* of the majesty of God's name in all the earth! ("O LORD, our LORD,/how majestic is your name in all the earth!").

II. **Cause for Praise** (verses 1-8)

    A. **Summary Statement** (verse 1) = The majestic Lord has displayed His splendor above the heavens ("You have set your glory / above the heavens").

    B. **Two Specific Illustrations** of His splendor (verses 2-8)[6]

        1. **Illustration 1** (verse 2) = God's glory is displayed in His use of children's praise to silence His strong enemies ("From the lips of children and infants / you have ordained praise / because of your enemies, / to silence the foe and the avenger").

        2. **Illustration 2** (verses 3-8) = God's splendor is also displayed in His use of "lowly man" to carry out God's dominion over His creation.

            a. (verse 3) The backdrop is creation, God's "fingerwork" ("When I consider your heavens, / the work of your fingers, / the moon and the stars, / which you have set in place").

            b. (verse 4) The amazing thing is that Creator God even thinks about us! ("What is man that you are mindful of him, / the son of man that you care for him?")

            c. (verses 5-8) Yet, God has granted man *glory and dominion* over God's created order (verse 5—made a little lower than God [angels]; verses 6-8—made ruler over all creation).

III. **Renewed Call to Praise** (verse 9) = Proclamation of the majesty of God's name in all the earth ("O LORD, our Lord, / how majestic is your name in all the earth!").

the unexpected examples of how God has displayed His majestic might in verses 3-8 are filled with irony and catch the reader off guard. The Israelites were "destabilized" and puzzled by such unusual and unanticipated examples of their mighty God using the weak (children, infants) to oppose the strong (enemies, foes, avengers) and dignifying the weak (man) to accomplish His appointed task. How does this all fit together? We must stop and ponder these unlikely combinations.

Perhaps this was exactly what David wanted us to do, to ponder the unfathomable ways that God works at times. As we meditate on God using little children's praise of Him (or of Jesus on Palm Sunday—see Matthew 21:15-16), we are awed that He would display His splendor through such humble means. We are struck that verse 2 pictures this childlike praise creating an audible bulwark or fortress. We are struck by God's grace to the weak and lowly.

But then we come to the second illustration, in verses 3-8, and the backdrop drastically changes. Suddenly we are staring at the astonishing immensity of God's created universe. However, the stunning part of this backdrop is that it is simply the result of God's "fingerwork," not even His "armwork"! He simply spoke and ordained the moon and stars into existence. God is incomprehensibly immense and incomparable in power and splendor! But then the hammer drops. Backdropped by the universe, who are we as puny little humans, motley men and women? Anyone who has stared at the heavens for any length of time on a clear, starry night surely has had this thought: *The universe is so large and we are so little. How can we have even a nickel's worth of value in such an overwhelming scheme of things?* This is exactly David's point in verse 4! How can a God who creates universes with His digits give even a thought to human beings? How are we worthy of even a flicker of thought?

This is where David's meditative time in Genesis 1–2 surely comes to fruition. He has a revealed answer, a biblical one, to the starry-night musings of millions of human beings. Yes, the universe is immense and God is unspeakably powerful. But He not only pauses to think about us, He also created us with dignity and honor. So much so that He has ordained that we function as co-rulers over the created order with Him (verses 5-8). Of all His creative masterpieces, He has placed us at the top of the heap! He willed that "lowly humans" would share in His rulership over His creation; in our weakness we experience His power. In our lowly frailty, we experience the majesty of co-reigning over God's creation at God's behest. Who could have guessed such an unexpected turn of events? Who can comprehend such gracious splendor and humble majesty on the part of our Creator God? Who can fathom how undeserving we are, yet how unrelenting God is in His grace toward us? We have but one cry appropriate for such moments as this:

O LORD, our Lord,
how majestic is your name in all the earth! (verse 9)

By the time we revisit the call to praise in verse 9, it is pregnant with new meaning and greater understanding. Perhaps we spoke of the majesty of God's name by rote in verse 1. But after we read David's two illustrations, we can never speak the same about how God has displayed His splendor in the universe. In light of how the all-powerful God uses the weak ones of the world (praising little children and puny little humans), we must marvel at His majesty and speak of His grace. We must praise His name in all the earth.

Let us now step back and ask if the information about the category and structure of Psalm 8 was helpful. Did learning that this psalm was one of "descriptive praise" and that it had a certain structure embalm the psalm and turn it to dust? Did this information destroy the rich emotionality of the psalm and make it seem mechanical and cold? Did we impede any emotional connection with God by mobilizing some information about this psalm? Or if we are honest with ourselves, can we admit that this little bit of information actually did help us to appreciate more fully what David wrote? Can we acknowledge that both our understanding and emotional connection were enriched by the extra insights about type and structure? I hope so.

But let's return to the suggested questions for the Psalms on page 143 and ask them of Psalm 8.

Our *primary question:* "What does this psalm tell us about how

God's presence and work connect with our deepest concerns and emotions in the midst of difficult or joyous circumstances?"

Psalm 8 powerfully connects two unusual bedfellows: our intense sense of smallness and insignificance in the universe and God's immense majesty and splendor. In the process, David heightens the distance between God's immensity and our insignificance before he stunningly brings them together in verses 5-8 in a mini-meditation on humans' role in the created order from Genesis 1–2. Apart from God's revelation of humanity's dignity and rulership in the Genesis creation account, we would never inductively conclude that we are of any significance in the universe.

This psalm revels in the dignity that we humans have in God's created order. However, in balanced fashion, the focus is not just on us humans as an end in and of ourselves. Rather, our dignity comes as a gift of God's grace. He has deeded us this dignity because of His creative relationship over us—we're made in His very image! We know who we are in light of who God is as Creator, and once we realize this, we end up praising His majestic name. While Psalm 8 is about us, it begins and ends with a call to praise God for *His* glory. Such is the balanced perspective of the Psalms. Real knowledge of who we are begins and ends with recognizing God for who He really is.

Our *secondary question*: "What does this psalm tell us about how we should pray, praise, and generally express our hearts' desires to God in individual and corporate worship?"

While Psalm 8 stirs us to ponder how we can better rule "over the works of [His] hands" (verse 6), this is not the main thrust of the psalm. Rather, it models God as Creator for us and beckons to us to praise Him because of the unexpectedly gracious ways that He has displayed His splendor above the heavens. In an age of evolutionary scientism, many believers hang their heads and shuffle their feet when the concept of God as Creator is raised. However, Psalm 8 calls on us not to forget what all the creatures of heaven, especially the twenty-four elders, sing to God:

> You are worthy, our Lord and God,
> to receive glory and honor and power,

for you created all things,
and by your will they were created
and have their being.
    (Revelation 4:11, NIV, emphasis mine)

Responding to David's example of praising God as Creator in Psalm 8 will give us a foretaste of heavenly psalms. Do you want to know the words to the songs of heaven ahead of time? Then learn the words of the Psalms because they are one of God's primary means of teaching our souls to sing.

Chapter Eight

TO BE WISE: PROVERBS AND THE WISDOM BOOKS

Hear, my son, your father's instruction,
And do not forsake your mother's teaching;
Indeed, they are a graceful wreath to your head,
And ornaments about your neck.

PROVERBS 1:8-9

Most say, "Oh, well, live and learn."
Wisdom says, "Know well, learn and live."

POPULAR SAYING

AS NEW COVENANT SAINTS, WHERE DO WE LOOK IN THE NEW Testament for spiritual guidance about lending or borrowing money? Or saving money? Or making friends? Or wrestling with life's inscrutable questions? Or addressing the seemingly random incidents of human suffering like the death of a child, the occurrence of disease, or a crippling injury? How about detailed discussions about training our children or disciplining them for godliness? Where could we look to get wise counsel about the meaning of work, play, success, or life in general? What about a theology of marital romance and sensuality? Obviously, if we limit our spiritual formation in these vital areas to the New Testament, our souls will be greatly impoverished.

However, the good news is that God has provided wonderful spiritual counsel for us in the Wisdom Literature of the Old Testament. While we're no longer functioning under the old covenant, we can still benefit greatly from the wisdom given there, wisdom that addresses many of the complex and difficult issues of life. This is found primarily in the four Old Testament books of Job, Proverbs, Ecclesiastes, and the Song of Songs (or Song of Solomon).

Because of the dearth of Wisdom Literature in the New Testament, as disciples of Jesus Christ we must continue to drink deeply from the well of these wisdom books if we are to be transformed in the realm of wise, practical living. We should approach them with a clear expectation of receiving profound, godly advice, even if some of it is not immediately transparent and requires thought-provoking meditation in order to grasp the intended thrust (for example, Ecclesiastes and parts of Job). However, the vast majority of this literature is straightforward and demands clear-cut, obedient responses. If you want to be wise and skillful during your days on earth, read on.

THE GENRE OF WISDOM LITERATURE

There is a lot of misunderstanding among Christians about the nature of the Wisdom Literature, especially about Proverbs. A few years ago, as pastor of a church, I was teaching an Old Testament survey course on Saturday mornings. One Saturday a few weeks into our survey we came to the Wisdom Literature, and I was teaching about the genre of "proverb," using Proverbs 22:6 as a well-known example:

> Train up a child in the way he should go,
> Even when he is old he will not depart from it.

I taught that this proverb, like others, was a wise saying and was not to be equated with a promise. If wise parents raised their children in the way that they should go (probably the way of the Mosaic covenant), the vast majority of the time these children would continue in that way throughout their lives. This was not an ironclad, 100 percent promise, but what wise parents do with their children.

At the end of this explanation, a distinguished and gracious older gentlemen, a godly man with grown children who was a relatively new member of our church, interrupted me. He was very distraught with me because I was countering what he had been taught about this passage and what he assumed to be the nature of Proverbs. It became apparent that some well-meaning person had taught him early in his Christian life that Proverbs 22:6 was a promise about child rearing that was to be "claimed" by Christian parents. He and his wife had been doggedly holding on to this "promise" for over thirty years with one of their children, claiming it hundreds of times when they faithfully prayed for a spiritually wandering adult son. One of the few comforts in their longstanding, painful situation was their hope in God's "promise" to them in this passage. You can imagine the horror, shock, and anger that this man felt when this young pastor tried to pry something so precious from his tightly clenched hands.

On the other hand, think of the decades of false hope from which this dear couple could have been saved simply with better attention to the genre of Proverbs and the Wisdom Literature. Additionally, think of the unnecessary anger and perhaps disillusionment from which countless parents could be saved regarding this one proverb alone if their preachers and teachers would rightly attend to genres when they teach the Bible. Multiply this misunderstanding by dozens of verses interpreted contrary to their genres, and we can only imagine the unneeded confusion and heartache. The stakes are far too high to ignore the Bible's genres.

GENERAL CHARACTERISTICS OF WISDOM LITERATURE

Let's observe a nonbiblical proverb to get some insight into the nature of Wisdom Literature in general, and proverbs in particular. This proverb was created a few years ago by a very wise man, my father, Bo Russell. Read it and ponder its characteristics:

> It's the still sow
> that eats the slop.

What do you notice about this little proverb? Perhaps you are struck by its brevity. It is only eight words long, and every word is absolutely necessary. Proverbs, including biblical ones, are short and pithy, utilizing the least number of words to communicate the thought in the most powerful manner. Speaking of power, note also the use of alliteration, the repetition of words beginning with the same consonant or syllable. In this case three of the eight words begin with *s*. Add to this the repetition of the *t* sound in six of the eight words. Note also the use of these repeated sounds in a rhythm of four beats per line. Additionally, all eight words are simple, one-syllable words, which gives the four-beat rhythm a short, staccato texture. All these sound features combine to help make the proverb more memorable, and this memorable quality is another characteristic of proverbs and wisdom literature.

In addition to the sound features, notice that the proverb is based on the observation of the world of nature and describes animal behavior that can be observed. The vivid imagery appeals to a common experience that anyone can observe and ponder on. Out of this observation of the ordinary or the general, a particular truth arises, which is stated with a voice of certainty. A proverb (and wisdom literature in general) does not waffle or hesitate to state particular, observational insights with a great sense of certainty. The voice of experience is one of authority!

While many proverbs and much wisdom literature utilize universal language, many of them are nevertheless dependent on understanding certain specific contexts that gave rise to the saying. For example, when I ask my hermeneutics classes at Biola University to interpret my father's proverb, those few students who were raised on farms have a lot less trouble understanding this wisdom saying than their city-dwelling friends! Also, students from other cultures who are limited in English vocabulary often struggle with two of the key words and totally misinterpret the proverb as a result. How does this happen?

"It's the still sow that eats the slop" is an observation my dad made as he fed the hogs on our farm when I was young. A "sow" is a full-grown, female pig, usually with a litter of baby pigs. My father observed over time that the quiet sows, the "still" ones, were the hogs that ate the most food. They would quickly get a good space by the feeding trough (or in it!) and would go about their business with little fuss. The sows that ran around the trough squealing and raising a ruckus, the noisy ones, drew a lot of attention to themselves, but got less of the food. However, many of our foreign students were not familiar with the term *sow* as a noun that referred to female pigs. Instead, they knew *sow* as a verb that referred to scattering seed in a field. Therefore, based on this misunderstanding of the proverb's original context, they would interpret it as a bad sowing of seed (a "still sow") that leads to eating bad food ("slop"). They totally misinterpreted the proverb!

Their city-dwelling classmates didn't do much better. They understood "slop" to be a bad or undesirable thing. They were interpreting within their own use of the word *slop* and its connotation of lousy or terrible food. Therefore, they understood being "still" as a bad thing that led to getting "slop." To get good food, a sow must be aggressive. Again, a wrong interpretation. By contrast, anyone who has ever fed hogs knows from experience that "slop" to hungry sows is the most desirable thing in the world! Therefore, to be able to eat the slop is not a penalty, but a reward. But proper understanding, as with many of the biblical proverbs and other types of wisdom literature, demands a little bit of contextual understanding.

I would note one last characteristic of this little proverb. It is obviously not just trying to communicate some insight about pig life. Rather, this observed insight about the eating habits of female pigs is *representational* of the habits of human beings. Wisdom Literature is designed to encourage us to transcend the insight or principle spoken of in the saying and apply it to our own experience. So, what significance do still sows eating most of the slop have for us humans? My father's intention in making this observation was to draw attention to the fact that this principle is also true with people. Many times the quiet, unassuming persons who do not draw attention to themselves are the ones doing the best job and actually accomplishing the desirable goals. However, to see these people we often have to look past the "squealers" and frantic folks who are attracting the majority of attention to themselves. Time will eventually reveal who is doing the job (that is, the fatter sows!), but more thoughtful observation can make it presently obvious. Therefore, a word of encouragement to you still sows: we see you, so stay in the trough and keep on eating!

HOW THE VARIETY OF WISDOM LITERATURE HELPS FORM US IN CHRIST

We have noted some of the general characteristics of Wisdom Literature: it is concise, memorable, simple, and profound; it observes life and reflects the voice of experience; it is thoughtful about human experience and designed to give us practical living skills for confusing circumstances. It also challenges us not to falsely spiritualize everything in life. Learning to live wisely and skillfully may be the most spiritual thing we can do in many circumstances! Therefore, we must assess the circumstances and wisely chart a course that honors God and respects our fellow humans. Moreover, when we read the wisdom books, we should be looking for practical, thoughtful contributions to our spiritual growth. We can summarize this in the following manner:

THE SPECIFIC CONTRIBUTION OF WISDOM LITERATURE TO OUR SPIRITUAL FORMATION

- **The Biblical Books:** Job, Proverbs, Ecclesiastes, and Song of Solomon.

- **Primary Contribution:** They directly (Proverbs) or indirectly (Job, Ecclesiastes, and Song of Solomon) instruct us how to make wise choices in the nitty-gritty, daily affairs of life and in the difficult, inscrutable events of life.

   Therefore, ask, "What does this passage tell us about what wise, skillful living would be in the area being discussed? What general pattern does this reveal for God's people, or what specific behaviors does it challenge us to embrace?"

Let's now examine briefly the specific characteristics and contributions made by each of the four books of this genre.

Job

This remarkable piece of Wisdom Literature addresses two issues foundational to our spiritual understanding:

- Why do the righteous suffer?
- Will they worship God even when they suffer?

Job is an ancient book about events that likely occurred during the patriarchal period (that is, before the Mosaic Law was given), although it was probably written during Solomon's reign (971-931 B.C.). Scholars give the writing this date because of Job's similarity with other Wisdom Literature written during this period (for example, Proverbs 8). The author is unknown, and the setting seems to be in and around the land of Edom, east of Israel. Job seems to be an historical person (he is mentioned as such in Ezekiel 14:14 and James 5:11), and nothing in the book suggests that he is merely a symbolic character.

The book of Job's interesting structure can be summarized as follows:

Chapters 1–2 = Prose Prologue: The testing of Job ("Will a person love God for nothing?" 1:9-11)

Chapters 3–37 = Poetic Dialogue: The false comfort of Job's friends

    Chapters 3–4 = first round of speeches

    Chapters 15–21 = second round of speeches

    Chapters 22–31 = third round of speeches

    Chapters 32–37 = Elihu's speeches   gradual degeneration

Chapters 38–42:6 = God's Poetic Dialogue: The climax of the book

Chapter 42:7-17 = Prose Epilogue: The vindication and restoration of Job

Job addresses the mystery of suffering in believers' lives and encourages us to think about and feel the depth of pain in life, rather than give naive or trite responses to suffering. Additionally, Job challenges us to be wise and to love God for who He is in spite of the inscrutability of our suffering. Even though we may not fully understand all our suffering, we must still choose to cling to God and His ways. Such wise encouragement is necessary in a world where not all of life's experiences can be fully explained this side of heaven. If our spiritual maturity is dependent on understanding and neatly categorizing everything we observe or experience in life, we will be sorely disappointed and probably end our days in skepticism or cynicism. The book of Job offers a bulwark against taking such a path. The wise person will love God in spite of the severe ups and downs of life that tend to be attributed to God's hand. The wise person *will* love God even when nothing makes sense![1]

Proverbs

What Job brings into central focus—the hard-to-understand, periodic calamities of life—the book of Proverbs barely touches at all; its focus is on the normal issues that we all confront almost every day in life. King Solomon wrote much of the book (10:1–22:16), and many of his other proverbs were also collected by "the men of Hezekiah, king of Judah" (chapters 25–29). This gives the book the following structure, according to its authors:

1:1-7	The Title, Purpose, and Motto of the Book (Motto = 1:7, "The fear of the LORD is the beginning of knowledge; / Fools despise wisdom and instruction")
1:8–9:18	A Father's Praise of Wisdom
10:1–22:16	The Proverbs of Solomon
22:17–24:34	Two Sets of Wise Men's Exhortations
25–29	Further Proverbs of Solomon (Hezekiah's collection)
30	The Words of Agur (musings on the idiosyncrasies of life)
31:1-9	The Words of King Lemuel (which his mother taught him)
31:10-31	An Alphabet of an Excellent Wife

What is the specific contribution of this book to spiritual formation? Clearly it was written to make us skillful in living amid life's many and varied situations and circumstances, as 1:1-7 sets forth:

The proverbs of Solomon the son of David, king of Israel:
To know wisdom and instruction,
To discern the sayings of understanding,
To receive instruction in wise behavior,
Righteousness, justice and equity;
To give prudence to the naive,
To the youth knowledge and discretion,
A wise man will hear and increase in learning,

And a man of understanding will acquire wise counsel,
To understand a proverb and a figure,
The words of the wise and their riddles.
The fear of the LORD is the beginning of knowledge;
Fools despise wisdom and instruction.

This section entails understanding wisdom and instruction for moral strength and practical relational skills (1:2-5) and also for mental insight into the complexities of life and spiritual truth (1:6). Foundational to gaining these moral, practical, and mental skills is the need to understand one truth: underneath all of creation and order is "wisdom," God's fixed and righteous course for life (1:7).[2] The wise person will embrace wisdom by knowing and following God's fixed eternal and righteous order that grants life to those who walk in it.[3] By tragic contrast, fools will reject it at their own peril. No other part of God's Word makes this contrast so stark. No other part of God's Word equips us so wonderfully to walk wisely in the world. How impoverished our spiritual life would be without this equipping.

Ecclesiastes
The exact genre of this piece of Wisdom Literature is one of the most debated literary topics of the Old Testament. Is it an expression of cynical wisdom that acts as a foil to true, biblical faith by advocating the ultimate meaninglessness of life (much like modern existentialism), a cynical contrast to what the Bible really teaches (acknowledged in the book's last two verses, 12:13-14)?[4] Or is Ecclesiastes really just a very honest, thoughtful explanation of the biblical perspective on the fruitlessness of trying to find the meaning of life ("under the sun") apart from trusting in a wise, good, and just God who alone holds the key to life?[5] These two very different understandings of this wisdom book lead to two starkly different readings. I personally lean toward the second perspective and will seek to justify it.[6]

Notice Solomon's preface to his book (see 1:1-3) and his conclusion (see 12:9-14). Let's see if we can gain some insight into the genre by putting together these "bracketing" parts of the book.

Preface

The words of the Preacher, the son of David, king in Jerusalem:

"Vanity of vanities," says the Preacher,
"Vanity of vanities! All is vanity."
What advantage does man have in all his work
Which he does under the sun? (1:1-3)

Conclusion

In addition to being a wise man, the Preacher also taught the people knowledge; and he pondered, searched out and arranged many proverbs. The Preacher sought to find delightful words and to write words of truth correctly.

The words of wise men are like goads, and masters of these collections are like well-driven nails; they are given by one Shepherd. But beyond this, my son, be warned: the writing of many books is endless, and excessive devotion to books is wearying to the body.

The conclusion, when all has been heard, is: fear God and keep His commandments, because this applies to every person. For God will bring every act to judgment, everything which is hidden, whether it is good or evil. (12:9-14)

While the preface announces the verdict that all of life is vanity, the conclusion counsels that, because God will judge all, we must fear Him and keep His commandments. Is such a conclusion contrary to or compatible with the preface? This gets us to the heart of the debate over the genre of Ecclesiastes. It seems that both the preface and conclusion can be simultaneously true if we understand that the book's purpose is to show that the Preacher searched for the key to life, but found that it could not be discovered under the sun. In other words, life does not hold the key to itself! We cannot inductively discover the sense or meaning of life by just living it (see 3:10-11; 7:14; 8:17). God has not allowed us to understand the enigmas and riddles of life. Instead, we are overtaken by time and chance (see 9:11).

But there is more. In spite of the reality that life seems meaningless, it is nevertheless a gift from God to be lived to the fullest (see 2:24-26; 3:12-13,22; 5:18-20; 8:15; 9:7-10). However, rather than this leading to a meaningless hedonism, this enjoyment is tempered by the realization that we must live our life by faith in God because of who He is. He is *wise* (3:1-11; 7:14; 8:17) and *good* (see 2:24; 3:13) and *just* (see 3:16-17; 8:11-13; 11:9-10). Therefore, even if we cannot fully comprehend life by observing or living it, we should still enjoy it and fear God because He will ultimately judge all. In Ecclesiastes, Solomon brings these seemingly contradictory facets together into a high-grade diamond.

But why this mixture of vanity and verity? Literary professor Leland Ryken explains:

> His mingling of negative and positive is realistic and faithful to the mixed nature of human experience. . . . The dialectical pattern of opposites is a strategy of highlighting: the glory of a God-centered life stands out all the more brightly for having been contrasted to its gloomy opposite.[7]

This means that the thoughtful believer will feel the depth of pain in experiencing the vanities of life, yet will also scale the heights of joy in clinging to God and His ways. Without Ecclesiastes being a part of our spiritual formation, we might never put these two opposites together.

The diagram on the next page attempts to capture this mixture of opposites. It seeks to illustrate how fully understanding the meaning of God's good gifts is obscured by the darkness of life's vanities. The result? We strive after the wind, seeking to make sense of life under the sun.

Song of Solomon

The five poetic books we group together in the middle of the Old Testament—Job, Psalms, Proverbs, Ecclesiastes, and Song of Solomon—run the gamut from the agony (of Job) to the ecstasy (of the Song of Solomon). Of course, much of life runs this gamut too, doesn't it? This is why the Old Testament includes writings that address both ends of life's spectrum. While we have had no trouble recognizing the agony dimension of Job, we cannot say the same about the ecstasy part of Song of Solomon—God's people have been unable to accept such a good gift from Him! Instead, this series of love poems has been wrongly allegorized or spiritualized throughout much of recent Jewish history and almost all of church history, resulting in the wrong conclusion that it is about God's love for Israel or Christ's love for the church. While many parts of God's Word proclaim these wonderful truths, the Song of Solomon is not one of them!

Rather, the most natural and literal way to understand this ecstatic part of the wisdom writings is to take it at face value and read it as it is: a series of love poems that not so much tell a story as establish a certain mood through the use of love lyrics. In this sense, *God has given us the Song of Solomon so that we might glory in the depths and riches of love and sexuality within the marriage relationship and might fully enjoy God's good gift of marital romance.* Ryken has said this well:

The style of the book is the most purely poetic thing in the Bible. It is one of the delights of the book, but most modern readers are scared off by the very abandonment of the poetic style. Is something this poetic really appropriate in the Bible? Yes, it is. The right way to read the Song of Solomon is to abandon oneself to the poetry. It is a poetry full of emotional and imagistic fireworks, but this is in keeping with the subject matter of the book. Not to abandon oneself to the poetry is to cut against the grain of the book.[8]

As married couples read how Solomon expresses his love for the Shulammite woman, they are to be emotionally swept along in the recounting of their love for their mate. God consecrates, even encourages, such romance within marriage! He does so by revealing His endorsement in one whole book of the Bible dedicated to marital love. Far be it from us to turn such ecstasy into something less than ecstatic. This would leave a void in this area of our spiritual formation that God in His grace intended to fill. Let's accept His kindness with gratitude.

Spiritually Formed by a Wisdom Passage: Proverbs 5
As bold and helpful as your parents' advice may have been, God's advice is even bolder and wiser. The first nine chapters of Proverbs exemplify this candidness and are called "A Father's Praise of Wisdom." Each chapter begins with the address, "My son (child)" (for example 1:8, 2:1, 3:1, 4:1, 5:1, 6:1, and 7:1). While the writer of these proverbs may have used parental language in his role as a teacher, it is just as likely that this section was really meant to function as fatherly or parental advice to a child.[9] What makes Proverbs 5 so powerful is that it is fatherly advice about the threat of adultery! This is one of the most straightforward and helpful discussions imaginable. Please join me as we sit at the feet of our heavenly Father and listen to Him explain about the lure of, price of, alternative to, and judgment of an adulterous relationship.

The Delicious Lure of Adultery (Proverbs 5:1-6)

My son, give attention to my wisdom,
Incline your ear to my understanding;
That you may observe discretion,
And your lips may reserve knowledge.
For the lips of an adulteress drip honey,
And smoother than oil is her speech;
But in the end she is bitter as wormwood,
Sharp as a two-edged sword.
Her feet go down to death,
Her steps lay hold of Sheol.
She does not ponder the path of life;
Her ways are unstable, she does not know it.

Our Father's advice in verses 1-3 is that the wise person will learn *before* he or she lives through an adulterous relationship. Wisdom in our spiritual formation demands that we recognize the unbelievable contrast between the deliciousness of an adulterer's lips (verse 3) and their simultaneous deadliness (verse 4)! There is a sensual allure in the words and kisses of an adulterer (7:13) — even eyelids can be deadly (6:25). However, wisdom demands that we consider the bitter end: *death* (5:4-6), signaled by the words at the beginning of verse 4, *"But in the end. . . ."* Wisdom persuades that we not live for the moment (as the foolish person does), but that we consider *the end result* of all our actions. The fool lives for the present lust, but the wise son or daughter ponders the ultimate end of an action. In this case that end is not the path of life, but the road of death (verses 5-6). As Derek Kidner insightfully notes, "Here it utterly reverses the promise: the delicious ends as the disgusting; the soothing, as the murderous."[10]

The Demanding Price of Adultery (Proverbs 5:7-14)

Now then, my sons, listen to me,
And do not depart from the words of my mouth.
Keep your way far from her,

And do not go near the door of her house,
Lest you give your vigor to others,
And your years to the cruel one;
Lest strangers be filled with your strength,
And your hard-earned goods go to the house of an alien;
And you groan at your latter end,
When your flesh and your body are consumed;
And you say, "How I have hated instruction!
And my heart spurned reproof!
And I have not listened to the voice of my teachers,
Nor inclined my ear to my instructors!
I was almost in utter ruin
In the midst of the assembly and congregation."

Wisdom demands that we physically stay away from those who tempt us to an adulterous relationship (verses 7-8). Keeping a distance is extremely important, and the naive violate this to their own destruction (for example, 7:6-23). Wise believers keep their distance not only from certain persons, but also from certain places and websites (compare 1 Corinthians 6:18 and 2 Timothy 2:22). Such flight is not cowardly, but wise and strategic!

Such wise distancing is important because the *result* of an adulterous relationship is giving our strength and wealth to strangers (verses 9-11). This may mean a shortened life (verse 9), but verse 10 also suggests our assets being devoured by others (divorce, child support, blackmail?). Additionally, our body at the end of life may be consumed by disease, perhaps venereal disease or, more recently, AIDS (verse 11). However, such physical results pale in comparison to the *emotional regrets* of an adulterous relationship: our ignorance and shame before the whole assembly (verse 12-14). We will say, "If only I had . . ." —but it will be too late! We have lived and learned (verses 12-13). But God says, "Learn and then live!" Wisdom will help us avoid the public disgrace of an adulterous affair (verse 14), which far exceeds the loss of wealth and health with the loss of our honor. The results and regrets of adultery are almost beyond comprehension. The wise son or daughter will learn and then live.

But There Is a Better Way to Go (Proverbs 5:15-20)
Drink water from your own cistern,
And fresh water from your own well.
Should your springs be dispersed abroad,
Streams of water in the streets?
Let them be yours alone,
And not for strangers with you.
Let your fountain be blessed,
And rejoice in the wife of your youth.
As a loving hind and a graceful doe,
Let her breasts satisfy you at all times;
Be exhilarated always with her love.
For why should you, my son, be exhilarated with an
adulteress,
And embrace the bosom of a foreigner?

Of course, the better way to go is marital sex. The writer views sex within the marriage relationship as full of overflowing blessing, not isolation (verses 15-17), and makes this point by comparing the wife to a cistern or well (verse 15), or fountain (verse 18). In the dry, arid land of Israel, a well or fountain brings life, refreshment, and pleasure. So wonderfully beloved is a wife. And her comparison to a fountain is one of the beautiful marriage metaphors in the Bible (compare Song of Solomon 4:12,15). The wise person will be faithful to her (Proverbs 5:15), wasting none of this priceless water in the street (fathering children outside of marriage—verse 16). This ensures that your children will be yours alone and raised in your home by the two of you (verse 17).

Moreover, sex within the marriage relationship should be a choice to be passionate and exhilarated with your lifelong marriage partner (fountain = wife) (verses 18-20). Such passion is a *choice*—a choice that is to be sustained (verse 18)! Marital love is not like a bathtub that we fall into or out of, but rather a choice we make and sustain in faithfulness! This demands that the husband choose to continue to view his wife as a beautiful and graceful deer and continue to be intoxicated by her body (breasts in verse 19). If the husband does this, the answer to the two rhetorical questions of verse 20 about being exhilarated by an adulteress becomes very obvious. Truly, the rich sexuality of love within the marriage relationship is the better way.

God's Recompense and Sin's Own Judgment (Proverbs 5:21-23)

For the ways of a man are before the eyes of the LORD,
And He watches all his paths.
His own iniquities will capture the wicked,
And he will be held with the cords of his sin.
He will die for lack of instruction,
And in the greatness of his folly he will go astray.

God is all-seeing and all-knowing (verse 21), and by its very nature sin is a trap that entraps its keeper (verse 22). The adulterer will personally experience the bondage of his or her own sin, as 1 Corinthians 6:18 similarly asserts: "Flee immorality. Every other sin that a person commits is outside the body, but the immoral person sins against his or her own body."[11] The end result in Proverbs 5:23 will be a life that is spinning out of control, heading to an unhappy end due to lack of instruction from a loving Father about the true nature and final cost of adultery.

In Proverbs 5 God rips back the curtain of the enticing mystery that enshrouds adultery. As a loving heavenly Father, He tells us in graphic terms where adultery leads—destruction—and where it ends—death! The wise son or daughter will absorb this wise advice, will see the end, and will choose the better way—a rich, full, sexually satisfying marriage. Such advice is absolutely necessary for our spiritual formation. God, in His infinite wisdom, meets this need in our lives by providing the Wisdom Literature of the Old Testament. How impoverished our lives would be without this sagacious portion of God's Word! We would be left with what most say after reaping the consequences of their foolish choices: "Oh, well, live and learn." By contrast, through the Wisdom Literature God tells us we can be spiritually formed by "learning first, and then living."

Chapter Nine

HEART FOR GOD:
THE PROPHETS

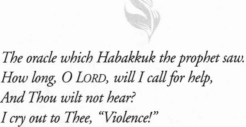

The oracle which Habakkuk the prophet saw.
How long, O LORD, will I call for help,
And Thou wilt not hear?
I cry out to Thee, "Violence!"
Yet Thou dost not save.
Why dost Thou make me see iniquity,
And cause me to look on wickedness?
Yes, destruction and violence are before me;
Strife exists and contention arises.
Therefore, the law is ignored
And justice is never upheld.
For the wicked surround the righteous;
Therefore, justice comes out perverted.

HABAKKUK 1:1-4

[God speaking] "Look among the nations! Observe!
Be astonished! Wonder!
Because I am doing something in your days—
You would not believe if you were told."

HABAKKUK 1:5

Then the LORD answered me and said,
"Record the vision
And inscribe it on tablets,
That the one who reads it may run.
For the vision is yet for the appointed time;
It hastens toward the goal, and it will not fail.
Though it tarries, wait for it;
For it will certainly come, it will not delay."

HABAKKUK 2:2-3

JUST MENTION "PROPHECY" OR "THE PROPHETS" AND IMAGI-
nations run wild with predictions of the future and exotic pictures
of flaming chariots (Ezekiel 1) or terrifying beasts with ten horns
(Daniel 7). However, the popular stereotype of the *seventeen books*
of the Old Testament that constitute the "prophetic" genre is somewhat misleading. While prophetic writers do employ fascinating and
picturesque images when trying to express what God revealed to
them, these portraits constitute a very small percentage of their writings. In fact, Fee and Stuart list several startling statistics about the
prophets:

- Less than 2 percent of the Old Testament prophecies
  speak about the Messiah.
- Less than 5 percent of the prophecies speak about the
  new covenant era.
- Less than 1 percent predict events that are yet to come.[1]

These statistics demonstrate that the prophetic books are something quite different from what we commonly perceive them to be.
Rather than primarily *foretelling* events in the future, the Prophets
are more correctly *forthtelling* truths and God's will concerning His
people; they mainly speak to concerns and issues that are *contemporary* to each of the prophets' lives. Because of this, they can
actually make a very different contribution to our spiritual formation
than we might initially think.

Specifically, reading and meditating on the prophetic books gives
us an enormous dose of *exhortation.* This is because the prophets
were mainly *covenant enforcers,* or people who spoke God's concerns
to His people on His behalf.[2] Thus the messages the prophets
preached were largely unoriginal; rather, they were calling the
Israelites back to fulfill their covenant responsibilities to God under
the clear guidelines of the Mosaic covenant. They did this through a
variety of exhortative means that underscored the covenant's stated
blessings for obedience and its curses for disobedience.

These exhortations are amazingly instructive to us who live
under the new or "better" covenant because we are as prone to wander as Israel was. Indeed, the words of the prophets are fraught with

significance as they point us to the tender, fatherly heart, yet firm, disciplining hand, of God. We also see the struggle of God's people with the expressions of the spiritual warfare of their day, and we are humbled. In the midst of our own warfare experiences, we can learn from the pervasive emphasis in almost all of the prophetic writings that weds beliefs about God with the tangible expressions of those beliefs in ethics and daily practices. The prophet Habakkuk will be our specific window into the richness of the contribution of the prophetic books to our spiritual growth. Let's learn from this courageous man of God.

SPIRITUALLY FORMED BY A PROPHETIC BOOK: HABAKKUK

Habakkuk is one of the most intriguing of the seventeen prophetic books because it wrestles with a pivotal issue for God's people throughout the ages: *How can God be all-powerful, all-loving, and just when evil exists and flourishes?* Habakkuk's prophecy is considered a "theodicy" (from the Greek *theos* = "God"; *dikê* = "justice") because it defends God's justice in the face of evil's apparent victory. Habakkuk's timing is crucial because he is writing at one of the lowest ebbs in the history of the divided kingdom of Israel and Judah. Within two or three years of his prophecy, vicious hordes of Nebuchadnezzar's Babylonian soldiers will plunder little Judah (in 605 B.C.), eventually destroying the land and exiling the people (in 587 B.C.).

What is so intriguing about Habakkuk's prophecy is the structure of his words and the unexpected response of God to his cry. The following is the flow of the argument of Habakkuk:

1:1-4 — **The prophet Habakkuk's** *first cry* **to God:** "What will You do about all of the evil and injustice in Judah?"
   1:5-11 — **God's** *first answer:* "I will send the Chaldeans (Babylonians) to crush you!"
1:12-17 — **Habakkuk's** *second cry* **to God:** "How can You, O God, use a more wicked people to judge Your own people and still be just?"
   2:1 — **Habakkuk's commitment** to wait for God's reply (the book's pivotal point).

2:2-20—God's *second answer* (to both questions)*:*
"My sure judgment will surely come."
- **2:4-8** *Woe 1*—upon *the proud* who plunder others; they will be plundered.
- **2:9-11** *Woe 2*—upon *the crooked;* they will be accused.
- **2:12-14** *Woe 3*—upon *the violent;* they will be foiled by God.
- **2:15-17** *Woe 4*—upon *the immoral;* they will be disgraced.
- **2:18-20** *Woe 5*—upon *the idolatrous;* they will be silenced.

3:1-19—**Habakkuk's prayer and resolution** in light of God's ultimate judgment of all unrighteousness and injustice.

3:1-15—**Habakkuk's prayer of faith:** "LORD, I have heard the report about Thee and I fear./O LORD, revive Thy work in the midst of the years,/In the midst of the years make it known;/In wrath remember mercy" (3:2).

3:3-15—His prayerful recounting of God's past trustworthiness in *an epic psalm.*[3]

3:3-7—God can be trusted because of His gracious presence and guidance when entering the land of Canaan in the conquest.

3:8-15—God can also be trusted because of His miraculous acts in the conquest of the land of Canaan.

3:16-19—**Habakkuk's resolution to remain faithful,** no matter what happens:

Though the fig tree should not blossom,
And there be no fruit on the vines,
Though the yield of the olive should fail,
And the fields produce no food,
Though the flock should be cut off from the fold,
And there be no cattle in the stalls,
Yet I will exult in the Lord,
I will rejoice in the God of my salvation.
The Lord God is my strength,
And He has made my feet like hinds' feet,
And makes me walk on my high places.

We see many of the typical characteristics of the prophecy genre in Habakkuk and will attend to them in a moment. However, first we need to see how God can use a prophetic book to form us spiritually. We note that Habakkuk, in his first complaint to God in 1:2-4 and even more strongly in his second cry in 1:12-17, was very open and bold in expressing his anger and frustration to God about the spiritual and social conditions in the land of Judah. Observe especially his honest but respectful challenge to the Lord in 1:12-13:

> Art Thou not from everlasting,
> O LORD, my God, my Holy One?
> We will not die.
> Thou, O LORD, hast appointed them to judge;
> And Thou, O Rock, hast established them to correct.
> Thine eyes are too pure to approve evil,
> And Thou canst not look on wickedness with favor.
> Why dost Thou look with favor
> On those who deal treacherously?
> Why art Thou silent when the wicked swallow up
> Those more righteous than they?

Notice how distraught and angry the prophet is toward God, yet he is never demeaning or disrespectful in his complaint. Rather, he first asserts what God's character is like in its holiness and how this must explain why God is using the Babylonians as His instrument of judgment and correction (verse 12). He then boldly expresses to the Lord what is on his heart, but he never violates God's honor when he questions God's actions. Habakkuk strikes a dynamic balance and gives us a wonderful model for expressing our concerns to God about what He has allowed to happen to His people. Central to our spiritual growth and well-being is this ability to speak freely, honestly, and yet reverently to God in our complaints and reasoning with Him. Habakkuk is unsurpassed in achieving this balance.

Second, we gain an important but painful insight into God's work in our lives as we observe how He worked in the lives of His people. For instance, God allowed Judah to fall into deep sin so that the Mosaic Law was ignored, justice was not upheld, the wicked overwhelmed the righteous, and justice was perverted (1:4). Habakkuk cried out to God as if it were God's responsibility to correct this situation. While the Lord was still involved with His people, it was not His will to rescue Judah this time. God had already mercifully done that for many generations! Instead, this time God intevened by using an evil, pagan people as an instrument of discipline on His people. This is a familiar pattern in His dealings with Israel (for example, during the period of the judges). God had even forewarned Israel in Moses' time that this would be one of the curses of disobedience to the Law (see Deuteronomy 28:25,33,49-57). Now the hypothetical curses of Deuteronomy 28 were going to become a stark reality for Judah.

In particular, God was allowing the barbarous Babylonians to triumph over little Judah. This seemed unjust to Habakkuk, given his spectrum of righteousness and justice. Sure, Judah was perverted in its behavior at present, but she wasn't in the Babylonians' league! How could God allow the greater evil to triumph over the lesser one? This seemed immensely unjust to Habakkuk. Perhaps it seems the same to us when we experience similar judgments as God's new covenant people. Our cry resembles Habakkuk's: "While we may have sin in our lives individually and collectively, Lord, we are certainly not as bad as the unbelievers around us!"

However, such a comparison did not impress God in Habakkuk's day, nor does it in ours. Rather, it seems that God *still allows* evil like sickness and death to discipline us (see 1 Corinthians 11:28-32). Moreover, He even allows evil people to persecute us as a part of His child training in our lives (see Hebrews 12:4-13). While these are painful truths, they are necessary in our spiritual formation. God deals with His children with both the right hand of joy and, if necessary, the left hand of sorrow. The book of Habakkuk is decidedly instructive about God's theology of the left hand.

Last, this prophetic book teaches us a remarkable lesson about how to trust God in the midst of terrifying circumstances. Habakkuk faced the overwhelming destruction of his people and his nation. He was confronted with the prospect of losing all that was dear to him on earth! Therefore, when he girds up his loins and seeks to trust God while facing such catastrophic circumstances, we would be wise to learn from his example how he could do that.

Habakkuk's prophecy ends with his trembling and quivering resolution to trust God no matter if the whole land is destroyed and there is nothing to eat (3:16-19). How did he get to this point of scared, but sure, trust? This is where the preceding verses of the prophecy are so important. In particular, God's faithfulness in the past, which Habakkuk recounts in 3:3-15 (in an epic song with two movements), is what emboldens him to place his trust in God. *Habakkuk must look to the past in order to face the future!* But this is typical of the perspective of the saints of both testaments. Their orientation was an *historical* one. Their faith in God was rooted not only in God's character as revealed in the Bible, but also in His deeds recorded in history. While we modern, Western believers are increasingly existential and live for the here and now, biblical believers were historically oriented and lived in light of God's plan in history. What an incredible contrast this makes when disaster and catastrophe strike! And this brings us to the heart of Habakkuk's orientation.

Notice that the epic psalm of 3:3-15 recounts God's presence and guidance (3:3-7) and His miraculous acts (3:8-15) that occurred during Israel's conquest of the land, about eight hundred years earlier. Now that's an historical orientation! We need to pause and drink in this remarkable perspective. Facing the total devastation of his nation, Habakkuk apparently drew extraordinary comfort from God's loving acts toward His people some eight centuries earlier! What does this tell us about his faith — and ours?

Some have compared Habakkuk's perspective, and that of the other Old Testament believers, to that of a person rowing a boat. When you row a boat, you face the rear of the boat. To see where you're heading (in the future), you periodically glance over your shoulder and look ahead. However, most of the time you're looking at where you've been. If you have kept a straight line from where you started, you can be sure that you will arrive at your desired destination. Do you see the analogy?

Old Testament believers primarily looked back at what God had done in creating the nation of Israel through the patriarchs (Abraham, Isaac, and Jacob) and in redeeming His people from Egypt and bringing them into the Promised Land. These events clearly defined who they were as God's people and powerfully expressed God's love and commitment to them. If they could stay focused on these beginnings, they could stay on course to where God wanted to lead them in the future. But if they lost sight of their past, they mortgaged the future. Great is the cost of losing sight of your history!

Habakkuk knew this and apparently drew great encouragement for the frightful future with his eight-hundred-year backward gaze. These ancient events had far more to say to him and his people about who they really were than the events that lay just ahead! To face the future he had to recount the past afresh. With this noteworthy orientation, Habakkuk has much to tell us about how we can face a future that may be uncertain, or perhaps disastrous. If we learn from him, then we can say with Habakkuk,

> Yet I will exult in the LORD,
> I will rejoice in the God of my salvation. (3:18)

THE ROLE OF PROPHETS IN A NONPROFIT ORGANIZATION!

Much of what Habakkuk says and does is typical of Israel's other prophets who wrote the seventeen prophetic books of the Old Testament. In particular, there are three key characteristics of biblical prophecies.

The Prophets Are Creative "Covenant Enforcers"

The Old Testament prophets speak to the people of Israel (and sometimes the surrounding nations) on behalf of God. What they say is what God wants them to say. Therefore, in some respects prophetic literature parallels the Bible's narrative literature:

Narratives/histories	**humans** = main characters, but God = the Hero of the narratives
Prophecies	**prophets** = main speakers, but God = the Source of prophets' words

In this sense the prophets' words are unoriginal because they are rooted in God's initiative and reflect what He wants to communicate to His people. But the prophetic literature is unoriginal in another sense, also. The prophets' basic role is to remind Israel of the provisions of her covenant relationship with God (for example, the Mosaic covenant) and to call her back to living faithfully within that relationship. Thus the title "covenant enforcement mediators." They are gifts of God's grace to His people to serve as "reminders" and "renewers" of Israel's relationship with Him.

The prophets' message was that Israel would reap *the blessings* of the Mosaic covenant if they obeyed God (see Deuteronomy 28:1-14) and *the curses* of the covenant if they disobeyed (see 28:15-68). Usually by the time the prophets began to speak to Israel on behalf of God, the divine curses had already begun to occur. As one might guess, this created a difficult context for their ministry.

Therefore, as Israel's history records, the prophets' reminding and renewing of the people was largely a thankless task! So much so that Jesus could summarize the continuity in suffering between the prophets' ministry and His own by saying,

> "Blessed are you when men hate you, and ostracize you, and cast insults at you, and spurn your name as evil, for the sake of the Son of Man. Be glad in that day, and leap for joy, for behold, your reward is great in heaven; for in the same way their fathers used to treat the prophets."
> (Luke 6:22-23)

Similarly, the writer of Hebrews speaks about the remarkable faith of the Old Testament prophets (and other heroes) with these stirring words:

Women received back their dead by resurrection; and others were tortured, not accepting their release, in order that they might obtain a better resurrection; and others experienced mockings and scourgings, yes, also chains and imprisonment. They were stoned, they were sawn in two, they were tempted, they were put to death with the sword; they went about in sheepskins, in goatskins, being destitute, afflicted, ill-treated (men of whom the world was not worthy), wandering in deserts and mountains and caves and holes in the ground. (Hebrews 11:35-38)

Tradition tells us that Isaiah was the one sawn in two at the orders of the evil king Manasseh. The prophet Zechariah was stoned to death (see 2 Chronicles 24:20-22; Matthew 23:35), as was Jeremiah. Therefore, these descriptions are not just rhetoric, but they actually happened to faithful servants of God. People in Israel were not standing in line to become prophets!

In spite of an unpopular role in Israel's history, the prophets went about their work with amazing creativity. They used numerous types of prophecy to communicate their passionate messages. For example, some have counted at least eleven types of messages in the prophetic books:[4]

- *Disaster Prophecy* (an imminent or future disaster is coming)
- *Salvation Prophecy* (future restoration announced)
- *Woe Speech* (specific judgment is coming for specific sins; for example, Habakkuk 2:4-20)
- *Prophetic Dirge* (a funeral lament over Israel as if she were dead)
- *Prophetic Hymn* (a psalm or hymn praising God, as in worship services)
- *Prophetic Liturgy* (two or more speakers respond to one another; for example, Habakkuk 1:2-17)
- *Prophetic Disputation* (a persuasive speech seeking the acceptance of some truth)
- *Prophetic Lawsuit* (Israel is on trial before God)

- *War Oracles* (assurances of the defeat of foreign nations by God)
- *Prophetic Vision Report* (reports of what the prophet saw in a vision about God's message)
- *Prophetic Narratives* (the prophet's commissioning, or taking instructions from God)

The main goal of reading the prophetic books is not identifying the various forms or devices the prophets use, but rather, noting the main divisions of the prophet's message. This means thinking in terms of "oracles" or units of prophetic thought,[5] especially in the longer prophecies. These books are not like narratives that tell a story or like laws that follow a pattern. Rather, biblical prophecies are generally a string of oracles or prophetic topics that God revealed to the prophet at various times. Our responsibility is to note when the topic changes significantly. If it does, then we have probably begun a different oracle given to the prophet by God at a different time.

For example, one of the best-known oracle beginnings starts in Isaiah 6:1: "In the year of King Uzziah's death, I saw the Lord sitting on a throne, lofty and exalted, with the train of His robe filling the temple." Notice that Isaiah gives the date of the prophecy as the year King Uzziah died (740 B.C.) and also how the prophecy begins (it starts with a vision of the Lord in His temple). Both the date and the setting signal the beginning of a new oracle or prophetic unit. These are the kinds of structural signals in the prophetic books that the reader should notice.

The Prophets Require Historical Background Study

Visualize a spectrum of the Bible's various genres. On one end would be those genres or types of literature that demand little knowledge of the human author, the recipients, and the historical setting of the period. These genres can be read quite well without undertaking much background research; they are not particularly historical context–dependent. The genres on the other end of the spectrum, though, demand more historical background knowledge to understand what is going on within the various passages. These

genres demand some knowledge of the author and the historical setting of the recipients, and information about what was going on in
the peoples' lives. Without this information, we would be greatly
handicapped when we read these genres. We could get some of the
author's thrust, but will miss much of it. A spectrum of some of the
biblical genres might look like this:

Background Information Is Less Significant		Background Information Is of Average Significance	Background Information Is Highly Significant
●─────────────	───────────	●────────	────────────●
Narratives	**Law**	**Psalms**	**Epistles**
Proverbs		**Gospels**	**Prophecies**
Wisdom Literature		**Acts**	**Parables**

You will notice that the prophecies genre falls near the end of
the spectrum where background information is *highly desirable*. To
appreciate fully what the prophets were addressing in the life of
Israel, we need to know about the historical setting and circumstances of that particular period—where the book falls within
Israel's history and what the people of Israel had done to stir God
to send this prophet. Consulting a Bible dictionary, handbook, or
encyclopedia will pay great dividends to the reader's understanding. Again, the principle of a little information greatly aiding our
spiritual transformation is valid and timely.

The Prophets Make Specific and Holistic Contributions

We can now summarize how God may want to use our reading of
the seventeen prophetic books in our lives. We always want to be
aware of the fact that we are reading about how the prophets of
Israel called their people back to faithful obedience to the *old
covenant with its blessings and curses*. While this is not our
covenant, these remarkable books still reveal to us God's steadfast
love and holiness and His people's tendency to wander from Him.

Additionally, the prophetic books emphasize both right belief
and right behavior. God had an exceedingly holistic emphasis for
His old covenant people as they lived a life of faithfulness. He did

not just want them to hold right beliefs in their hearts, but also to employ right practices in their interaction with other people in business dealings, religious acts, family relationships, social relationships, and so on. Every area of their lives was to showcase the reality of their faith in the God of Abraham, Isaac, and Jacob. While there are dozens of examples of this, let's examine a representative one from the prophet Amos:

> Hear this, you who trample the needy, to do away with the
> humble of the land, saying,
> "When will the new moon be over,
> So that we may buy grain,
> And the sabbath, that we may open the wheat market,
> To make the bushel smaller and the shekel bigger,
> And to cheat with dishonest scales,
> So as to buy the helpless for money
> And the needy for a pair of sandals,
> And that we may sell the refuse of the wheat?" (8:4-6)

Unlike the neighboring pagan peoples, the Israelites were to have tender hearts for the poor that aided, not exploited, them. Time and again God rebukes His people through the prophets for their dishonest manipulation of the needy and the exploitation of those in vulnerable states. This was not to occur in a land where the God of Mercy reigned! It is the prophets who remind Israel of such mercy and who call their people back to just and merciful behavior toward the poor and disadvantaged. While there is some emphasis on similar issues of social justice in the New Testament (for example, James 5:1-6), it is relatively rare. For this emphasis and the tenderness of heart that it brings, we must read the Old Testament prophets.

Therefore, we derive remarkable edification from investing time and energy in reading, studying, and applying this part of God's Word. No other part of the Bible addresses these specific issues. God designed the prophetic books to do this. Any spiritual diet that excludes them will be unbalanced and may lead to spiritual anemia. He who has ears, let him hear!

THE SPECIFIC CONTRIBUTION OF THE PROPHETS TO OUR SPIRITUAL FORMATION

■ **The Biblical Books:** Isaiah, Jeremiah, Lamentations, Ezekiel, and Daniel (called the Major Prophets); and Hosea, Joel, Amos, Obadiah, Jonah, Micah, Nahum, Habakkuk, Zephaniah, Haggai, Zechariah, and Malachi (called the Minor Prophets).

■ **Primary Contribution:** To exhort us about the rewards of covenant obedience and warn us of the discipline of disobedience under the old covenant so that we are challenged to maintain our heart for God and our just treatment of others as we live under the new covenant.

> **Therefore, ask,** "What does this passage or oracle tell us about Israel's behavior in her covenantal relationship with God and about God's response to His people, and those areas that we may also be susceptible to neglect within our new covenant relationship?"

■ **Secondary Contribution:** To give us glimpses into the immediate future of God's people or into the distant future of the messianic/new covenant era and the superseding blessing of life in this climactic era.

> **Therefore, ask,** "What does this passage or oracle tell us about God's plans for Israel (now past) or His plans for His new covenant people (now present or still future)?"

A BRIEF WORD REGARDING PROPHECIES ABOUT THE FUTURE

While many of the announcements of the Old Testament prophets were of events that were future to them, few of those events extend into our era. In other words, most of the events that God told them to announce *were future to them but are now past to us.* For example,

Habakkuk's prophecies about the coming of the Chaldeans (Babylonians) in 1:5-11 occurred within two or three years of his announcement. Therefore, whatever part of the prophet's message was "foretelling" was primarily significant to his immediate hearers. This fits with the prophets' basic emphasis on "forthtelling."

Remember, less than 2 percent of Old Testament prophecies speak about Messiah, and less than 5 percent speak about our new covenant era. However, while not large, these percentages are significant because of the central importance of the coming of the Messiah and His inauguration of the better covenant that God had long promised.

This is a fascinating area of study and has its own marvelous contribution to our spiritual growth. In particular, studying these prophecies offers us enormous encouragement regarding God's working in history. Seeing how the coming of Jesus the Messiah was rooted and grounded in the history of Israel over a period of fifteen hundred years tremendously boosts our recovery of an historical orientation as modern believers. God is the God of history, which includes our history! Our souls will be strengthened as we recognize our historical connection to God's kingdom plan. This study will forever strengthen one's foundation in this area. However, focusing on the messianic and new covenant prophecies within the seventeen prophetic books is beyond our scope. Therefore, let me simply recommend three remarkable books for studying this topic.

- (An old classic!) E. W. Hengstenberg, *Christology of the Old Testament (and a Commentary on the Messianic Predictions)* (Grand Rapids: Kregel, 1970; reprint of the 1847 translation from the German original). It has 600 pages on messianic prophecies in eleven of the Old Testament prophets.
- (A recent gem!) Gerard Van Groningen, *Messianic Revelation in the Old Testament* (Grand Rapids: Baker, 1990). This has 518 pages on the messianic concept in the Prophets.
- For the new covenant prophecies within "the seventeen," I recommend: (A classic of sorts!) Alva J. McClain, *The*

*Greatness of the Kingdom: An Inductive Study of the
Kingdom of God* (Winona Lake, Ind.: BMH Books,
1974). McClain has about 125 pages on the concept of
the kingdom of God in the prophetic books.

Closer to home is our abiding interest in the 1 percent of Old
Testament prophecies that announce events yet to come, what we
call "end-time events." Zechariah, who prophesied after Judah was
carried into exile in Babylon in 587 B.C., provides a stirring example of this sort of prophecy. Apparently, Zechariah was one of the
Jewish remnant who returned to Israel to rebuild the land. He prophesied around 520, alongside the prophet Haggai, to motivate the
people of Israel *to finish rebuilding the temple.* Listen to his words
about the Lord's return to the land in Zechariah 14:4-9:

> And in that day His feet will stand on the Mount of Olives,
> which is in front of Jerusalem on the east; and the Mount of
> Olives will be split in its middle from east to west by a very
> large valley, so that half of the mountain will move toward
> the north and the other half toward the south. And you will
> flee by the valley of My mountains, for the valley of the
> mountains will reach to Azel; yes, you will flee just as you
> fled before the earthquake in the days of Uzziah king of
> Judah. Then the LORD, my God, will come, and all the holy
> ones with Him! And it will come about in that day that there
> will be no light; the luminaries will dwindle. For it will be a
> unique day which is known to the LORD, neither day nor
> night, but it will come about that at evening time there will
> be light. And it will come about in that day that living
> waters will flow out of Jerusalem, half of them toward the
> eastern sea and the other half toward the western sea; it will
> be in summer as well as in winter. *And the* LORD *will be
> king over all the earth; in that day the* LORD *will be the only
> one, and His name the only one.* (emphasis mine)

The Lord gave these prophecies to Zechariah to encourage and
strengthen the people of God in his day. They now fortify us as the

people of God in our day as we await the return of Jesus the Messiah to the Mount of Olives. We believers in Jesus are mentioned in this prophecy! (Can you find it?) We will have a phenomenal view of these earth-shattering events!

Although these prophecies certainly enlighten us about our future, that is not their major value to us. As in Zechariah's day, they were given to encourage God's people to persevere in faithfulness to Him in the midst of difficult circumstances. In light of our glorious future with Messiah, we should choose to trust Him *in the midst of today's circumstances.* This is the desired impact of many of the future prophecies. Their goal is to encourage and strengthen us for the tasks immediately before us. Drink in this encouraging picture and absorb it into the depths of your soul. Be strengthened! *In that day* He will be King over all the earth!

Chapter Ten

DISCIPLESHIP 101:
THE GOSPELS

"And why do you call Me, 'Lord, Lord,' and do not do what I say? Everyone who comes to Me, and hears My words, and acts upon them, I will show you whom he is like: he is like a man building a house, who dug deep and laid a foundation upon the rock; and when a flood rose, the torrent burst against that house and could not shake it, because it had been well built. But the one who has heard, and has not acted accordingly, is like a man who built a house upon the ground without any foundation; and the torrent burst against it and immediately it collapsed, and the ruin of that house was great."

LUKE 6:46-49

Christ's statements are either cosmic or comic.

JOHN BLANCHARD[1]

ROCHELLE IS A TYPICAL MEMBER OF HER CHURCH. SHE IS committed to Christ and faithful to the programs of her church. She came to know Christ personally in junior high, but did not really start growing until she went to summer camp just before her senior year in high school. Since that time she has been growing fairly steadily as a Christian. Most of those who went to school with Rochelle or work with her now know her to be a Christian. She even brings her Bible to work and finds a quiet place during her lunch break to read the Scriptures.

However, Rochelle is beginning to encounter some difficulties—some storms—in her life. Most of them can be traced to her dating relationship with a wonderful guy she recently met at a business function. He is kind and thoughtful to Rochelle, fun-loving, but not a Christian. Also, he parties with a group of friends that push way beyond the limits that Rochelle has adopted since she has been a Christian. She now feels caught in the midst of a very confusing situation. It is complicated by the fact that she thinks she might be falling in love with this man. All of this confusion motivates Rochelle to cry out for the Lord's help in her disarray.

This particular day during her lunch break, Rochelle is reading in the Gospel of Mark. One of the elders at church suggested that she read about Jesus because He so readily came to the aid of those who sought His help during His ministry. Rochelle is impressed with Jesus' compassion as she reads the early chapters of Mark. But when she gets to Mark 4:35-41, she becomes riveted by Mark's account of Jesus calming the storm on the Sea of Galilee for His disciples. She is deeply touched by this story. She identifies with the fearful disciples who think they are going to drown as they row in the midst of the storm. She remembers a talk on this passage by one of her youth leaders a few years before, and the speaker's main point comes rushing back to her with a vivid freshness. She feels a sense of comfort and peace as she ponders the thrust of this story.

Jesus wants to calm the storms of her life just as He calmed the storm on the Sea of Galilee. Jesus wants to rescue her from her storms just as He did His disciples. Jesus is saying to Rochelle what the disciples heard Him say— "Hush, be still." She feels a wonderful comfort this particular day. She knows that Jesus is in the boat with her and that He will not let her drown.

The story of Jesus calming the Sea of Galilee in Mark 4:35-41 is well known (with parallels in Matthew 8:18, 23-27, and Luke 8:22-25). Teachers generally relate it to our spiritual lives by asserting that it teaches that Jesus cares about our individual ships of faith and wants to calm the storms of our lives before we sink in overwhelming problems. This is Rochelle's understanding of the story, and it agrees with her youth pastor's interpretation. In fact, it agrees with that of thousands of pastors, youth pastors, Sunday school teachers, Bible study leaders, and retreat and camp speakers who derive the same type of application from this passage.

I would suggest, however, that *this interpretation is popular not because it is accurate, but because it reflects our cultural glasses!* It is rooted in an increasingly existential view of the world and also in a misunderstanding of the genre of the Gospels. Such an interpretation makes for nice emotional comfort, but it is simply not the meaning nor an appropriate application of the passage! In fact, it is a radical *distortion* of the emphasis of this passage in particular, and of the Gospels in general. So, I suggest we start over to determine what this story means. What is the point of Jesus calming this storm on the Sea of Galilee?

BEING SPIRITUALLY FORMED BY A GOSPEL PASSAGE: MARK 4:35-41

And on that day, when evening had come, He said to them, "Let us go over to the other side." And leaving the multitude, they took Him along with them, just as He was, in the boat; and other boats were with Him. And there arose a fierce gale of wind, and the waves were breaking over the boat so much that the boat was already filling up. And He Himself was in the stern, asleep on the cushion; and they awoke Him and said to him, "Teacher, do You not care that we are perishing?" And being aroused, He rebuked the wind and said to the sea, "Hush, be still." And the wind died down and it became perfectly calm. And He said to them, "Why are you so timid? How is it that you have no faith?" And they became very much afraid and said to one another, "Who then is this, that even the wind and the sea obey Him?"

This incident occurs at an interesting point, roughly midway, in Jesus' three-and-a-half-year ministry. He has been preaching to great response all over Galilee, the northern part of Israel. After a healing, for example, the enthusiastic former leper spreads the word about Jesus "to such an extent that Jesus could no longer publicly enter a city, but stayed out in unpopulated areas; and they were coming to Him from everywhere" (Mark 1:45).

Such popularity drew the hasty attention of the religious leaders of Israel, and they began to investigate Jesus and challenge His claims. In fact, Mark 2:1–3:6 recounts *five successive conflicts* between Jesus and the Pharisees that immediately follow the healing of the leper. In these conflicts, Mark contrasts Jesus' valuing of paralyzed, ritually unclean, and disabled Israelites with the Pharisees' valuing of their oral traditions. The conflicts escalate and reach their climax in Mark 3:6: "And the Pharisees went out and immediately began taking counsel with the Herodians against Him, as to how they might destroy Him." These odd bedfellows, normally on opposite ends of the religious spectrum, are now united in their desire to kill Jesus.

In response to this growing opposition among the leaders (not the masses), Jesus withdraws with His disciples (Mark 3:7-12) and then officially chooses twelve of them to be with Him and to be sent out to preach (Mark 3:13-19). At this juncture a pivotal event in Jesus' ministry occurs. Mark 3:20-35 records that Jesus' family comes to him and tries to put Him away because they think He is crazy (Mark 3:20-21,31-32). Right on their heels come the scribes (the theologians) from Jerusalem, who give their theological judgment of Jesus' ministry: "He is possessed by Beelzebul," and "He casts out the demons by the ruler of the demons" (Mark 3:22).

What an assessment! After seeing all of Jesus' miracles and hearing all of His teaching over the previous months, they conclude that He is a demonized man who harnesses *Satan's* power. They think He is a sorcerer! However, in correcting them, Jesus also points out that they are making the eternally fatal mistake of attributing the work of the Holy Spirit to the Devil (Mark 3:23-30). Additionally, Jesus redefines who Messiah's family is: "For whoever does the will of God, he is My brother and sister and mother" (Mark 3:35). Moreover, this unofficial rejection by the religious leaders of Israel motivates Jesus to change the way He teaches. He now begins to instruct in parables so that those with hardened hearts will not understand and those with receptive hearts will receive the truth (Mark 4:1-34).

This is where our passage begins. At evening, after an incredible day of rejection and teaching in parables ("And on that day, . . ." in Mark 4:35), Jesus directs His disciples to go over to the other side of the Sea of Galilee. Probably they are traveling from the west side to the eastern shore, in a small fleet of boats, to get away from the multitudes (Mark 4:36). Frequently, squalls or storms suddenly arise from the south or southwest and pummel small craft making this six- to seven-mile crossing. These winds, in addition to the strong prevailing westerly winds, caused the waves to break over the sides of these small boats (verse 37). However, because of the full and unusually stressful day, Jesus peacefully remained asleep in the elevated stern of the boat on the cushion by the helmsman's seat (verse 38).

By contrast, Jesus' disciples are panic-stricken, and they finally wake Him with a rebuke: "Teacher, do You not care that we are perishing?" (verse 38). Jesus graciously addresses the problem by rebuking the wind and telling the sea *to be still* (verse 39). A virtually identical rebuke occurs in 1:25 when Jesus casts a demon out of a man in the synagogue in Capernaum. Could this storm be demon-driven, a strategic attack from Satan? It's very possible, for Jesus seems to treat it as such.

Additionally, Jesus challenges His disciples with two questions: "Why are you so timid? How is it that you have no faith?" (verse 40). From these questions we can assume that Jesus expected His disciples to have adequate faith at this point to handle a crisis. He had already given them as kingdom insiders the special privilege of the explanation of His parables (Mark 4:11,34). Because they had been with Him for some time and had recently been officially chosen as His twelve representatives (Mark 3:13-19), Jesus expected more faith from them than from the masses. However, at this point the Twelve were disappointing. They did not yet have this kind of faith.

What the disciples did have was fear! We now encounter the third occurrence in this story of the Greek word *mega*, which means "great or large." The first was the *mega* wind in verse 37, which was followed by the *mega* calm in verse 39. But verse 41 has the climactic *mega:* "And they feared a *mega* fear" (my literal translation). Perhaps the disciples' previous fear of drowning was now exceeded by their incredulous fear of Jesus: "And [they] said to one another, 'Who then is this, that even the wind and the sea obey Him?'" (verse 41). Note that they are not questioning Jesus' identity. Their question is about Jesus' status or honor within the hierarchy of powerful beings in the universe. Because God Himself controls the wind and the sea (Psalm 107:29), then Jesus must possess the Father's direct authorization to overtly display this control. This was a scary thing indeed! No wonder this reality induced a *mega* fear in them.

However, there is more to this story than the stilling of the sea and the disciples' fear. Lurking in the background are the Old Testament prophecies about what God's kingdom would be like when Messiah came. The Old Testament prophets foretold of miraculous changes in at least nine major aspects of the world when the Messiah came to Israel:

1. The prophets foretold beneficial changes in the earth's climate and natural elements (Isaiah 30:23-26; Ezekiel 47:1-12; Joel 2:21-26; Zechariah 14:8).
2. The Messianic Kingdom would be characterized by unprecedented growth and fruitage of trees (Isaiah 41:17-20; Ezekiel 36:8-11,29-30; 47:6-7,12; Joel 2:21-26).
3. The prophets declared that there would be great productivity of animals, including a huge multitude of fish, during the Messianic Kingdom (Jeremiah 31:10-12; Ezekiel 36:11; 47:8-10).
4. The Messianic Kingdom would be blessed with a superabundant supply of food (Psalm 72:16; Isaiah 30:23-24; Jeremiah 31:10-14; Ezekiel 34:25-30; 36:29-30; Joel 2:21-26; Zechariah 8:11-12).

5. According to the prophets, wine would be abundant in the Messianic Kingdom (Jeremiah 31:10-12; Joel 2:21-26; Amos 9:13; Zechariah 8:11-12).
6. Unprecedented changes in the animal world during the Messianic Kingdom were predicted (Isaiah 11:6-9; 65:25).
7. The prophets asserted that the Messianic Kingdom would be free from ordinary hazards (Isaiah 11:8-9; 65:23-25; Ezekiel 34:25-29).
8. There will be healing of physical diseases and deformities (Isaiah 29:18; 33:24; 35:5-6).
9. The prophets foretold that the Messianic Kingdom would be marked by great longevity of life (Isaiah 65:20-22).[2]

As Showers puts it, "The primary purpose of Jesus' miracles was to demonstrate the fact that He was the Messiah promised by God to Israel through the prophets."[3] In other words, every one of Jesus' miracles corresponds to one of the nine aspects of change mentioned above. Every one of His miracles was to prove that He was the Messiah, because each miracle fulfilled one of these areas of prophetic anticipation. While these miracles point in some sense to Jesus' deity, they primarily point to His identity as Messiah (which includes deity). This is what the Gospel writers were trying to convince their readers of—that Jesus is the long-promised Messiah of Israel!

This background is crucial to understanding Mark 4:35-41 and Jesus' calming of the wind and the sea. Because these are ordinary hazards that threaten the safety of humans, they correspond to the seventh category above. By stilling the wind and the sea, Jesus proved that He, and He alone, had the authority from the Father to bring about the safety from the hazards of nature that would be found in the messianic kingdom. In other words, only Jesus of Nazareth could command the wind and sea as God does. Therefore, only Jesus of Nazareth could be the prophesied Messiah!

The disciples' realization that Jesus had such colossal power frightened them. However, knowing the context of the messianic prophecies, we can better appreciate why they questioned His status. Moreover, the timing of their newfound awe about Jesus as Messiah was crucial. Remember, earlier that same day they probably had a ringside seat to hear Jesus' family reckon Him insane (3:20-21) and Israel's theologians declare Him demonized! Surely, these accusations shook their faith and confidence in Jesus to some degree. Therefore, Jesus' powerful manifestation of His messianic authority over nature was timely and compassionate. It must have more than offset the fallacious accusations of those family members and religious leaders who should have known better.

Having read this short passage in light of the larger context, we can better determine its contribution to our spiritual growth. Does it teach that Jesus wants to calm the storms of our lives? Does it comfort us about the things that rock our boat? While other passages do give this kind of comfort, Mark 4:35-41 is not one of them! If this is what this incident is about, then it actually teaches that Jesus is asleep and we need to wake Him up and rebuke Him to motivate Him to give attention to our wind and waves! Of course, this is not the thrust of the story, nor its application to us.

Rather, this remarkable story tells us of Jesus' unmistakable authority over nature as the Messiah. For some reason, His authority in this area seems to be of a greater magnitude than even His authority over disease, or over demons, or over the multiplying of food. This authority seems more spectacular and more intimidating. It inspires a greater sense of awe about Jesus, rather than comfortable familiarity with Him. This passage stretches our perspective about Jesus beyond our well-known sense of Him as "Gentle Jesus, Meek and Mild."

And this is likely how God wants to use this and similar Gospel passages in our lives. Perhaps we have a shrunken view of Jesus. Perhaps we have "domesticated" Him so much that there is no sense of awe or godly fear about His person. Perhaps our sense that Jesus is only meek and mild is lopsided and not the whole story. Perhaps our view of Jesus is too small. Perhaps we have contoured our view of Him in such a way that He doesn't threaten our way of life or the choices we want to make in our lives. Seeing the disciples' response startles us into this realization. He *is* gentle and He *is* meek. But He is *also* the reigning and ruling *King of kings* and *Lord of lords* who has absolute authority over all things, including the wind and sea—and our lives!

Is this the Jesus you know and love? This is the real Jesus—the one presented to us in the Gospels. Knowing Him in all of His messianic fullness is absolutely necessary to our spiritual formation. This is why we must read the Gospels as they were intended to be read. Distorting them leads to a distorting of Jesus. It makes the Gospels just another source of insight about ourselves rather than a dynamic picture of Jesus the Messiah. Therefore, we must learn to read them, and Him, correctly!

SIX PRINCIPLES FOR READING THE GOSPELS FOR SPIRITUAL FORMATION

Unfortunately, we need to counter widespread bad habits in interpreting the Gospels. To that end, the following principles offer some helpful advice for reading the Gospels with sensitivity to their genre and intended focus.

1. Because the Gospels are narratives (like the Old Testament histories), we should emphasize the broader context when reading.

While the exact genre of the Gospels has been hotly debated for several generations, they appear to be biographical in nature and fit most cleanly into the genre of *lives of famous persons*. Many such literary "lives" of well-known people in the Greco-Roman world have been preserved from the time of Jesus. The four Gospels fit quite well into this genre and underscore that the focus of the Christian faith is on the life and person of Jesus of Nazareth. The Gospels are first and foremost about Jesus.

Additionally, because of the story nature of the Gospels, we should always think about the broader sweep of the narrative when we read, constantly relating the various events and teachings to those that precede and follow them. In our reading of Mark 4:35-41, we sought to identify the context of the calming of the sea within the life of Jesus as recorded by Mark in chapters 1–4. Mark himself tells us this is important by beginning 4:35 with the phrase, "And on that day," which sends a signal that what happened earlier "that day" is important and should be noticed. This is notable because, in one sense, the heart of a narrative lies in *the interrelation of the various events and teachings to one another.* To ignore this interrelation is to miss the basic meaning of the narrative. Therefore, when reading the Gospels, always think of the broader flow of the story and establish the context of the event or teaching within that flow. This process reveals the emphasis that the Gospel writer is making in the narrative. It also puts our spiritual formation from the Gospels on a more certain foundation.

2. The Gospels demand some background information regarding history and culture.

It is more relevant to understand the culture, values, and worldview of the people on the pages of the Gospels than to know the specific author or recipients. This is especially true of Westerners because Western culture is so far removed from the biblical culture. People from Asia, Latin America, or Africa are already familiar with some of the basic elements and structures of first-century Mediterranean culture and probably understand something about the importance of group identity, honor-shame concerns, and strong kinship relationships. These core values give essential clues to New Testament culture.

The necessity of these cultural clues can be illustrated in Mark 3:20-35. In this unusual incident, Jesus' family comes to take Him out of the public eye because they have concluded that "He has lost His senses" (3:21). We can all understand the pain Jesus must have felt to be rejected in this manner by His own mother and brothers. But as the firstborn in His family—His "father" Joseph had apparently died—Jesus had assumed the primary, cultural responsibility to defend and advance His family's honor within their community and beyond.[4]

However, Jesus had also incurred the wrath of Israel's religious leaders (2:1–3:6), so much so that they were plotting to kill Him (3:6). Within His cultural context, this means that Jesus is on the brink of shaming His entire family. They are probably at risk of being booted out of the synagogue because of Him. So they spring into immediate action and try to take Him away from His public ministry and quietly keep Him at home. They have a sense of urgency because the religious leaders are right behind them and are ready to declare their own conclusion about Jesus: He is a demonized man (3:22-30)! Such a declaration would most certainly shame Jesus' family and ensure their rejection by their entire community. This is why Mark intertwines Jesus' rejection by His family with the religious leaders' rejection in the same passage (3:20-30). These events that may seem unrelated to Westerners are clearly interrelated within their Middle Eastern cultural context!

Additionally, understanding these concerns about honor and shame and kinship identity helps us make sense of Jesus' seemingly cryptic response to His family's request to get Him to come outside the house where He is teaching and see them (3:31-32). In His response, Jesus rejects both His family's and the religious leaders' conclusions about Him. As Messiah, He is also redefining who will be in *His* family:

> And answering them, He said, "Who are My mother and My brothers?" And looking about on those who were sitting around Him, He said, "Behold, My mother and My brothers! For whoever does the will of God, he is My brother and sister and mother." (3:33-35)

All of this interaction comes to full light when we understand these important historical and cultural aspects of the Gospels.[5]

3. The focus of the Gospels is on Jesus, not on us!

It is almost embarrassing to have to make this statement, but it is absolutely necessary. Why? Because the increasing tendency in our reading of the Gospels is to reduce them primarily to sources of insight about ourselves. For example, we read about Jesus calming a storm on the Sea of Galilee, and we think it is about the storms of our lives. Or we read about Jesus being rejected by His friends and family in the Nazareth synagogue (Luke 4:16-30), and we think it is primarily about our possible rejection by those around us when we take a stand for Christ. Or we read in John 6:1-15 about Jesus miraculously feeding the five thousand in the wilderness with the boy's five barley loaves and two fish, and we think it is about what we should be giving to Jesus! You get the idea.

While this tendency is both a problem of our worldview glasses and a symptom of our narcissistic woundedness, its impact is still tragically the same: We end up knowing more about ourselves and less about Jesus. We become theologically impoverished in our knowledge about the only One who can really transform us! We become ignorant of our Master, whom we should be seeking to please with all our being.

Perhaps a word of balance would be appropriate here. When I say that the Gospels are about Jesus, this does not mean they do not give us any insight into ourselves or have significance and application to our lives. Of course they do. However, the Gospels were primarily written to tell us about who Jesus is, what He did, and why He is the only, true object of our faith. If we change this focus, we distort the very essence of the Gospels. By making the Gospels more about ourselves, we ironically lessen their transforming impact on our lives, because the more we learn about Jesus Christ, the more we will entrust ourselves to Him as His disciples. We will trust Him more in new circumstances and be able to make increasingly hard decisions to live as His child in the ups and downs of life. However, to exercise more faith in the Lord Jesus, we must have an accurate and full knowledge of Him. And that knowledge helps feed a growing intimacy with Him. The four Gospels are the main source of this knowledge. The stakes are high; the cost is great. We must learn to read the Gospels better!

4. One of the primary goals of the Gospel writers is to prove that Jesus is the Messiah, not to prove that He is God.

Does Jesus' miracle of calming the wind and the sea prove that He is God? Many Christians interpret it in that light, along with most of the rest of Jesus' miracles. We automatically think of them as reflecting His deity. Is this accurate? Actually it is not. As we mentioned above, all of Jesus' miracles attest the fact that He is the Messiah—the Anointed One who was long prophesied and long awaited by the people of Israel. Because the Gospel writers share this *historical perspective* with the Old Testament writers, they seek to prove that Jesus of Nazareth is the One about whom the Law, Prophets, and Writings (that is, the entire Old Testament) spoke. Their accounts of Jesus include the fact that He preexisted as Deity as the second person of the Godhead (see John 1:1-18), but this is not their primary emphasis.

In other words, the Gospel writers and the people to whom they wrote did not seem troubled with the idea that God could step into history as the God-man named Jesus. They did not have the antisupernaturalistic worldview that has developed since 1650. Rather, what the people of Israel wanted to know was whether Jesus of Nazareth was the One anointed, appointed, designated, empowered, and solely authorized to fulfill God the Father's bidding on earth. Was Jesus the One who would bring about God's kingdom on earth? Was Jesus the Messiah?

In addition to Western culture's anti-supernaturalism, six centuries of controversies about the Trinity and the person of Christ (second to seventh centuries A.D.) also shape our reading of the Gospels. Christians have been sensitized to oppose those with false doctrine who attack the deity of Christ, and many of us go to the Gospels to seek proof that Jesus is God. Again, while there is some proof of Jesus' preexistence as the second person of the Trinity in the Gospels, this was not the main concern nor central focus of the Gospel writers. They lived before the centuries of theological controversies and had a different goal: to prove that Jesus was the Messiah of Israel. Properly understanding this emphasis gives our relationship with Jesus more of an historical texturing. We will not think of Him in vague, ethereal terms as the second person of the Trinity, but rather as the God-man who walked the earth and now sits in His resurrected and glorified state at the right hand of the Father. In other words, we will have a more historical and biblical view of Jesus. The impact on how we relate to Him will be more specific and therefore more profound.

5. With four different Gospels, we should do comparisons of the various Gospel accounts when appropriate.

While all four Gospels share the central focus on Jesus, each writer nevertheless has a distinctive emphasis regarding the person of Christ. *This is why each Gospel should be read as a literary whole!* We must avoid the temptation to blur one Gospel account together with the other Gospels when they contain the same story. For example, Matthew, Mark, and Luke all have slightly different *purposes* for including the account of Jesus' calming of the storm on the Sea of Galilee. By comparing these purposes we can gain insight into *the unique emphasis of each Gospel.* But when we blend the three accounts together, we lose something unique and precious: the distinctiveness of each Gospel writer's *intention* and the emphasis the Holy Spirit wants to make in our lives through the God-breathed emphasis of each Gospel account.[6]

Therefore, while we remain cautious in comparing the Gospels, doing so is helpful. The tool for studying the four Gospels side by side is called a *synopsis.* The best one is edited by Kurt Aland and entitled *Synopsis of the Four Gospels* (United Bible Societies, 1975). This book lists the Gospel accounts in parallel columns and is of great value. If two or more Gospels have the same incident or teaching, you can easily compare them. Again, this comparison is always secondary to studying each Gospel as a literary whole to determine what the author was emphasizing within the passage. So the primary reason for consulting a synopsis is to gain additional insight into what Matthew, Mark, Luke, or John was seeking to say in a specific passage. Synoptic study helps underscore their uniqueness and common traits.

6. We need to understand the centrality of the kingdom of God in the Gospels.

Mark's Gospel records this statement about the beginning of Jesus' ministry in Galilee:

And after John [the Baptist] had been taken into custody, Jesus came into Galilee, preaching the gospel of God, and saying, *"The time is fulfilled, and the kingdom of God is at hand;* repent and believe in the gospel." (1:14-15, emphasis mine)

Notice that Jesus' announcement about the kingdom of God being at hand is an integral part of his preaching of the gospel. One cannot be separated from the other. All of Galilee must have been buzzing at that announcement! The Jewish people had been waiting centuries for the inauguration of Messiah's kingdom; they must have been ecstatic thinking that the moment was at hand.

However, Jesus would disappoint the typical Jewish person's expectations about the form this kingdom of God would take; most Jews believed the present age would end and the kingdom of God would come immediately *in all of its full power and glory when Messiah came:*

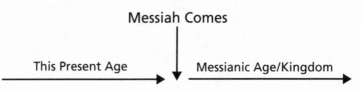

Messiah Comes

This Present Age   Messianic Age/Kingdom

However, as Jesus would explain in His teaching (for example, Matthew 13, the kingdom parables), the messianic kingdom of God was not coming in the form the Jews expected—at least, not at the present time—but was going to begin in an unexpected form. Even more stunning, Messiah's kingdom would be inaugurated, but would not be consummated until He returned. In the meantime (the "in-between time"), Messiah's kingdom would overlap with and run concurrently with this present age! In other words, the kingdom of God would have an "already, but not yet" dimension to it between Messiah's first and second comings.

Once Jesus is unofficially rejected by the religious leaders of Israel (see Matthew 12; Mark 3), He begins to explain about His messianic kingdom coming in this unexpected form (Matthew 13; Mark 4). This does not negate the expected form of the messianic kingdom in all of its glory (Matthew 24–25; Mark 13). But that larger form of Messiah's kingdom must await His return.

Understanding the kingdom of God is essential when reading the Gospels. Living obediently as a citizen of the kingdom presupposes our correct understanding of its nature.

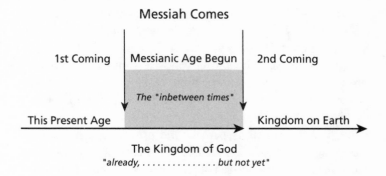

THE GOSPELS AND SPIRITUAL FORMATION: BE DISCIPLED BY JESUS

If the Gospels focus on the life of Jesus Christ, how does this relate to *the believer's* spiritual formation? In the last couple of generations, some have read the Gospels as "discipleship manuals" that tell us how to instruct our "disciples" as we place ourselves in the discipler role of Jesus. Unfortunately, this is both a misunderstanding of the genre of the Gospels and of the meaning of "disciple."[7]

As we have already noted, many Christians read the Gospels as stories about themselves, freely inserting their own issues and concerns into the text. However, the genre of the Gospels also judges this kind of reading as out of bounds and an inappropriate distraction from the focus on Jesus. Which leaves us with the lingering question: How *do* the Gospels relate to our spiritual formation?

In particular, the Gospels are unrelenting in emphasizing and proving that Jesus is the Messiah, come to offer a universal kingdom to all who believe in Him. Critical to our spiritual reading of the Gospels is this profound understanding of the messianic World

Ruler we love and follow. To read the Gospels as metaphorical stories about ourselves is to impoverish His identity and our growth in understanding who He really is and who we should be following!

Another issue relevant to the messianic identity of Jesus is His unique relationship with His disciples. While the Gospels clearly focus on the person of Jesus, they focus on Him *in intimate relationship with His followers.* Because of His resurrection, Jesus is still living and still gaining followers as we speak. So we ask: How is He shaping *us,* His present disciples?

One of the most significant ways He forms us spiritually is through the relationships we disciples have with one another. However, this is never to be confused with the relationship that Jesus also wants to have *with each of us.* It seems that reading and meditating on the Gospels is perhaps the primary means of Jesus continuing to disciple us through the experience of the original disciples. In other words, instead of putting ourselves into Jesus' place and learning how to disciple others as we read the Gospels (a secondary emphasis), *we should put ourselves into the disciples' place by identifying with them in their relationship with Jesus.* In doing this, we avail ourselves of His masterful teaching. By seeing what Jesus did in their lives, we learn what He may want to do in our lives:

- Through His *teaching in discourses,* we learn *faith lessons* about how we can walk in the lifestyle of His currently-unseen kingdom by making direct, obvious applications today.
- Through His *parables* we learn *perspective lessons* about the unique viewpoint of His kingdom that we should cultivate in the midst of the prevailing culture.
- Through His *conflicts with Israel's religious leaders,* we learn *values lessons* about how we can traffic in God's gracious, kingdom authority, not in manmade religious traditions.
- Through His *life* we learn *incarnate lessons* about God's great love for us and what He designed us to look like apart from the tyranny and ravages of sin.

- Through His *constant, sacrificial choices,* we learn *lessons of the will* about how we can, in the choices we face, find our life through losing it for the sake of God's kingdom.
- Through His *mentoring of His disciples,* we learn *lessons about process* as we observe His training genius and patience with us as we stumble toward godly maturity.

Reading as one of the disciples is a powerful benefit in reading the Gospels for spiritual formation. And it functions quite appropriately within the generic boundaries of the Gospels. The unique and beautiful life of the God-man, Jesus, continues to transform those who enter His presence. We are discipled by Jesus Himself through the accounts of His life. While others are important in our formation, no one can take His place. In large part Jesus fills His place in our lives as we read, study, and meditate on the Gospels. Do you want to be discipled by Jesus? Then read the Gospels! Be transformed by our loving Savior.

We can now summarize the basic contribution of this part of God's Word to our spiritual formation.

THE SPECIFIC CONTRIBUTION OF THE GOSPELS TO OUR SPIRITUAL FORMATION

- **The Biblical Books:** The Gospels of Matthew, Mark, Luke, and John.

- **Primary Contribution:** To teach us about who Jesus the Messiah is and give us the opportunity to be discipled by Him as we observe Him and His disciples; also, to observe Him modeling life in the kingdom of God and listen to Him about how we should live in the kingdom and be transformed in areas of sinful resistance.

Therefore, ask, "What does this passage tell us about who Jesus is and about how I should respond to being His disciple? How then should I live as a citizen of the kingdom of God?"

continued on next page . . .

■ **Secondary Contribution:** To give insight into how we may encourage fellow disciples.

Therefore, ask, "Are there certain principles or methods of ministry that Jesus is modeling as He ministers to His disciples or others that would be appropriate for us to imitate in our ministries?"

Chapter Eleven

OUR PURPOSE: THE ACTS OF THE APOSTLES

And so when they had come together, they were asking Him, saying, "Lord, is it at this time You are restoring the kingdom to Israel?" He said to them, "It is not for you to know times or epochs which the Father has fixed by His own authority; but you shall receive power when the Holy Spirit has come upon you; and you shall be My witnesses both in Jerusalem, and in all Judea and Samaria, and even to the remotest part of the earth."

ACTS 1:6-8

Fanaticism consists in redoubling your effort when you have forgotten your aim.

GEORGE SANTAYANA[1]

LET ME INTRODUCE YOU TO A CONTEMPORARY NOVEL, PERHAPS being written in your area even as you read this. It's called *A Tale of Two Churches* (with apologies to Charles Dickens), and it's a contrast between two sincere and committed churches. The first body of believers is called the Church of Devoted Fanaticism. Because its members have forgotten the aim or purpose of the church, they double and redouble their efforts in church activities and religious programs every year or two. The members joke among themselves that when you join the Church of Devoted Fanaticism, you never see home. There are an overwhelming number of church services, home Bible studies, committee meetings, planning meetings, and men's and women's ministry meetings to attend several nights each week. There are meetings for the Christian school that the church sponsors, social action meetings that relate to the broader community, and numerous group meetings for alcohol, food, money, power, and sex addictions. There is no end to meetings at the Church of Devoted Fanaticism! In large part this is because this church has forgotten its purpose and is redoubling its efforts.

By contrast, the members of the second church, the Church of Focused Purpose, appear to be much less active. The members of the first church consider them less spiritual because they aren't at the church building several nights each week. Instead, they spend more time with their families, their neighbors, and the broader community. This is because the activities of the Church of Focused Purpose are fewer and less varied. The members seem to give themselves to a handful of activities like training in how to discover and use their spiritual gifts, how to study the Bible effectively, how to understand the Christian faith more profoundly, and how to minister to family, friends, neighbors, and those from other cultures who live in the community. As a result, over the years the Church of Focused Purpose has developed, supported, and sent out several teams of missionaries to unreached people groups in various countries and in large urban areas of the United States. The church has grown as it has consistently led people to Christ and helped these new Christians use their gifts to fulfill God's purpose for the church. While regularly tempted to change its name and emphasis, this community of Christians has persisted as the Church of Focused Purpose.

Which church would you like to belong to? Perhaps the Church of Devoted Fanaticism sounds all too familiar to you! If it does, then spending time being spiritually formed by the book of Acts is definitely for you. This unique part of the Word of God is specifically crafted to teach us *what God is doing in history at the present and how this informs the purpose of the church.* No other book of the New Testament models this purpose in such vivid and passionate terms. No other biblical book helps us sharpen our aim on what we should be doing and encourages us to focus our attention on a clarified purpose. No other book of the Bible can form us in the specific areas that the book of Acts does. Notice the uniqueness of its contribution.

THE SPECIFIC CONTRIBUTION OF THE BOOK OF ACTS TO OUR SPIRITUAL FORMATION

■ **The Biblical Book:** The Acts of the Apostles.

■ **Primary Contribution:** To teach us what God is doing in history at this present time under the kingship of Jesus the Messiah and to model for us what our corresponding purpose is as God's new covenant people; it also explains our roots, as well as some of the fruits of our identity as the church as we fulfill our purpose in the world.

Therefore, ask, "What does this passage tell us about our purpose and focus as God's people and how I should respond to being a part of the church and living as a citizen of the kingdom of God?"

■ **Secondary Contribution:** To give us methods and techniques for ministry to others.

Therefore, ask, "Are there certain methods or techniques of ministry that the apostles or others are modeling as they minister to others that would be appropriate for us to imitate in our ministries?"

THE GENRE OF THE BOOK OF ACTS: PORTRAYING OUR PURPOSE

The book of Acts is narrative literature like the Gospels and was written to enrich Christians in our purpose and identity as the people of God. Acts models for us how to live out that purpose in a hostile environment. It is a continuation of the story of the Gospel of Luke, traditionally attributed to Dr. Luke, Paul's traveling companion on several of his mission journeys. He wrote Acts to a man named Theophilus, who perhaps was a Gentile patron of the church in some area Luke and Paul visited or possibly a key government official. Notice how Luke introduces each volume of his Luke-Acts narrative:

> Inasmuch as many have undertaken to compile an account of the things accomplished among us, just as those who from the beginning were eyewitnesses and servants of the word have handed them down to us, it seemed fitting for me as well, having investigated everything carefully from the beginning, to write it out for you in consecutive order, most excellent Theophilus; so that you might know the exact truth about the things you have been taught. (Luke 1:1-4)

> The first account I composed, Theophilus, about all that Jesus began to do and teach, until the day when He was taken up, after He had by the Holy Spirit given orders to the apostles whom He had chosen. (Acts 1:1-2)

Luke's purpose in both his Gospel and Acts was to prove that the kingdom offered to both Jews and Gentiles by the resurrected Jesus of Nazareth was always designed by God to be a universal kingdom. This kingdom may be entered by anyone who humbles himself or herself and exercises faith (believes) in Jesus Christ as the sacrificial substitute for his or her sins. Luke goes to great lengths to demonstrate that the identifying mark of those who have entered this kingdom is the indwelling, empowering presence of the Holy Spirit, not the traditional identity marks of Judaism (circumcision and Law observance).

The book of Acts is Luke's account of the universal spread of this universal gospel to the far reaches of the Roman Empire from A.D. 33 to 62. Acts covers this twenty-nine-year period in a selective manner in order to show the transition of God's people from a small group of Jewish Christians huddled in an upper room in the Jewish capital of Jerusalem (Acts 1) to a largely Gentile people who were penetrating the Gentile capital city of Rome (Acts 28). The universal gospel of Jesus Christ was being accepted by Jews and Gentiles alike all across the Mediterranean world.

If the narratives of the Old Testament teach us about individual believers and their faith in God, about the destiny and work of the children of Israel, and about the eternal, universal plan of God, can we expect to find parallel values in the Acts narrative? Definitely! Additionally, if the Gospel narratives tell us about who Jesus the Messiah is, can we find a similar emphasis in Acts? Certainly! Acts tells us what the resurrected, ascended, reigning Messiah Jesus is *continuing to do* in and through His people (implied in Acts 1:1). In such light, this book records the Messiah's ongoing discipling of His people beyond His earthly ministry with the Twelve.

All of this is to say that the narratives of Acts are very important for our spiritual growth! It appears that God may want to use them in ways similar to how He uses the other narrative literature of the Bible. *In fact, apart from Acts, no other narratives in the New Testament provide as clear a description of God's purpose in human history being worked out through the church under the authority of King Jesus.* In our spiritual journey, we can turn to Acts for a definitive and bold statement of our purpose in the world: we are to be about proclaiming the good news of the crucified and resurrected Messiah Jesus to all the peoples of the world. However, an important question remains.

IS ACTS ABOUT OUR ROOTS OR OUR FRUITS?

In clarifying our purpose as the church, what is the specific relationship of the book of Acts to our spiritual development? Is it simply about *our roots*—the history of the first generation of the church as a crucial part of our identity? Or is Acts also about *our fruits*—the kinds of things we should still be doing and experiencing as the church of God? In other words, is Acts just about our past, or does it also model for us ideas for our present experience as Christians? Should we read Acts and expect to accomplish things similar to what Peter, Stephen, Philip, and Paul did? Or should we simply admire these early heroes of the faith and be encouraged that we are on the same team and have the same purpose?

Let's apply this roots/fruits question to a few key issues in the book. For example, should a local church use Acts 1:8 as its blueprint for ministry? Should we structure for local ministry (Jerusalem), regional ministry (Judea and Samaria), and worldwide impact (to the remotest parts)? Should a local church hold all its members' assets in common like the Jerusalem church seemed to do (2:44 and 4:32)? Should we include baptism as an absolute necessity for the salvation of everyone, as some argue from Peter's statement to the Jews on the Day of Pentecost (2:38)? Should we regularly expect as stringent a response to believers lying about their giving to the Lord as when Ananias and Sapphira lost their lives (5:1-11)? What about choosing "deacons" in our local churches as the apostles chose helpers to oversee the distribution of food to Greek widows (6:1-6)? How about using 13:1-3 as the blueprint for choosing missionaries to send out from our churches like the church in Antioch did? Is this a pattern we should reproduce? All of these questions are decisive for the life of the church and our formation in Christ! And, as one would expect, these important issues about interpreting the book of Acts have spawned two diverse answers in recent generations.

So, how are we to determine which behaviors of Christians in the book of Acts are to be normative for us today? I recommend two important criteria for this. The first is: *the behavior or emphasis must be repeatedly emphasized within the broader narrative of Acts.* Rather than micro-interpreting every incident in a narrative as something that is normative for us, we readers should weigh *recurring themes* of the narrative. It is in these recurring behaviors and events that narrative emphases are established and the main points of the story are communicated. Luke may have included many different events in order to give a full historical account of what happened, but they are only *incidental information* to the prescriptive behaviors. However, those events that are part of a recurring pattern are far more likely to be teaching prescriptive behavior to us because they represent the human and divine authors' main concerns about the kinds of choices we should be making as God's people.

In seeking to derive some normative behavior from the Acts narrative, we fly in the face of well-respected interpreters who argue the opposite. For example, Fee and Stuart state this interpretive assumption about reading Acts and other parts of Scripture:

> Our assumption, shared by many others, is that *unless Scripture explicitly tells us we must do something, what is only narrated or described does not function in a normative way—unless it can be demonstrated on other grounds that the author intended it to function in this way.* There are good reasons for making this assumption.[2]

In my opinion, the very fact that *the behavior or emphasis is repeatedly emphasized within the broader narrative of Acts,* is one of the author's signals that normative or prescriptive behavior may be in view.

However, before one can be certain, a second criterion must also be met: *to be considered normative, the recurring patterns of behavior must also closely align with Luke's main purpose.* In other words, if something is of such significance that all Christians everywhere should do it, then surely it will be closely related to the author's main purpose for writing. And Luke's specific purpose in Acts is this: to provide certainty that God's eternal purpose is to create a people by seeking and saving persons universally through faith in Jesus Christ without Judaistic attachments so that God's people will respond in humble, Spirit-empowered obedience to the Son's directing of this universal mission—even though it may lead to suffering.

In short, for a behavior or action in Acts to be considered normative or prescriptive behavior for us, it must first be a recurring theme and then also closely align with Luke's emphasis on a universal, Law-free identity for God's people. Now, let's test our criteria and see if they help in reading Acts.

Example 1: Is meeting on the first day of the week (Sunday) prescribed behavior for God's people in Acts? (One wonders if this question is ever asked before we establish our Saturday evening meeting times!) Acts 20:7 says of Paul at Troas, "And on the first day of the week, when we were gathered together to break bread . . ." The Gospels record that Jesus was raised on the first day of the week (see Matthew 28:1; Mark 16:2; Luke 24:1; John 20:1,19). Additionally, Paul instructs the church at Corinth (as he did the churches of Galatia) to set aside their financial pledge for the collection for the poor saints of Jerusalem on "the first day of every week" (1 Corinthians 16:1-2). To honor Jesus' resurrection from the dead and perhaps to distinguish themselves from Judaism and its Saturday meeting time, it appears that the early church had its assembly on Sunday. However, it does not appear that the book of Acts emphasizes this as normative behavior because it is only mentioned once (see Acts 20:7). Additionally, the early chapters of Acts record the church meeting "day by day" (Acts 2:46-47). Therefore, according to our two criteria, meeting on Sunday for our assemblies does not seem to be *prescribed* in the book of Acts (although it may be elsewhere in the New Testament).

Example 2: Is being of one mind or of one accord a prescribed behavior for God's people in Acts? According to our two criteria of repeated emphasis and aligning closely with Luke's purpose, being unified or "of one accord" (Greek, *homothumadon*) is definitely to be normative behavior for God's people. Note the following occurrences of this dynamic when the church gathered in Acts (emphasis mine):

- 1:14 (while waiting in the upper room): "These all *with one mind* were continually devoting themselves to prayer."
- 2:46 (of the earliest Christian meetings): "And day by day continuing *with one mind* in the temple, and breaking bread from house to house, they were taking their meals together with gladness and sincerity of heart."

- 4:24 (in response to the Sanhedrin's threats): "And when they heard this, they lifted their voices to God *with one accord* and said . . ."
- 4:32 (after their prayer about the Sanhedrin's threats): "And the congregation of those who believed *were of one heart and soul.*"
- 5:12 (after Ananias and Sapphira's deaths): "And at the hands of the apostles many signs and wonders were taking place among the people; and *they were all with one accord* in Solomon's portico."
- 15:25 (the Jerusalem Council's unity in their letter to the Gentiles): "It seemed good to us, *having become of one mind,* to select men to send to you with our beloved Barnabas and Paul."

These examples clearly demonstrate with their repetition of certain phrases and emphases that such unified behavior is a desirable—and prescribed—behavior for God's people. Certainly, if the peoples of the world are going to be reached with the good news of Jesus Christ, then God's people will need to place a very high value on becoming of one mind or one accord.

As one might guess, using these criteria will probably yield few prescriptive behaviors in Acts. Many different behaviors will be modeled, but few of them will be deemed normative for all of the church by meeting our two criteria. Why is this so? It seems that Luke's emphasis in Acts is one of freedom and flexibility for God's people. In other words, it seems that God's desire is to give His church minimal restrictions and maximum freedom and flexibility under the leadership of the Holy Spirit in order to spread the gospel most rapidly and effectively to every different people group in the world. Such minimal universal or transcultural behaviors will expedite the ability of Christians to enter new cultures and emphasize the main contours of the gospel without getting enmeshed in behavioral or cultural issues that could derail the preaching of the gospel. While there are clear-cut prescribed behaviors in Acts, these seem to be only those that are essential to our life in Christ and of minimal hindrance in most of the cultures of the world. Minimal restriction and maximum freedom—can we handle such grace?

In this light, let's examine an interesting event in Acts 11:27-30 that should give some insight into what the book of Acts has to say about the use of our money. This will also help shed light on whether the earlier passages in Acts where the believers "had all things in common" (for example, Acts 2:43-47) are normative for us. Hopefully we will gain some insight into whether communal living out of a common purse is prescribed for the church.

SPIRITUALLY FORMED BY AN ACTS PASSAGE: ACTS 11:27-30

Now at this time some prophets came down from Jerusalem to Antioch. And one of them named Agabus stood up and began to indicate by the Spirit that there would certainly be a great famine all over the world. And this took place in the reign of Claudius. And in the proportion that any of the disciples had means, each of them determined to send a contribution for the relief of the brethren living in Judea. And this they did, sending it in charge of Barnabas and Saul to the elders.

The historical context of this incident is important, as it is in any narrative passage. Luke mentions the Roman emperor Claudius, who ruled as Caesar from A.D. 41 to 54. According to one of the best New Testament chronology experts, Jesus was crucified, resurrected, and ascended in April of 33.[3] The events of Acts 1–7 in Jerusalem covered the years 33-35, after which the church was dispersed throughout Judea and Samaria. Acts 8–12 records the Judean and Samaritan witness and apparently covers the years 35-48. Agabus's famine prediction and the relief visit with the collected funds were during this period. The visit itself was probably in the autumn of 47. Therefore, historically, Acts 11 occurs within the first fifteen years of the church.

Luke specifically emphasizes geography in Acts. As Jesus commands in 1:8, the eyewitness testimony about Him is to begin in

Jerusalem; expand to the surrounding region of Judea and its neighboring region to the north, Samaria; and then burst forth to all the world. Luke gives specific markers as to how this threefold geographical progression is occurring:

- *Acts 1–7—the witness in Jerusalem:* ends with the persecution of the Jerusalem church at Stephen's death, when "they were all scattered throughout the regions of Judea and Samaria, except the apostles." (Acts 8:1, A.D. 33-35)
- *Acts 8–12—the witness in Judea and Samaria:* ends with the sending of Paul and Barnabas as missionaries by the church in Antioch to the ends of the earth in Acts 13:1-3 (A.D. 35-48).
- *Acts 13–28—the witness to the ends of the earth:* begins with Paul and Barnabas's first missionary journey, continues through two more trips by Paul, then concludes with Paul's five-year imprisonment in Caesarea and Rome (A.D. 48-62).

In addition to the historical setting, the context of Acts 11:27-30 within the flow of the narrative of the book is also important. In particular, expanding the section about the witness in Judea and Samaria in Acts 8–12 may prove helpful to appreciating the immediate context.

- The witness of Philip (8:4-40) reaches half-breed Samaritans and the first Gentile (the Ethiopian eunuch).
- The commissioning and witness of Saul (9:1-31) establish him as apostle to the Gentiles.
- The witness of Peter (9:32-11:18) expands to Samaria (9:32-43) and Gentiles (10:1-11:18).
- The witness of some dispersed Hellenists in Antioch (11:19-30) plants the first church outside of Israel, which becomes the new sending center led by Barnabas and Saul.
- The opposition of kings (Herod) leads to the suffering of saints (12:1-25).

We can see from the context of Acts 11:27-30 that the church in Antioch is extremely significant because *it is the first church with a largely Gentile membership* (11:20-21). The very existence of a Gentile majority in a local church *this early* is an historic event in the spread of the gospel throughout Judea and Samaria. In fact, Antioch sits over three hundred miles north of Jerusalem, well outside the land of Israel and the provinces of Judea and Samaria. However, the persecution that began at the death of Stephen (8:1-3) not only scattered the church throughout Judea and Samaria, but also as far north as Antioch (11:19). Therefore, the beginning of the Antioch church resulted from the spread of the gospel into Judea and Samaria.

Also significant in the context of this Acts narrative is the sequence of events that precedes the establishment of the Antioch church. Note that we see remarkable ethnic and cultural barriers crossed in chapters 8–11. The hated, half-breed Samaritans are added to God's people along with the first Gentile in chapter 8. Saul/Paul, the primary missionary to the Gentiles in the early church, is encompassed in God's people in chapter 9. Even Peter, the apostle to the Jews, crosses barriers in Samaria (9:32-43) and particularly with Gentiles (10:1–11:18). Each of these significant events sets the stage for the appearance of the first Gentile church in 11:19-30.

To provide mature, stable leadership for Antioch's fledgling congregation, the Jerusalem church sent faithful Barnabas, a Hellenistic Jewish Christian, that is, a Jew born outside the land of Israel (11:22-24). Because "considerable numbers were brought to the Lord" (11:24), Barnabas soon traveled the 115 miles from Antioch to Tarsus to recruit Paul to join him in the work (11:25-26). "And it came about that for an entire year they met with the church, and taught considerable numbers; and the disciples were first called Christians in Antioch" (11:26). Such a ministry would have far-reaching consequences because this city of about 500,000 people was the third-largest in the Roman Empire, smaller than only Rome and Alexandria. Additionally, Antioch was the capital of the Roman province of Syria and also had a significant Jewish population, estimated to be about one-seventh of Antioch's total population. Providentially, God chose this particular city to become the new sending center for the next thrust of the church—to the ends of the earth (13:1-3).

We note in 11:27-30 that some prophets came from Jerusalem "down" to Antioch (lower than elevated and revered Jerusalem, but north on the map!). Agabus, one of these prophets, prophesied about the coming famine that would blight the Roman Empire. We know from Roman and Jewish historians that several bad harvests occurred during Claudius's reign (A.D. 41-54), and there was a particularly severe famine in Israel between 45 and 47.[4] The important point that Luke seems to be making is that the church in Antioch had specific information from the Holy Spirit (through the prophet Agabus) about the suffering of their fellow believers in Jerusalem. This information is ironic because the Antioch church was founded by Christians who had been driven from Jerusalem by the persecution that arose when Stephen was martyred (11:19; 8:1-4). However, rather than focusing on their past persecution, this largely Gentile church responded with a generous heart to help those Christians who had remained in Jerusalem when their founders had fled:

> And in the proportion that any of the disciples had means, each of them determined to send a contribution for the relief of the brethren living in Judea. And this they did, sending it in charge of Barnabas and Saul to the elders [of the Jerusalem church]. (11:29-30)

We can gain several significant insights from these verses. First, the Christians were also called "disciples." These terms are synonymous; equating a "disciple" to a supercharged Christian is a recent misunderstanding. But also note that the standard for giving to the need was not a certain percentage (for example, 10 percent), but rather was *in proportion to the means or resources that each believer had.* This is the clear New Testament standard for giving that is modeled (for example, the widow's mite in Luke 21:1-4) and taught (see 1 Corinthians 16:1-2; 2 Corinthians 8–9). The practice of the Christians in Antioch aligns perfectly with this broader practice and teaching.

Additionally, their giving is less radical than the holding of all things in common that we saw in the Jerusalem church (see Acts 2:44-45 and 4:32). If the standard is to operate out of a common purse, then the response of these Antioch Christians is not commendable. Yet, Luke seems to commend them and hold them as models worthy of imitation. Therefore, their response must be the typical, desired response, and the more radical sharing of the Jerusalem church must be very admirable, but not normative. Why is this so?

The Jerusalem church's radical financial approach was demanded by a unique and desperate economic crisis. Thousands of Jewish pilgrims from all over the Mediterranean world had come to faith in Christ on Pentecost and shortly thereafter (three thousand in Acts 2:41 and five thousand in Acts 4:4). They apparently extended their stay in Jerusalem to learn about their newfound faith in Jesus the Messiah, and in the process apparently used up their food, money, and clothing. Out of brotherly love and Middle Eastern hospitality, the "host" Jerusalem church felt responsible to care for their needs. This demanded liquidating all of their available assets because of the thousands of pilgrims who were involved and because of the urgency of the hour. Therefore, while immensely commendable, this early pooling of finances is not prescriptive, nor is it repeated in the book of Acts.

What is the point of recounting the Antioch believers' giving in Acts 11:27-30, and what significance does it have for our spiritual formation? First, the genuineness of the faith of these new believers is demonstrated by their sharing of their possessions. While the Jewish Christians in Jerusalem may have accepted the new Gentile Christians in Antioch with some hesitancy, the act of generosity by these believers is one of the most tangible signs that they had a genuine faith in Messiah Jesus. In fact, the idea that *sharing our possessions proves the genuineness of our faith* is a common theme throughout Luke and Acts. Note examples of this in Luke 3:7-14; 6:27-37; 10:25-37; 16:1-13; 19:1-10; 21:1-4, and Acts 2:44-45; 4:32; 11:27-30. Most certainly Luke's first point is that the believers in Antioch had genuine faith because they freely shared their possessions. Such a point should challenge us to do likewise with our possessions. When our faith in Christ includes our pocketbook, then we know that we have the real thing! This proves the sincerity of our love (see 2 Corinthians 8:8).

However, Luke makes a second point in Acts 11:27-30, which we have already alluded to. The giving by the Christians in Antioch was *on an international basis.* It transcended their local setting, their own region, and even their own ethnicity. They gave to others who were not only removed from them geographically, but also ethnically. This is significant because such giving is one of the main ways of uniting the body of Christ internationally. This is what Paul teaches in 2 Corinthians 8–9 when he exhorts the Corinthian church to give to this same need. One of his main points is that God *desires that there be equality between abundance and want on an international basis among the people of God* (2 Corinthians 8:13-15). This is exactly what we see modeled by the new believers in Antioch. They understand that God's heart transcends geography and ethnicity. Because it does, they respond accordingly. It appears that Luke wants us to ponder their behavior and imitate their faith.

OUR SPIRITUAL FORMATION BY ACTS: SOME PRINCIPLES

In being spiritually formed as we read Acts, the following three principles have proven helpful to many of God's people. They are given, not to restrict, but rather to unleash the riches of this remarkable and transforming part of God's Word.

1. Grasp the whole to understand the part.

Read all of Acts to get the sense of the whole narrative when you start to spend time in this book. Set aside an hour or hour and a half to read the whole book in one sitting. This will also give you a more solid grasp of Luke's purpose in writing this narrative. Acts is a remarkable story and should be read in a continuous manner like any narrative.

2. Emphasize Luke's emphases for maximum spiritual impact.

We can definitively say that Luke emphasizes at least four things in the book of Acts:

a. The overt geographical spread of the gospel (Acts 1:8 = the outline)
b. The intentional crossing of racial and cultural barriers as the gospel is boldly proclaimed[5]
c. The church living in loving community as it proclaims the gospel and plants local churches where there was no previous testimony to the name of Jesus Christ
d. The living out of the baptism of the Holy Spirit through the repeated filling of the Holy Spirit, who empowers believers to proclaim the gospel and cross racial, cultural barriers[6]

Emphasizing these recurring concerns in Acts will help you major in the majors (prescriptive behaviors) and keep the minor points (options for behaviors) in proper perspective.

3. Be impacted by the godly models and imitate their faith.

This is a slightly different concern from reading for prescriptive principles or behaviors. The point here is to get to know the people in the book of Acts and to meditate on and deeply ponder the lives of the godly models. Thinking long and hard about Peter, Barnabas, Philip, Stephen, Paul, and the rest will transform our souls. Again, if we learn over 95 percent of all we will ever know by imitating models, then the transforming impact of this kind of meditation will be far-reaching. We should make these models our friends — and our mentors!

Being rightly informed of the nature of the book of Acts should give us better expectations as to how God may want to use this wonderful part of His Word to transform us. Aligning more obediently with God's purposes for Acts may also greatly aid our spiritual formation by helping us align more obediently with God's purposes in human history. Without this kind of nurture from Acts, we would be greatly impoverished in discovering His purpose for us in the world, and we would be in danger of lapsing into inappropriate religious fanaticism—redoubling our efforts because we lost sight of our purpose.

Chapter Twelve

COMMUNITY:
THE EPISTLES

I, therefore, the prisoner of the Lord, entreat you to walk in a manner worthy of the calling with which you have been called, with all humility and gentleness, with patience, showing forbearance to one another in love, being diligent to preserve the unity of the Spirit in the bond of peace. There is one body and one Spirit, just as also you were called in one hope of your calling; one Lord, one faith, one baptism, one God and Father of all who is over all and through all and in all.

EPHESIANS 4:1-6

There is no life, but life in community.

T. S. ELIOT[1]

READING THE EPISTLES OF THE NEW TESTAMENT COULD BE considered a rude gesture in many homes. Why? Because we are reading someone else's mail—letters addressed to others, not to us. How, then, can we read these twenty-one letters written to other churches and individuals and not only avoid rudeness, but also read them for our own spiritual growth? How applicable are they to us?

READING SOMEONE ELSE'S LETTERS?

First, the issue of reading someone else's letters. While it is true that these Epistles are addressed to others, there is no evidence that they were intended to be read only by the original recipients; they were also to be re-read to others in neighboring places. The Epistles offer several indications of this re-reading intention (for example, 2 Peter 3:14-16), but the clearest is the apostle Paul's instruction to the church at Colossae: "When this letter *is read among you, have it also read* in the church of the Laodiceans; and you, for your part read my letter that is coming from Laodicea" (Colossians 4:16, emphasis mine).

It is reasonable to assume that the authors of the Epistles intended and expected their letters to be re-read because of the time and effort spent writing and delivering them and because of the oral environment of the first century. Because only about 5 to 10 percent of the people in the Roman Empire could read, the vast majority of them would have *heard,* not read, the original letters. The American obsession with privacy would have gone out the window from the very beginning of this process! The lines of what was written *to others* rather than *to us* would have been blurred from the outset due to the culture. Thus, these letters could easily be read in sister churches. Reading the Epistles of the New Testament as a secondary reader is not a rude, unusual, or distorting thing to do. Rather, it appears to have been *intended and expected* by the authors. They wrote their letters with readers *and re-readers* in mind. Therefore, in a real sense, they are our mail also and appropriate for our spiritual formation.

This leads us to a second, important issue in reading the Epistles for spiritual development. If the Old Testament Wisdom

Literature, especially Proverbs, is the least context-specific type of literature in the Bible, the Epistles are at the other end of the scale. These letters are a type of dialogue that demands that we know as much as possible about both the sender's and the recipients' lives. Isn't this obvious when you read any letter? Of course. The letters of the New Testament are no exception. To read these Epistles for personal impact demands that we do more historical context and background work than we might do when reading the other genres of the Bible. The genre qualities of letters increase the need to be informed about their setting before we can be transformed by their content in our formational reading of them. Let's revisit the chart on the importance of background information:

Background Information Is Less Significant		Background Information Is of Average Significance	Background Information Is Highly Significant
Narratives	Law	Psalms	Epistles
Proverbs		Gospels	Prophecies
Wisdom Literature		Acts	Parables

Of all the genres of the Old and New Testaments, none so intensely demands background information as the Epistles or "letters." I wish it were not so, but it is. The good news, though, is that taking the time to find such information allows us to make far better application of this material to our lives. Indeed, background information will actually increase the impact of the Epistles on our spiritual formation. We can see even more specifically what God was saying to the readers and to us as the re-readers about our identity and behavior as the church.

APPLICATIONS FROM THE EPISTLES IN SPIRITUAL FORMATION

We must understand what God said to the original recipients of an epistle in light of their specific historical context because the applications the readers were to make are part of what God intended to communicate. In other words, applications are not totally free choices that we make as readers. Rather, *they are a part of the meaning of the passage.* As readers, we must work within the intentions or boundaries established by the author.

THE SPECIFIC CONTRIBUTION OF THE EPISTLES TO OUR SPIRITUAL FORMATION

■ **The Biblical Books:** Romans, 1 and 2 Corinthians, Galatians, Ephesians, Philippians, Colossians, 1 and 2 Thessalonians, 1 and 2 Timothy, Titus, Philemon, Hebrews, James, 1 and 2 Peter, 1, 2, and 3 John, and Jude.

■ **Primary Contribution:** To teach, exhort, and model our identity as the church and how we are to live it in the community of God's people by making godly choices in a myriad of practical areas in order to fulfill our purpose.

Therefore, ask, "What does this passage tell us about our identity in Christ and about specific choices we should make to underscore that identity or enhance our unity and ministry as God's primary means of ministry in the world?"

The way to prove this is to ask, "Are there wrong applications that we can make from a passage?" Of course there are. Do we have the right as readers to decide that we're not going to connect emotionally with fellow believers when we read Romans 12:15 ("Rejoice with those who rejoice, and weep with those who weep")? No, that would be a wrong application because the only authority we can appeal to is the authority of the author's intended meaning. This is because the human and divine authors of Scripture intended as a part of their meaning that a certain range of applications be made. Sometimes the range is narrow and sometimes it is broad, depending on the biblical genre. But there is a definite range of appropriate or desired applications established by the author when he chooses a certain type or category of meaning.

Therefore, not all applications are equal or good. Some are inappropriate, and some are just wrong!

This is an especially pertinent point to remember in reading the Epistles. We have to understand what the author was saying to his original recipients and what his intended application was before we can make that same application to our setting—a setting that may be somewhat different from the original one. The following diagram attempts to picture an appropriate application process for us:

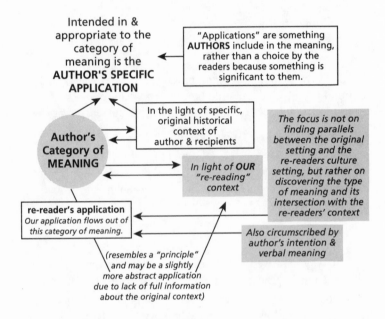

This discussion about application and context is important for reading the Epistles because, of all the genres of the Bible, this one is most directly applicable to our life within the community of God's people. Therefore, the applications that the writers of the Epistles intended for us to make directly affect the lives within our local churches. The original recipients of these letters were either local churches or their leaders, and the issues addressed in them are those of daily life in the body of Christ. The ramifications to our spiritual growth are very direct and very evident. That's why we have to get it right! In reading the epistle genre, we have to spend a little extra time being rightly informed in order to be rightly transformed.

Perhaps the best way to unpack the diagram on page 236 and to illustrate how to read a passage from the Epistles for spiritual formation is to model the process in a specific passage. Reading, contemplating, and applying Ephesians 4:25-32 should give a vivid example of the growth in Christ that can occur when we humbly do our job. These exhortative words from the apostle Paul give us much to ponder about the centrality of relationships for our spiritual life in the midst of community with God's people. Just as there is no life but life in community, so there is no spiritual formation but spiritual formation in community. It is this that the New Testament Epistles address.

SPIRITUALLY FORMED BY AN EPISTLE PASSAGE: EPHESIANS 4:25-32

Therefore, laying aside falsehood, speak truth, each one of you, with his neighbor, for we are members of one another. Be angry, and yet do not sin; do not let the sun go down on your anger, and do not give the devil an opportunity. Let him who steals steal no longer; but rather let him labor, performing with his own hands what is good, in order that he may have something to share with him who has need. Let no unwholesome word proceed from your mouth, but only such a word as is good for edification according to the need of the moment, that it may give grace to those who hear. And do not grieve the Holy Spirit of God, by whom you were sealed for the day of redemption. Let all bitterness and wrath and anger and clamor and slander be put away from you, along with all malice. And be kind to one another, tender-hearted, forgiving each other, just as God in Christ also has forgiven you.

The context and structure of this passage are remarkable. But first, a word about the context within the entire letter. In Ephesians

1–3, Paul emphasizes that God offers *specific blessings and purposes* in building a new body called "the church." While the church is in continuity with the old covenant people, Israel, it also has elements of discontinuity. In particular, Paul emphasizes in chapters 1–3 that the church is not a geopolitical and ethnic entity like Israel, but rather an organic, international body comprised of Jews and Gentiles who believe in Jesus as their Savior and Lord (2:1-10). Each group maintains its ethnic identity, yet both are to work to maintain the oneness that Jesus Christ created between them when He made the two into one people at His death (2:11-22). In and through this new people God is now making known His will and purpose for this age (3:1-13). Because the majesty of God's grace and purposes exceeds whatever we could hope or think, we need the strengthening work of the Holy Spirit in our inner person to help us comprehend the riches of His love toward us in Christ (3:14-21).

It is at this point that Paul usually makes a familiar shift in his letters from instruction to exhortation or challenge. In fact, Ephesians 4–6 is called the "Moral Exhortation" section of the letter. In these chapters Paul emphasizes that in light of God's gracious purposes for Christians, we have *specific responsibilities* in order to reflect what God's new building (the church) is like. We are to walk (live) in unity (4:1-16) and purity (4:17-24), and to enhance the unity of the body of Christ by dealing with personal areas of sin in our lives (4:25-32). This means walking differently than we used to walk (5:1-21), now walking in submission in marriage (5:22-33), in the home (6:1-4), and in working relationships (6:5-9). Finally, Paul exhorts the people of God to stand strongly in spiritual warfare (6:10-20). In light of God's incredible kindness (chapters 1–3), Christians are privileged with the responsibility of walking in a manner worthy of our high calling in Christ (chapters 4–6).

In the more immediate context of Ephesians 4, Paul introduces the idea of our "worthy walk" by first emphasizing that the believers must *preserve* the unity that the Holy Spirit has created in the church. He does this in the following manner:

Ephesians 4:1-16: The church is one new body of people with a *unity* (4:1-6), yet this unity is based on a stunning *diversity* of grace-gifts that individual believers have (4:7-10), which need therefore to be coordinated or *arranged* by certain gifted individuals for the unity to be preserved (4:11-16).

Ephesians 4:17-24: The pattern of our *purity* as Christians is to be in contrast to that of our former identity as nonChristians ("lay aside the old self") and consistent with our knowledge of our new identity in Christ ("put on the new self").

Ephesians 4:25-32: Paul now weaves together the two previous themes of *unity* and *purity* in this paragraph by setting forth *five specific areas* where Christians must replace sins that disrupt the unity of the body and destroy its purity with edifying (building-up) traits that preserve the unity of the body and enhance its purity.

In addition to noting the interesting context of Ephesians 4:25-32, we should also mention its fascinating internal structure. Passages like this should inspire our awe at the literary brilliance of the Word of God! While Paul's earlier exhortations about our unity (4:1-16) and purity (4:17-24) are somewhat general, his exhortations in 4:25-32 are specific and focused. In particular, notice that Paul follows a pattern in each of the five troublesome areas mentioned in 4:25-32: he mentions the disruptive sin, then gives the unifying trait that should replace it, and finally gives a reason or rationale for such a replacement. After re-reading the passage, study the chart on the next page for a moment.

Like so many passages in the exhortative parts of the New Testament Epistles, the applications the author intended the original readers to make are fairly obvious. In Ephesians 4:25-32, even for a re-reader, there is no real mystery or difficulty in understanding Paul's desired applications. While we may not know the specific problems in Ephesus (or in the neighboring churches of Asia) that precipitated these corrective exhortations, we know with strong certainty the responses that Paul intended his readers and re-readers to make. Ephesians 4:25-32 is a good passage to illustrate *how the desired applications reside as a part of the meaning that the author intends in a passage.* (See diagram on the next page.)

Verse	Divisive Sins	Replace with Unifying Traits	Replacement Rationale	The Application Paul Wants Us to Make
25	Lying	Speaking truthfully	We are members of one another (one Body).	Stop lying & speak truthfully to one another.
26-27	Explosive, sinful anger that remains	Righteous wrath that is quickly reconciled	The Devil will exploit unresolved and sinful anger (cause divisions).	Let the day of our anger be the day of our reconciliation.
28	Stealing	Working with our own hands	So we can share with others who have needs	Stop stealing & start working so we can share.
29-30	Unwholesome, worthless words	Edifying (building up) words	We will benefit those who hear and not grieve the Holy Spirit.	Stop speaking worthless words & edify with words of grace to one another.
31-32	Bitter, divisive feelings and actions	Being kind, tender-hearted, and forgiving toward one another	God forgave us!	Stop these bitter, divisive feelings and actions & be kind, tender-hearted and forgiving instead.

The intended applications are more overt and obvious in exhortative material than in the other parts of New Testament Epistles, or in other biblical genres. However, greater subtlety in the nonexhortative passages does not mean the applications desired by the author are not also controlled by the author's intended meaning. Rather, it just takes a bit more thoughtfulness and meditative work by the reader to determine the desired application. *Perhaps nothing we do in all of our spiritual formation is as strategic as this contemplation of the intended application of a biblical passage!* In this process we must continue to seek to place ourselves under the authority of the Holy Spirit, who also superintended and then "breathed out" these applications as part of the meaning of the passage (see 2 Timothy 3:16-17). As we align our thoughts and interpretations with His purpose and intentions as expressed in the biblical passage, we experience more of His power in the transforming process. In other words, we are changed more profoundly because we are focused on the truth and response that the Holy Spirit coauthored and wants to implement in our lives! Crassly put, we then meet the Spirit both coming and going, on both sides of the transforming process!

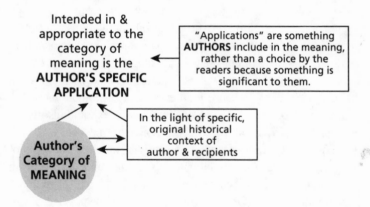

This brings us to the challenge we have as re-readers of a New Testament letter (or any part of the Bible). What must we be aware of in order to be humble, faithful, and accurate appliers of God's Word? We revisit the bottom half of the above application diagram to answer this question:

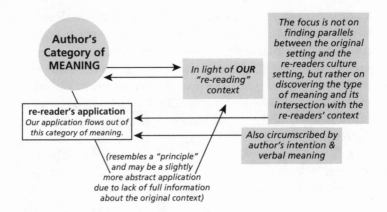

We note from this diagram that because our re-reading context is different from that of the original readers, we may not be privy to all the specific historical and cultural details they had. However, this should not discourage us because we still have what the original readers/hearers had: the meaning of the passage! This meaning is of a certain type or category of expression. The category of meaning in Ephesians 4:25-32 is exhortations about relationships within the body of Christ and the unifying qualities needed to make them work. We can immediately sense this category of meaning, even if we don't know all the particulars Paul had in mind when he wrote this passage. Why? Because Paul expressed his intentions within this category of meaning, and this is where we should also focus our intentions. What we share in common in this passage with Paul (in addition to the help of the Holy Spirit!) is knowledge of the public things like genres (a letter), types/categories of meaning (exhortations about edifying relationships), and interests and concerns about the same sorts of things discussed in the passage. These things work in tandem to assist our understanding of the passage and its desired application.

However, the focus in deriving the application is mainly on the category of meaning in the passage, and not on any cultural setting. While the issue of culture may be relevant in certain difficult passages (for example, 1 Corinthians 11:1-16 and women's head coverings), we should not focus *primarily* on it in making applications. Rather, we focus on the category of meaning in the passage to determine the application that should flow out of that meaning. This focus keeps us centered in the biblical text and on the author's intentions expressed in the passage.

In presenting what may seem to be a narrower view of application, we appear to be flying in the face of the popular adage about biblical passages: "one interpretation and many applications." While the "one interpretation" part of the saying is true, the "many [or unlimited] applications" part is not. Rather, the author intends a certain *range of applications* or responses to the passage appropriate to the genre of the passage and the category of meaning expressed. This range of applications may be quite narrow ("Thou shall not murder") or a little broader (that is, the response to a narrative passage). The point is that the applications from a passage are not open-ended or infinite, depending on the judgment of the reader. Instead, they are also intended by the author and then perceived and entered into by the readers or re-readers.

At this point, we need to make an important clarification because there may be confusion about this limiting of our "rights" as readers. While the author determines the applications that are intended in his or her meaning, the readers determine *the significance* of that meaning to their lives or to anything to which they want to relate it. Literary critic E. D. Hirsch Jr. helps us in this matter with his definition of *significance* in relation to *meaning:*

> *Meaning* is that which is represented by a text; it is what the author meant by his use of a particular sign sequence; it is what the signs represent. *Significance,* on the other hand, names a relationship between that meaning and a person, or a conception, or a situation, or indeed anything imaginable.[2]

Most of what we call *application* when we respond to a biblical passage is more properly called *significance*. It is the relating of the meaning of the passage to something in our lives or in the world around us. This is certainly a good and appropriate thing to do. However, we should be aware that sometimes our judgment as readers of *the significance* of the meaning of a passage to our lives may have nothing to do with *the application* that the biblical author desired us to make in response to the passage! *We can certainly do both.* However, as a rule, it is best to try to determine the application of a passage before determining its significance in our lives. Starting with the application gives clear guidelines as to how the author intended the passage to impact us. *However, God in His grace also uses His Word in our lives when we glean instances of significance from it.* Let me give an example of this from my own life.

In the summer of 1973, I was engaged to a lovely young woman named Marty Megarity. We were exactly six weeks away from our August wedding day when I began to have significant doubts and fears about getting married. My doubts related to my development in the past of an unrealistic and fleshly view of women set forth by Hollywood and the media. In other words, my physical ideal for my wife was air-brushed perfection! Of course, this was a lousy perspective fraught with sinful elements.

One day God convicted me of my sinful grid as I was reading through 1 Corinthians—in particular, when I came to chapter 5 and the discussion about a man in the church at Corinth who was having sexual relations with his stepmother. I was struck by the apostle Paul's statement in 5:6-7: "Your boasting is not good. Do you not know that a little leaven leavens the whole lump of dough? Clean out the old leaven, that you may be a new lump, just as you are in fact unleavened. For Christ our Passover also has been sacrificed."

Now this discussion is about cleaning out a sinning Christian who represents the leaven in the lump of dough represented by the church in Corinth. I knew this was what Paul was intending to say. The application he desired was for the church to discipline this sinning brother, even to the point of excommunication (verse 13). However, I saw *significance* and an analogy to my situation as an individual believer. If my life was the lump of dough, then my fleshly perspective about what I wanted my wife to look like was the leaven that was permeating my dough. I needed to clean it out because of its negative effect on all of my life. I took Paul's meaning about leaven when he was relating it to the whole church in Corinth, and I found great *significance* in relating that meaning to my individual life.

I knew this was not Paul's application; it was my relating of his meaning to the great turmoil in my life. I was finding *significance* apart from the application of the passage. By the way, this instance of significance helped me make a very life-changing decision. Marty and I recently celebrated our twenty-sixth wedding anniversary!

In short, we should primarily seek to discover the intended application in a biblical passage. This should be our first priority in seeking to relate the passage and its impact to our spiritual formation. It is absolutely essential if any real, meaningful spiritual transformation is to occur! Determining the application lets us know how the human author and God wanted the meaning of the passage to impact us. This should be our first order of business in applying the Word of God to our lives.

However, it is certainly still appropriate to derive specific significance from biblical passages as we relate the meaning of the passage to various aspects of our lives in ways other than the author intended in the application. God can and does still use His Word in these instances to communicate to us. However, at the end of the day, the search for significance should be secondary to the search for the passage's application. Always remember, it is the application, not the significance, that is clearly a part of the God-breathed meaning of the passage.

SOME PRINCIPLES FOR BEING SPIRITUALLY FORMED BY THE EPISTLES

1. Read the whole epistle in one sitting to get the big idea of the letter and its main contours.

If meaning comes from the top down, from the whole to the parts of the letter, then reading in a similar fashion will give you a clearer and more helpful idea of the thrust of the whole letter. This is a discipline that must be cultivated! However, it will pay enormous dividends spiritually in your life. Having a more accurate sense of the whole of the epistle will give you far greater understanding of the various parts of the letter as you read them in more depth.

Read the whole letter in one sitting and then write down the big idea or main theme of the book. Reading it again a short time later and improving your big idea statement will enhance your understanding geometrically. Cultivate this discipline and your understanding will escalate dramatically.

2. Think in terms of the paragraphs being the main units of thought.

While the chapter and verse divisions are very helpful street addresses, they are not the best guides to the units of thought in a New Testament epistle. Following the paragraph divisions from a literal translation (NASB, KJV, NKJV, RSV, and so on) is a far better path to understanding the message of a letter. Beware of isolating verses from the context of their paragraph. As we saw in chapter 3, this can easily lead to distorting the Word of God and missing the real meaning of a passage.

3. Knowing the structure of epistles helps you know where you are in the letter.

Ancient letters, like modern ones, had three main parts in their structure: greeting, body, and closing. The apostle Paul generally adds two sections to this basic structure, and his thirteen New Testament Epistles usually have five parts: greeting, *thanksgiving*, body, *moral exhortation*, and closing. Structurally knowing where you are in the letter will help you follow the flow of the argument a bit more easily. Each section generally begins with and is characterized by traditional terminology, just as our letters are (for example, "dear," "sincerely,"). Additionally, there is a wide variety in the types of letters in the ancient world, and many of these types are found in the New Testament.[3]

4. Do some background reading in order to understand better the epistle's main concerns and its historical and cultural setting.

As we discussed earlier, because the epistle is the most personal of all the biblical genres, it demands the most information about the authors and their original readers. If there is a bad short-cut that most Christians take in their spiritual formation, it is failing to get adequate information about a biblical passage or book. This may prove very costly when reading the Epistles! However, rather than collecting a whole library of books, the following two volumes should prove invaluable for supplying historical and cultural background information when reading the New Testament letters: for Paul's thirteen Epistles, see Gerald F. Hawthorne, Ralph P. Martin, and Daniel G. Reid, eds., *Dictionary of Paul and His Letters* (Downers Grove, Ill.: InterVarsity, 1993); for the eight general Epistles, see Ralph P. Martin and Peter H. Davids, eds., *Dictionary of the Later New Testament and Its Developments* (Downers Grove, Ill.: InterVarsity, 1997).

CONCLUSION

As with every other genre of God's Word, the New Testament Epistles make a distinctive contribution to our growth in Christ. In particular, no part of the Bible seems so directly and intentionally applicational as these twenty-one letters. Many, if not most, of the issues that first-century Christians wrestled with are still in vogue today. Take the struggles of the church in Corinth: divisions, misunderstanding the gospel, lack of church discipline, lawsuits between Christians, sexual immorality among believers, questions about marriage and divorce, conflicting cultural views among Christians, the dress of women, the Lord's Supper, tongues and prophecy, the resurrection of Jesus, and so on. This list sounds like tomorrow's agenda in many of our churches. No wonder we read the Epistles with such interest!

However, the New Testament letters are also valuable in unpacking what our life in community with one another should look like. They set forth the ideal and correct the less-than-ideal. They reveal how much God cares about our life together in unity and harmony in the body of Christ. Perhaps this is one of the most important yet neglected contributions that the Epistles can make to our growth in Christ. While there is no life but life in community, so there is no growth but growth in the community of God's people. We desperately need one another to help bring about our wholeness as God's people. After asserting that this is our group goal as the church in Ephesians 4:13, Paul paints this marvelous picture of what we should look like as we move together toward maturity in Christ:

> As a result, we are no longer to be children, tossed here and there by waves, and carried about by every wind of doctrine, by the trickery of men, by craftiness in deceitful scheming; but speaking the truth in love, we are to grow up in all aspects into Him, who is the head, even Christ, from whom the whole body, being fitted and held together by that which every joint supplies, according to the proper working of each individual part, causes the growth of the body for the building up of itself in love. (4:14-16)

May God give you great joy as you experience this formative journey with His people in Christian community.

Chapter Thirteen

LIVING EXPECTANTLY: REVELATION

The Revelation of Jesus Christ, which God gave Him to show to His bond-servants, the things which must shortly take place; and He sent and communicated by His angel to His bond-servant John, who bore witness to the word of God and to the testimony of Jesus Christ, even to all that he saw. Blessed is he who reads and those who hear the words of the prophecy, and heed the things which are written in it; for the time is near.

REVELATION 1:1-3

"Therefore be on the alert, for you do not know which day your Lord is coming. . . . For this reason you be ready too; for the Son of Man is coming at an hour when you do not think He will."

MATTHEW 24:42,44

As I READ THE MORNING NEWSPAPER ONE DAY RECENTLY, I was amazed at a large ad with the following headline: "Eight Compelling Reasons Why Christ Is Coming 'Very, Very Soon.'" The advertisement was subtitled, "How to Be Prepared for History's Greatest Event," and the body of the advertisement began with these statements: "The evidence for the soon return of Jesus Christ is overwhelming. It could be any moment. One scholar lists 167 converging clues just in the last few years of this millennium. The following are eight. . . ."

The article-like advertisement then listed the "clues," with some biblical references and explanation to support each point: (1) Israel's rebirth, (2) plummeting morality, (3) famines, violence, and wars, (4) an increase in earthquakes, (5) explosion of travel and education, (6) explosion of cults and the occult, (7) the new world order, and (8) an increase in both apostasy and faith. Additionally, the article set forth evidence of the "Angel Factor," or verified accounts of recent visits by angels who say, "He is coming very, very soon."[1]

How should we respond to such claims about the end of the world? We might want to quibble with *the certainty* that Christ is coming soon in light of Jesus' statement to His disciples, "It is not for you to know times or epochs which the Father has fixed by His own authority" (Acts 1:7). But we can deeply appreciate the desire to persuade people to place their faith in Jesus Christ as their Savior because He is going to return to planet Earth and carry out His appointed judgment as World Ruler *at some point.* Moreover, Revelation does not leave the timing of Jesus' return totally open-ended; it emphasizes that Jesus is revealing "the things which must *shortly* [or *speedily*] take place" (1:1, emphasis mine). In other words, we *are* to have a sense of urgency about the end of this age, even if we don't know *the exact time* it will occur!

How about you? Wouldn't you like to know the end of the story, even if you won't know exactly when it will end? Wouldn't you rather be informed than be scared or startled or totally surprised by the future? And wouldn't you like to be *encouraged* by the end of history that God has designed? If so, then the book of Revelation is must reading for you.

THE END OF THE STORY

At the risk of taking away the drama of life, God has told us the end of the story of history! Of course, this includes the end of each of our own individual stories. And amazingly, God in His revelation has given us a pretty full picture of what the end will look like. We know roughly how the world as we know it now will end:

- what will happen to the currently powerful kingdoms of the world at the end
- what will happen to all the armies that opposed God
- what will happen to all people, be they great or small, at the end of the world
- what will happen to those who love God and believe in His Son, Jesus Christ
- what will happen to those who have rejected Jesus and die separated from God

We even know what will happen to us because of the deeds we have done in faith:

- how we who have believed in Jesus will be spending much of eternity
- how those who have rejected Jesus Christ will be spending their eternity
- what will happen with all the time, money, and energy we have invested in the advancement of God's kingdom
- what will happen to all the wealth, fame, and power people have falsely gained
- what will happen to Satan and his demonic followers
- and many other fascinating things beyond these

You see, we do know a lot about the end of the story of planet Earth, and we know it because God has graciously revealed it to us. Most of the end He has told us in the last book of the Bible, The Revelation of Jesus Christ to the Apostle John. What a wonderfully important and encouraging biblical book this is because of all the ultimate endings it gives us. The irony, though, is that for many Christians Revelation ranks right up there with Leviticus as the least-read book of the Bible. For many, this is because this book seems scary, intimidating, alien in its perspective, or all of the above! This is in spite of the incredibly important endings that Revelation shows us and in spite of the blessing attached to reading it. It is the only book of the Bible with such a promise: "Blessed is he who reads and those who hear the words of the prophecy, and heed the things which are written in it; for the time is near" (1:3).

To fear the book of Revelation is to misunderstand its designed purpose in our spiritual formation. Jesus Christ gave this continuous revelation to John in order to encourage him and, specifically, the seven churches of Asia (1:4) to overcome difficult times. These churches in the Roman province of Asia (now the western quarter of the modern nation of Turkey) were being persecuted by the civil authorities near the end of the first century (95-96). By revealing God's ultimate triumph over Satan in establishing Christ's kingdom and the new heavens and the new earth, Jesus intended to encourage them to overcome in the midst of the persecution.

Revelation 2–3 is His specific message in the form of a letter to each of these seven churches. As with the Epistles, these letters were apparently written to be re-read by Christians throughout the age until the end comes. Paralleling His purpose with these specific churches, Jesus' purpose is also *to encourage us to be overcomers in the midst of whatever persecutions and difficulties we may be having.* Revelation teaches that the ironclad confidence Christians should have is that God will ultimately triumph in human history through His Son, no matter how bleak circumstances are or how unlikely that triumph may seem at times. Jesus has been appointed the Ruler of History at His resurrection from the dead (see Romans 1:3-4), and all ultimate authority and power have already been given to Him (see Matthew 28:18). Therefore, Christians should choose *to overcome* (that is, persevere in faith and faithfulness to Christ), no matter how difficult the circumstances may be, because God's triumph in Christ is sure.

In light of the purpose of Revelation, we can now suggest the following enrichment of our growth in Christ by reading this biblical book.

THE SPECIFIC CONTRIBUTION OF THE BOOK OF REVELATION TO OUR SPIRITUAL FORMATION

■ **The Biblical Book:** The Revelation of Jesus Christ to John.

■ **Primary Contribution:** To encourage and exhort us to overcome through continued faith and faithfulness in the difficult times by revealing God's ultimate triumph over Satan in establishing Christ's kingdom and the new heavens and new earth.

> **Therefore, ask,** "What insights into God's ultimate triumph does this passage give us and how does it encourage us to live faithfully and courageously today in the face of opposition to and persecution of the church?"

■ **Secondary Contribution:** To inform us of some of the specific events signaling the end of the age.

> **Therefore, ask,** "What can we learn about where God is going to take history and glorify Himself as we see what events He will sovereignly allow at the end of the age?"

THE GENRE OF THE BOOK OF REVELATION

Revelation is a *prophetic account in letter form* of the ultimate ending of this age in *apocalyptic terms* that are culturally foreign to most of us. In other words, this biblical book is a creative blending of the three genres of apocalyptic, prophecy, and epistle:

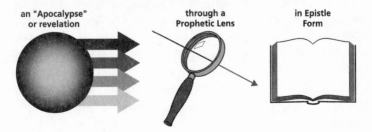

| an "Apocalypse" or revelation | through a Prophetic Lens | in Epistle Form |

Apocalyptic literature appears in the ancient world during times of persecution and great suffering. It is usually written in symbolic language to protect both the writer and the readers, lest it fall into the hands of their persecutors. The symbolic language also helps conceal the truths of the revelation from unbelievers while revealing the desired content to believers. Like all communication, apocalyptic literature seeks to communicate in specific circumstances in an understandable way. While it may seem alien and oblique to us, it was not to its original readers/hearers. *Apocalyptic* was a beloved genre readily recognizable in the first century.

Usually apocalyptic literature was connected to an historical situation. In Revelation's case, this appears to be the Roman emperor Domitian's persecution of Christians at the end of the first century. While most apocalyptic works were written by pseudonymous authors (authors writing under a pen name), the apostle John claims to be the author of Revelation on four different occasions (1:1,4,9; 22:8). Apparently, Jesus Christ gave this revelation to him while John was exiled for his Christian faith on the little island of Patmos, forty miles off the western coast of Asia Minor (modern-day Turkey) (1:9). As with most apocalypses, the message here is presented through a series of visions that contain an element of prediction. There is also a strong use of the dramatic element for vividness in communicating these visions. Revelation is particularly vivid because of the symbols drawn from the rich, oriental imagination of the Mediterranean world. This imagery was John's attempt at capturing the remarkable revelation that Jesus Christ was giving him. While it was written to represent accurately this divine revelation, the symbolic imagery may have also provided some protection against those who were persecuting the church.

No wonder we struggle in reading this biblical book! However, learning to read and interpret this climactic book in the manner it was intended will bring the encouraging message of Revelation much closer to us. It will also give us a sense of *the historical ending* that God is bringing to human history, rather than an existential orientation to the world. As you may recall from our discussion of worldviews in chapter 1, this is one of the main issues that the Word of God—and especially the book of Revelation—addresses in our lives.

Additionally, not trying to understand Revelation may limit our spiritual formation to an earthbound view of Jesus as "Gentle Jesus, Meek and Mild." As Revelation asserts from beginning (in 1:9-20) to end (in 19:11-16), this Sunday school representation of Jesus is not the real picture of who He is as the resurrected, ascended, reigning, ruling King! Studying Revelation should help dispel this limited vision of Him and give us a richer, deeper, and more majestic view of the One about whom John said, "Behold, He is coming with the clouds, and every eye will see Him, even those who pierced Him; and all the tribes of the earth will mourn over Him. Even so. Amen" (1:7).

THE INTERPRETATION AND STRUCTURE OF REVELATION

The Interpretation of Revelation

As you might guess with a biblical book that is a creative blend of apocalyptic, prophecy, and letter, a range of different approaches to the interpretation of Revelation have emerged through the centuries. At least four main interpretive approaches can be identified throughout the history of the church:

1. **The *allegorical approach* (also called idealistic or spiritualist) sees Revelation as one great allegory about good and evil, which are in eternal conflict in every era. Therefore, the symbols and events of the book are not tied to any particular historical events.**[2]

The spiritualizing of Scripture has generally been rejected as a viable approach to interpretation. The stated future significance of Revelation (see 4:1) is ignored in this view. Also, one is hard pressed to understand the binding of Satan for the thousand years in chapter 20 and the significance of new heavens and the new earth in chapters 21–22 as allegory. Are these not real events rather than allegorical symbols?

2. The *preterist approach* sees Revelation as a record of conflicts of the early church with Judaism and paganism in the first century A.D. Therefore, all events were fulfilled in the past.[3]

While there may be some similarities to first-century events, again, this view ignores the stated future significance of the book in 4:1. Additionally, the city of God in chapters 21–22 has never been realized in history, and certainly not in the first century A.D.

3. The *historical approach* sees Revelation as a picture book of the continuous history of the church from the first century to Christ's second coming at the end of time.[4]

This view seems vulnerable to the criticism that it focuses only on the history of the church in the Western world. There is no meaningful agreement among those who hold this view as to how the events of Revelation relate to church history. Therefore, it makes Revelation's prophecies unclear and difficult to understand.

4. The *futurist approach* sees Revelation 4–22 as describing events that were future to the author and that still await fulfillment.[5]

This is the most literal of the interpretations of the specific prophecies of the book and takes the language most naturally from 4:1 to the end of the book. There is no historical data to verify the accuracy of this view (because it is future), and some think it makes the book less applicable to our present situation. However, it appears to be the most obvious understanding of the genre and fits the language and structure of the book most naturally.

While godly, committed Christians may hold one of the other approaches, for the reasons stated above, the *futurist approach* will be the one followed in this chapter.

The Structure of Revelation

Some advocate a literary structure marked by the repetition of certain phrases like "in the Spirit." Others assert that Revelation is marked by a recapitulation of thought (for example, chapters 4–11 and 12–19 are parallel accounts of the coming of the kingdom of God). However, the outline suggested by the command of Jesus in 1:19 seems the most obvious and pleasing and sets forth *a threefold historical progression:* "Write therefore [1] the things which you have seen, and [2] the things which are, and [3] the things which shall take place after these things." Revelation 4:1 ("Come up here, and I will show you what must take place after these things") seems to signal the beginning of the third phase, as the following chart of Revelation pictures:

Revelation's Purpose: to encourage the church to overcome in difficult times by revealing God's ultimate triumph over Satan in establishing Christ's kingdom and the new heavens and the new earth.				
(Revelation 1:19) Jesus says to John, "Write therefore . . .				
the things which you have seen,...	and the things which are,...	and the things which shall take place after these things."		
(Revelation 1)	(Revelation 2–3)	(Revelation 4–22)		
(PAST)	**(PRESENT)**	**(FUTURE)**		
		in heaven	**on earth**	**in heaven**
John focuses on the majesty of Christ's authority when He commissioned him to write down the revelation.	Jesus focuses on the state of the seven churches of Asia, giving His warnings, solutions, and rewards to those who overcome.	(Revelation 4–5) All heaven worships God as Creator (chapter 4) and Jesus as the Lamb (chapter 5).	(Revelation 6–20) In a series of three judgments (seals/trumpets/bowls), God destroys the false kingdom Babylon and establishes the kingdom of His Son.	(Revelation 21–22) A new heaven and earth will be established by our God!

SOME GUIDELINES FOR BEING SPIRITUALLY FORMED BY REVELATION

1. Don't shy away from the book of Revelation because of its distinctive genre.

Feeding only on epistles, psalms, or narratives will deprive us of the rich challenge of this book and its message to a suffering church.

While the apocalyptic elements of the book may seem alien at first, reading and re-reading Revelation will help overcome the cultural or literary distance we may initially feel. God wants to form distinctive elements in our souls that only Revelation can address. Without it, we would lose our sense of history and would have an incomplete understanding of the identity and purpose of God and His plan for planet Earth.

2. Remember that this book is ultimately about Jesus Christ, not Satan or the Antichrist!

In a very real sense, we cannot fully know Jesus if we do not know Him in His present status as ascended, reigning, ruling Lord. Only Revelation can give us this complete picture. The rest of the New Testament points to these aspects of Jesus, but only this climactic book fleshes out this information and picture. While the Devil and his coworkers are prominent in Revelation, they are the vanquished, not the conquerors! Missing this will give us a shrunken and cowering view of Messiah Jesus' majestic lordship. Hopefully, this will become vivid in the passage we will examine shortly.

3. Because Revelation is in large part a prophetic word to the church, expect to be exhorted to holy living today by this vivid picture of God's future triumph through Christ.

This part of God's Word is not primarily to satisfy our curiosity about *the end times,* but rather to encourage us to persevere in faithfulness during *the hard times.* In this sense, Revelation is exhortative and challenging to both our human-centered view of the world and our inappropriate strategies to fulfill our own needs above all other things. No book of the Bible so confronts us with the reality that this world is about God being glorified through the rule of His Son over God's kingdom. While we play an important part in His kingdom, it is *His* kingdom, not ours! We desperately need Revelation's unique emphasis on final things that underscores the Messiah-oriented and God-centered purpose of human history.

4. Because Revelation is about the end of history, it is not meant to be surrealistic or unrealistic, but rather a realistic glimpse of the future in order to inform godly choices today.

To call the prophetic scenes in Revelation "realistic" does not mean that every detail of every prophetic picture is meant to be fulfilled in a woodenly literal manner. Rather, these scenes are *pictures* of the future reality. Fee and Stuart write, "The pictures express a reality but they are not themselves to be confused with the reality, nor are the details of every picture necessarily to be 'fulfilled' in some specific way."[6] Others have expressed this concept in a similar manner: "The prophecies predict literal events, though the descriptions do not portray the events literally."[7]

In other words, the genre of Revelation with its exhortations to its readers/hearers to overcome suffering circumstances with persevering faithfulness to Christ was probably best served with more of a "broad-brush" sketching of these future events. I suggest that it is neither proper nor edifying to press the minute details of the various prophetic scenes of Revelation for correspondences to present-day "fulfillment." While some of these correspondences may ultimately be accurate, we need to avoid making the text's secondary emphases our primary ones. Let's be careful not to reduce the future supernatural manifestations of God's wrathful vindication of His Name and His people that are sketched in Revelation to mere naturalistic means with which we are familiar. To do so is to miss the encouraging and exhortative thrust of Revelation.

5. Revelation is filled with over three hundred allusions to the Old Testament; therefore, it is really intended to function as the capstone of all of Scripture and to complete the picture of what God has been doing in human history.

God's purpose is to establish His kingdom on earth, as revealed in various ways throughout the books of both the Old and New Testaments. One last time we revisit our diagram of a biblical view of history:

SPIRITUALLY FORMED BY A PASSAGE IN REVELATION: 19:1-16

We are jumping into the book near the end of the story of history, so we need a bit of context to orient ourselves to the events that Messiah Jesus has already revealed. After His introduction to John in Revelation 1 and His letters to the seven churches of Asia in chapters 2–3, Jesus unfolds the series of judgments that will culminate history. These *three sets of judgments in 4–19* are punctuated with two heavenly interludes. The first is of God on His throne and the Lamb receiving the scroll of inheritance in chapters 4–5. In this heavenly scene we see God's majesty as Creator (chapter 4) and Jesus the Lamb's humility as our substitutionary sacrifice (chapter 5). These two images are important because they show us exactly what those who dwell on earth have rejected and why the judgments that will soon occur on earth are absolutely necessary.

Moreover, as these judgments begin in chapter 6, we are given the second encouraging heavenly interlude in chapter 7. In this picture we see two groups distinguished from one another by ethnicity: the 144,000 sealed bond-servants of God from *the nation of Israel* (7:1-8) and the innumerable multitude of *Gentiles* from every nation, tribe, people, and tongue who come out of "the great tribulation" (7:9-17). Both heavenly interludes underscore that a Sovereign God and compassionate Savior will continue to redeem people, even as horrifying judgments are poured out on the earth on those who reject God as Creator and Jesus as Savior. Revelation unblinkingly portrays God's vindication of Himself and His people through these earthly punishments.

This is why the main story line of Revelation is carried forward by each of the sevenfold judgments of *seals* (chapter 6), *trumpets* (8–9), and *bowls* (15–16). As these widespread judgments escalate, we have additional earthly interludes after the second set and before the last series of judgments:

- the little scroll of judgment (chapter 10)
- the two witnesses like Moses and Elijah (chapter 11)
- the war against the woman Israel and her son, the Messiah (chapter 12)
- the beast and his mouthpiece (chapter 13)
- the 144,000 singing in heaven and the harvesting of the earth in judgment (chapter 14)

These earthly interludes remind us that God is working out His plan and purposes in human history, even in the midst of seemingly chaotic judgments and terrifying destruction. Additionally, as God continues to empower His people to be righteous and holy in the midst of increasing evil, the contrast between God's ways and the trajectories of self-reliant humans is dynamically heightened.

Climaxing the three sets of judgments is the second coming of Jesus the Messiah in Revelation 19. However, before Jesus reveals the details of His return, He shows us the particulars of the destruction of the great city and system called "Babylon the Great" in chapters 17–18. Babylon has been the epitome of man-made religion since Genesis 11:1-9, and continued as a classic representative of human pride through Jeremiah's day (see Jeremiah 50–51). It is thus not surprising to see "Babylon" as the name of the vastly negative moral and religious system in Revelation 17, where it is called "Babylon the Great, the mother of harlots and of the abominations of the earth" (verse 5). This city on seven hills (verse 9; possibly Rome?) is the center of a great system that opposes God through her false religions that captivate peoples, multitudes, and nations all over the world (verse 15). Therefore, she must be judged for her evil deceptions.

Additionally, Babylon the Great represents a commercial system in Revelation 18 through which "the merchants of the earth have become rich by the wealth of her sensuality" (verse 3). Therefore, God will also judge this great commercial city and system: "Woe, woe, the great city, Babylon, the strong city! For in one hour your judgment has come" (verse 10). God will judge this great deceiver for her deception of the nations and to vindicate the suffering of His people at her hands: "And in her was found the blood of prophets and of saints and of all who have been slain on the earth" (verse 24). The Great Vindicator is now ready to return to His wayward domain.

Revelation 19:1-16 is one of the most exciting passages in the whole Bible because it recounts the pinnacle of human history in the return of Jesus the Messiah. Notice how it follows on the heels of Babylon the Great's destruction:

> After these things I heard, as it were, a loud voice of a great multitude in heaven, saying, "Hallelujah! Salvation and glory and power belong to our God; because His judgments are true and righteous; for He has judged the great harlot who was corrupting the earth with her immorality, and He has avenged the blood of His bond-servants on her." And a second time they said, "Hallelujah! Her smoke rises up forever and ever." And the twenty-four elders and the four living creatures fell down and worshiped God who sits on the throne saying, "Amen. Hallelujah!" (19:1-4)

Observe how heaven and its citizens are not the least bit hesitant about celebrating this exercise of God's justice and His avenging of His people's mistreatment! There will be a time and a place (not yet!) when such exuberant celebrations will be perfectly appropriate. However, in the meantime the apostle Paul rightly encourages us to be loving and not vengeful: "Never take your own revenge, beloved, but leave room for the wrath of God,

for it is written, 'Vengeance is Mine, I will repay,' says the Lord"
(Romans 12:19). What we see in the destruction of Babylon the
great harlot and in the return of Jesus the Messiah is the long-
awaited repaying that God has promised. And the celebration that
follows will be well worth the wait!

> And a voice came from the throne, saying, "Give praise
> to our God, all you His bond-servants, you who fear
> Him, the small and the great." And I heard, as it were,
> the voice of a great multitude and as the sound of many
> waters and as the sound of mighty peals of thunder, say-
> ing, "Hallelujah! For the Lord our God, the Almighty,
> reigns. Let us rejoice and be glad and give the glory to
> Him, for the marriage of the Lamb has come and His
> bride has made herself ready." And it was given to her to
> clothe herself in fine linen, bright and clean; for the fine
> linen is the righteous acts of the saints. And he said to
> me, "Write, 'Blessed are those who are invited to the
> marriage supper of the Lamb.'" And he said to me,
> "These are true words of God." And I fell at his feet to
> worship him. And he said to me, "Do not do that; I am a
> fellow servant of yours and your brethren who hold the
> testimony of Jesus; worship God. For the testimony of
> Jesus is the spirit of prophecy." (Revelation 19:5-10)

The marriage supper of Jesus the Lamb and His purified
bride stands in stark contrast to His previous destruction of the
spiritually promiscuous Babylon, the great prostitute. In many
respects this is a contrast between the destiny of those who gave
themselves spiritually to the immoral Babylon and those who
saved themselves in spiritual purity for their heavenly husband,
Jesus Christ. Therefore, these dear saints who have suffered so
greatly at the hands of Babylon's malevolent spiritual and commercial systems can now enter into the joy of official union with
Jesus the Messiah at the magnificent heavenly wedding celebration of the Lamb. Banquets such as this were pictured by the
prophets of Israel when they spoke of the celebration that would

erupt when the messianic kingdom came in all of its glory (for example, Isaiah 25:6-9).

This righteous bride who waited for the Lord to save her is also dressed in stark contrast to unrighteous Babylon. The great harlot was dressed in the flashy clothes of earthly wealth: "fine linen and purple and scarlet, and adorned with gold and precious stones and pearls" (Revelation 18:16). Vastly different and stunningly simple, the bride of the Lamb is clad in "fine linen, bright and clean; for the fine linen is the righteous acts of the saints" (19:8; this is just like the high priest's all-linen clothing when entering the Holy of Holies in Leviticus 16:4). In other words, the moral and spiritual acts or choices of the saints will be reflected in our appearance at the time Jesus Christ completes His union with us. What a motivation to make choices today that will be pleasingly manifested in our appearance on our heavenly wedding day! However, our wedding dress is also going to be our battle dress, as the next passage unfolds:

> And I saw heaven opened; and behold, a white horse, and He who sat upon it is called Faithful and True; and in righteousness He judges and wages war. And His eyes are a flame of fire, and upon His head are many diadems; and He has a name written upon Him which no one knows except Himself. And He is clothed with a robe dipped in blood; and His name is called The Word of God. And the armies which are in heaven, clothed in fine linen, white and clean, were following Him on white horses. And from His mouth comes a sharp sword, so that with it He may smite the nations; and He will rule them with a rod of iron; and He treads the wine press of the fierce wrath of God, the Almighty. And on His robe and on His thigh He has a name written, "KING OF KINGS, AND LORD OF LORDS." (19:11-16)

Earlier I mentioned that our primary view of Jesus Christ as "Gentle Jesus, Meek and Mild" is terribly lopsided if we do not read the book of Revelation to round out this picture a bit. Jesus' revelation of Himself upon His return is just the kind of passage to give us a full-orbed, biblical view of our Messiah. However, in saying that, the description of He who is called "The Word of God" is really a *culmination* or gathering of earlier things said about Jesus or others in Revelation:[8]

- His white horse (19:11; compare 6:1-2).
- His *many* crowns or diadems (19:12; compare 12:3, 13:1).
- His eyes like a flame of fire (19:12) and the sharp sword proceeding from His mouth (19:15) are described in 1:14 and 16.
- His striking of the nations with the sword of His mouth (His word) and thereby ruling over them with a rod of iron (19:15) was prophesied in 12:5 and promised in 2:25-27.
- "He treads the wine press of the fierce wrath of God, the Almighty" (19:15) is used of the angelic judging of the nations in 14:17-20 (the imagery of Isaiah 63:1-6).
- "He is clothed with a robe dipped in blood [from His enemies]" (19:13) is also the imagery of Isaiah 63:1-6, especially verse 3.
- The many diadems Messiah wears (19:12) point to His absolute authority, expressed by the name on His thigh, "KING OF KINGS, AND LORD OF LORDS" (19:16), and echoing His title in 17:14.
- The armies from heaven riding on white horses with King Jesus, "clothed in fine linen, white and clean" (19:14), are surely the recently married bride of the Lamb (believers) whose clothing is described previously with exactly the same words (19:8; compare 17:14).
- Messiah Jesus returns from a now-opened heaven, "and in righteousness He judges and wages war" (19:11) and strikes the nations with the wrath of God (19:15) in this anticipated expression of His messianic authority (see Psalm 2).

To get the remainder of the story of Christ's return, you absolutely must read the rest of Revelation 19 and all of Revelation 20. Don't stop reading until the birds are eating, the beast is burning, the abyss is unlocking, the saints are reigning, Satan is deceiving and then burning, and the great white throne is judging! But back to the return of Jesus Christ. How does a passage like Revelation 19:1-16, with its focus on Christ's return and the remarkable end of history, contribute to our spiritual formation? I would suggest at least two ways. First, as we have already noted, no other narrative-like passages in the Bible recount the messianic splendor of Jesus Christ like passages from the book of Revelation. While He is our dearest friend, closest companion, and most intimate confidant, He is still the KING OF KINGS AND LORD OF LORDS! We desperately need to see Him in His messianic power and splendor to be able to relate to Him for who He really is. God in His wisdom has supplied the book of Revelation to fill this gap in our spiritual lives. To neglect Revelation is to end up with a shrunken view of Jesus. To read, study, and ponder the truths of Revelation is to grow in our knowledge and love of Jesus our Savior. We need to send our love for Jesus to the school of Revelation so that it can abound still more.

Second, this passage allows us to see the future clearly so that we can live in the present wisely. The future that God has designed for His people includes the destruction of those who oppose Him, the vindication of His persecuted people, and the rewarding of those who have persevered in faithfulness to Him. We see all these central themes of the Bible in Revelation 19:1-16: the destruction of immoral Babylon, the blessing of the bride of Christ (believers), and the establishing of Jesus' absolute rule over the peoples of the earth. This is our future! This is our grace-filled legacy. God reveals it to us throughout the Bible, but He specifically brings it all together in a coherent whole here. This means that we can know the end of the story—the end of history. The result should be that we live expectantly in light of the end. The book of Revelation challenges us to this very task.

Conclusion

GET CLOSE TO
THE FLAME!

IT WAS NOT UNTIL I HAD LOGGED TEN OR TWELVE YEARS AS a Christian that I realized the Word of God was written to be understood by humans and was designed to be life-changing when applied to our lives. Up to that point, I viewed reading the Scriptures like singing the national anthem at a sporting event. It is usually a very solemn, heart-touching moment when we experience the anthem. It can even bring tears to our eyes and vivid images about past heroes and past victories to our thoughts. However, when the anthem is over, the crowd cheers because now we can get on with the game—the real reason we came together!

My experience with the Bible in several churches was a mirror image of singing the national anthem. Like singing the anthem, the Scriptures would be read at the beginning of the event (a Bible study, Sunday school class, worship service, youth rally, and so on). However, also like singing the anthem, the Bible would then have absolutely nothing to do with the study, class, service, or rally! We would simply get on with the game of life with no meaningful relationship to the Scriptures and certainly no profound informing of the game by their truths. No wonder I had so little understanding and appreciation for the power and purpose of the Bible in the life of a Christian.

You may have been in the same state when you picked up this book. Our goal has been to equip and motivate you to read and apply the various genres of the Bible according to the manner in which they were intended to be read and applied in your spiritual formation. We believe that reading the Word of God in this manner will be life-changing to you. The living God of the universe stands behind this boast! It is not the quality of what we have written that gives us such confidence. Rather, it is the nature and quality of the book of life—the Holy Scriptures. God will use it to change your life. All that He asks is that you read it humbly in the power of the Holy Spirit and in accordance with the "many portions and many ways" He has revealed it to us.

This book is structured to help facilitate this sensitivity to the multifaceted nature of God's revelation through the many genres of the Bible. Our goal has been to persuade you not to level the genre distinctions as you read the Bible, but rather to show sensitivity to the unique emphasis of each type of literature therein. This is the opposite of pulling every biblical book and passage through the same interpretive keyhole, no matter how spiritual the keyhole may be. Instead, we should glory in the remarkable variety of the genres and in the various impacts each one has on our spiritual formation. In that light, the following summary attempts to capture the diversity of all the genres of the Bible and how each genre gives us something very unique and specific to our growth in Christ.

A SUMMARY OF WHAT EACH BIBLICAL GENRE CONTRIBUTES TO OUR SPIRITUAL FORMATION

Each Biblical Genre's Specific Contribution to Our Spiritual Formation

- **O.T. Narratives/Histories:** Chapter 5.

- **Primary Contribution:** to inform and shape our worldview about the eternal plan God is working out universally in human history and also to underscore our continuity with the children of Israel as the people of God.

- **Secondary Contribution:** to give us positive and negative models of old covenant believers making choices to trust God.

- **The (Mosaic) Law:** Chapter 6.

- **Primary Contribution:** to explain how God relates to us within a covenantal relationship and how His holiness and Israel's sin could be reconciled through Israel's obedience to the covenant (Law). Within this covenantal relationship, the Law also demonstrates the concrete, practical, multifaceted areas in which God's people should obey and be transformed.

- **Secondary Contribution:** to give us ethical and moral illustrations of godly responses to a wide variety of life's situations.

- **The Psalms:** Chapter 7.

- **Primary Contribution:** to model what a God-centered view of life is like, through expressions of worship and prayer, and the way believers may express their deepest needs, pains, and concerns to God in passionate prayer and worship.

- **Secondary Contribution:** to give us models of how we are to worship God.

- **Proverbs/Wisdom Literature** (chapter 8)

- **Primary Contribution:** to they directly (for example, Proverbs) or indirectly (for example, Job, Ecclesiastes, and Song of Solomon) instruct us how to make wise choices in the nitty-gritty, daily affairs of life and in the difficult, inscrutable events of life.

- **The Prophets:** Chapter 9.

- **Primary Contribution:** to exhort us as to the rewards of covenant obedience and warn us of the discipline of covenant disobedience under the old covenant so that we are challenged to maintain our heart for God and our just treatment of others as we live under the new covenant.

- **Secondary Contribution:** to give us glimpses into the immediate future of God's people or into the distant future of the messianic/new covenant era and the superseding blessing of life in this climactic era.

- **The Gospels:** Chapter 10.

- **Primary Contribution:** to teach us about who Jesus the Messiah is and give us the opportunity to be discipled by Him as we observe Him and His disciples. Also, to observe Him modeling life in the kingdom of God and listen to Him about how we should live in the kingdom and be transformed in areas of sinful resistance.

■ **Secondary Contribution:** to give us insight into how we may encourage fellow disciples.

■ **The Book of Acts:** Chapter 11.

■ **Primary Contribution:** to teach us what God is doing in history at this present time under the kingship of Jesus the Messiah and to model for us what our corresponding purpose is as God's new covenant people; it also explains our roots, as well as some of the fruits of our identity as the church as we fulfill our purpose in the world.

■ **Secondary Contribution:** to give us methods and techniques for ministry to others.

■ **The Epistles:** Chapter 12.

■ **Primary Contribution:** to teach, exhort, and model our identity as the church and how we are to live it in the community of God's people by making godly choices in a myriad of practical areas in order to fulfill our purpose.

■ **Revelation:** Chapter 13.

■ **Primary Contribution:** to encourage and exhort us to overcome through continued faith and faithfulness in the difficult times by revealing God's ultimate triumph over Satan in establishing Christ's kingdom and the new heavens and new earth.

■ **Secondary Contribution:** to inform us of some of the specific events signaling the end of the age.

Is it a lot to ask that we read the Bible with a bit of sensitivity to the various genres and what they may contribute to our spiritual formation? Not really. However, there is a bit of work involved in the process. Have you ever done anything in life that was the least bit worthwhile and fulfilling that didn't involve a bit of work? The same is true of reading and contemplating the Word of God.

Actually, the effort you expend in reading the Bible well is even more valuable than with other things. This is because of the nature of the Bible—it is playing with fire!

It is a burning, raging, purging, cleansing, purifying, transforming, sanctifying, glorifying fire!

Get close to the flame! Eternity will attest to the effects this holy fire will have on you. The Father will use it to make you like His Son, Jesus Christ. Come, get close to the flame!

Appendix 1

THE TRANSLATION
SPECTRUM

"Formal Equivalency" or "Literal"	"Dynamic Equivalence"	"Free" or "Paraphrase"
NASB RSV NRSV KJB NKJB MLB	NIV JB NAB NJB NEB REB NLT	GNB(TEV)　　LB PHILLIPS MESSAGE
Emphasis on original language's wording and word order	Emphasis on finding equivalent concepts in the translated language	Emphasis on simplicity and clarity of the translated work over precision

For example,

note the translations of the difficult term *sarx* (flesh) in Galatians 5:24:

("Now those who belong to Christ Jesus have crucified the flesh with its passions and desires.")

LITERAL TRANSLATIONS
(PASS ON THE DIFFICULTY TO THE READER)

New American Standard Bible	"the flesh"
King James Bible/New King James Bible	"the flesh"
Revised Standard Version/New Revised Standard Version	"the flesh"

DYNAMIC EQUIVALENT TRANSLATIONS
(FIND EQUIVALENT CONCEPT IN ENGLISH)

New International Version	"the sinful nature"
New Living Translation	"of their sinful nature"
New English Bible	"the lower nature"
Revised English Bible	"the old nature"
New Jerusalem Bible	"self"

PARAPHRASES
(SEEK TO BRING MAXIMUM CLARITY WITH ADDITIONAL WORDS)

Today's English Version (Good News Bible)	"their human nature"
Living Bible	"their natural evil desires"
PHILLIPS	"their old nature"
MESSAGE	"everything connected with getting our own way and mindlessly responding to what everyone else calls necessities"

Appendix 2

HOW TO INTERPRET
THE BIBLE

STEP 1:
IDENTIFY THE GENRE OF THE BIBLICAL PASSAGE.

(A **genre** = a type of literature like a narrative, parable, law, prophecy, Gospel, epistle, and so on.)

In our culture, we do this automatically without even thinking. However, the Bible contains writings from another culture, and although the writers used the genres of the literature of their day, we don't instinctively know these genres. Thus we must make sure we understand what the genre of a given passage is before interpreting it because specific rules of interpretation apply to each genre. As we begin to read or study a passage, we must first identify the type of literature we are reading and then interpret our passage in light of the rules that apply to that genre of Scripture.

STEP 2:
DETERMINE THE "BIG IDEA" OR *MAIN THEME* OF THE PARAGRAPH OR EPISODE.

(The **"Big Idea"** is the statement of the controlling idea of the passage, like a topic sentence in a paragraph.)

It is a God-given ability that our minds automatically develop an initial understanding of what someone is starting to say or what we are beginning to read. In other words, we quickly develop *an understanding of the whole* that gives meaning to *every part* of the dialogue we are having or the passage we are reading. Normally, we should first do this with the entire biblical book, getting a proper understanding of the whole book in which our specific passage fits. However, for the sake of time, we generally skip this very crucial first step and move directly to stating the main theme of the paragraph or episode we are studying. When studying an individual verse or portion of a paragraph, determine the controlling idea of the whole paragraph or episode *by reading and re-reading the paragraph and its surrounding paragraphs several times!* (It really helps to use a Bible that has paragraphs indicated in it.) This is a basic requirement for Bible study. Now, here's the punch line! Because we already have some sort of big idea of the passage (otherwise we couldn't understand it), *write the "Big Idea" or main theme in one concise sentence!*

STEP 3:
MAKE OBSERVATIONS ABOUT THE STRUCTURE AND THE "PEOPLE ASPECTS" OF THE PASSAGE.

What kind of *"skeleton"* has the author chosen that supports the muscles or the meat of the passage? Is it repetitive or argumentative or storylike or something else? Look for these kinds of structural clues within the broader context of the passage and within the passage itself. How does the biblical author put together his argument and make his case? Is it subtle or straightforward? Does he hit us with a feather or a sledgehammer? Add any "people" insights that may be drawn from an understanding of *the history* or *the culture* of the biblical period. Some good Bible reference tools are great for this step! We should write down our observations as we read.

STEP 4:
INTERPRET THE MEANING OF THE PASSAGE AS WE MEDITATE ON IT AND ON OUR OBSERVATIONS.

Our goal is twofold: (1) to discover the meaning of the passage (a public thing) and (2) to get that meaning into our own soul (a private act). We not only want to understand the content of the passage, we also want to internalize the meaning and the desired response to this passage that God has given us. Therefore, we enter into the act of interpretation humbly, prayerfully, and submissively as we place ourselves under the authority of God the Holy Spirit. *Good interpretation is both an intellectual and a spiritual act!* It is both a mental and spiritual discipline and an aesthetic and spiritual art! Thus the interpretive process must be rooted in and grounded on the very best of intellectual work before we begin to meditate and get God's Word into our soul.

STEP 5:
FINALLY, *APPLY* THE PASSAGE TO OUR LIFE
AND TO THOSE AROUND US.

This is actually part of the interpretation process because application is part of the meaning of a passage! Therefore, first establish the thrust of the original application intended by the author. Then, in light of our own needs and those of our group or culture, make a contemporary application that does not violate the boundaries of the original application. Our goal is to get both the meaning of the passage and its significance into our soul and into the souls of those we love.

NOTES

Chapter One: Playing with Fire
1. Philip Cushman, "Why the Self Is Empty: Toward a Historically Situated Psychology," *American Psychologist* 45 (1990): p. 600.
2. Cushman, p. 600.

Chapter Two: Transformation Through Information
1. Calvin Miller, *The Table of Inwardness* (Downers Grove, Ill.: InterVarsity, 1984), p. 83.
2. M. Robert Mulholland, Jr., *Invitation to a Journey: A Road Map for Spiritual Formation* (Downers Grove, Ill.: InterVarsity, 1993), p. 111.
3. Robert Polzin, *Biblical Structuralism* (Philadelphia: Fortress, 1977), p. 75. Quoted in Tremper Longman III, *Literary Approaches to Biblical Interpretation* in *Foundations of Contemporary Interpretation*, 6 vols. in 1 (Grand Rapids: Zondervan, 1996), p. 126.
4. Susan Annette Muto, *A Practical Guide to Spiritual Reading*, rev. ed. (Petersham, Mass.: St. Bede's Publications, 1994), p. 5.
5. M. Robert Mulholland, Jr., *Shaped by the Word: The Power of Scripture in Spiritual Formation* (Nashville: Upper Room, 1985), pp. 55-56.
6. Adrian van Kaam, cited in Mulholland, *Shaped by the Word*, p. 60.
7. See E. D. Hirsch, Jr., *Validity in Interpretation* (New Haven and London: Yale University Press, 1967), pp. 24-126, for one of the most helpful and persuasive discussions of the nature of genres and genre ideas. See also D. Brent Sandy and Ronald L. Giese, Jr., eds., *Cracking Old Testament Codes: A Guide to Interpreting the Literary Genres of the Old Testament* (Nashville: Broadman & Holman, 1995), especially chapter 2 ("Literary Forms and Interpretation") and chapter 14 ("Literary Forms in the Hands of Preachers and Teachers").
8. For a fuller defense of the need to read and interpret the Bible with sensitivity to genres, see Walter B. Russell III, "Literary Forms in the Hands of Preachers and Teachers," chap. 14 in *Cracking Old Testament Codes*.

Chapter Three: Illumination: Truth from the Top Down
1. Thomas à Kempis, *The Imitation of Christ*, book 1, section 5, quoted from the Clarion Classics edition (Grand Rapids: Zondervan, 1983), p. 11.
2. For a defense of the view that illumination equals help in applying the Bible, see Daniel P. Fuller, "The Holy Spirit's Role in Biblical Interpretation," in *Scripture, Tradition, and Interpretation*, ed. W. Ward Gasque and William Sanford LaSor (Grand Rapids: Eerdmans, 1978), pp. 189-198. For the traditional view that illumination equals help in both understanding and applying the Bible, see Millard J. Erickson, "The Role of the Holy Spirit in Biblical Interpretation," in *Evangelical*

Interpretation: Perspectives on Hermeneutical Issues (Grand Rapids: Baker, 1993), pp. 22-54. First Corinthians 2:14 teaches that a "natural man" (nonChristian) does not "welcome" or "accept" the things of the Spirit of God because he or she cannot understand their spiritual nature. It does not seem that such persons cannot comprehend the words or concepts, but that they do not understand because they do not accept them as truth. Therefore, they will not welcome them into their lives nor live by them. This seems to be more of a moral issue than an intellectual one, which the Holy Spirit solves in the Christian's life. However, a person cannot totally separate one from the other. In this sense, the refusal to accept the Word of God as truth would eventually erode and oppose the nonChristian's understanding of such truth. Therefore, on the back end (as opposed to the front end), nonChristians' intellectual understanding of Scripture would be diminished by their sinful orientation. It is these kinds of moral issues (with intellectual ramifications) that the ministry of Holy Spirit illumination seems to address in the lives of believers.

3. Clark H. Pinnock, "The Role of the Spirit in Interpretation," *Journal of the Evangelical Theological Society* 36 (1993): p. 494. This short article (pp. 491-497) is an excellent summary of how the Holy Spirit aids us in interpreting and applying the Bible to our lives.

Chapter Four: Ingesting the Fire

1. Eugene Peterson, *Living the Message* (San Francisco: Harper, 1996), p. 14.
2. Joel B. Green, Scot McKnight, and I. Howard Marshall, eds., *Dictionary of Jesus and the Gospels* (Downers Grove, Ill.: InterVarsity, 1992), p. 565.
3. M. Robert Mulholland, Jr., *Invitation to a Journey: A Road Map for Spiritual Formation* (Downers Grove, IL: InterVarsity Press, 1993), p. 112.
4. For solid evangelical guidance, see Dallas Willard, *The Spirit of the Disciplines* (San Francisco: Harper & Row, 1988), especially chapters 2, 8–9. Also see Susan Annette Muto, *A Practical Guide to Spiritual Reading,* rev. ed. (Petersham, Mass.: St. Bede's Publications, 1994), for an excellent guide and bibliography in spiritual reading that combines reading both biblical and classical texts in spiritual formation. Also helpful is Michael Casey, *Sacred Reading: The Ancient Art of Lectio Divina* (Ligouri, Mo.: Ligouri/Triumph, 1996).
5. Mulholland, pp. 112-115, adds two very helpful steps to these four classical ones. At the beginning he adds silence, to prepare our hearts for receptivity, and at the end he adds the step of incarnation, which expresses the commitment to embody the truth of the text in who we are and in what we do.
6. See Gordon D. Fee, "To What End Exegesis? Reflections on Exegesis and Spirituality in Philippians 4:10-20," *Bulletin for Biblical Research* 8 (1998): 75-88, for a passionate defense of the dual intention of Scripture.
7. For a stirring defense of the biblical role of the mind, see J. P. Moreland, *Love Your God with All Your Mind* (Colorado Springs, Colo.: NavPress, 1997), especially chap. 3, "The Mind's Role in Spiritual Transformation."
8. For excellent help regarding busyness, see the two practical books by Richard A. Swenson, *Margin* (Colorado Springs, Colo.: NavPress, 1992) and *The Overload Syndrome* (Colorado Springs, Colo.: NavPress, 1998).
9. Willard, pp. 176-177.

Chapter Five: God's Plan: Old Testament Narratives

1. *The Christian Educator's Handbook on Spiritual Formation,* ed. Kenneth Gangel and James C. Wilhoit (Wheaton, Ill.: Victor, 1994), p. 74.
2. While beyond the focus of this chapter, it is important to the Christian faith that the events that the Bible presents as "history" or "fact" actually did happen like it says they did. The postmodern (post-Enlightenment) assertion that it does not matter as long as

they are "factlike" or "true-to-life" or "artistically true" is, in the face of classic Christianity and its standards, totally incompatible and should be rejected from the outset! Rather, the whole faith of Israel and the church is built on God's revelation of Himself within history through both His words and His deeds. For a very readable defense of this historicity and a helpful rebuttal of the challenge of postmodernism to the historicity of biblical narratives and histories, see V. Phillips Long, *The Art of Biblical History* in *Foundations of Contemporary Interpretation*, 6 vols. in 1, Moisés Silva, gen. ed. (Grand Rapids: Zondervan, 1996), especially chap. 3 in Long's volume, "History and Truth: Is Historicity Important?" pp. 338-357.

3. The line breaks in this passage have been altered from their placement in the NASB to allow me to better make my point.
4. Gordon D. Fee and Douglas Stuart, *How to Read the Bible for All Its Worth*, 2nd ed. (Grand Rapids: Zondervan, 1993), p. 92.

Chapter Six: Good Boundaries, Good Neighbors: The Law

1. To complicate matters a bit, sometimes the Pentateuch, these four books plus Genesis, is called the Book of the Law (see Joshua 1:8). Additionally, sometimes the whole Old Testament, all thirty-nine books, is also called the Law. However, because we are focusing on the genres of biblical books, we will refer only to the four biblical books of Exodus, Leviticus, Numbers, and Deuteronomy when we speak of the Law. The Law actually begins in Exodus 20 and runs through Deuteronomy 33.
2. William W. Klein, Craig L. Blomberg, and Robert L. Hubbard, Jr., *Introduction to Biblical Interpretation* (Dallas: Word, 1993), p. 278.
3. This terminology, which is also used in the preceding diagram, comes from the helpful work by Thomas Edward McComiskey, *The Covenant of Promise: A Theology of the Old Testament Covenants* (Grand Rapids: Baker, 1985).
4. Klein, Blomberg, and Hubbard, p. 279.
5. See David A. Dorsey, "The Law of Moses and the Christian: A Compromise," *Journal of the Evangelical Theological Society* 34 (September 1991): pp. 325-329, for the following five reasons why the 613 regulations of the Mosaic Law are not binding on Christians:
   1. The corpus was designed to regulate the lives of a people living in the distinctive geographical and climatic conditions found in the southern Levant, and many of the regulations are inapplicable, unintelligible, or even nonsensical outside that regime. . . .
   2. The corpus was designed by God to regulate the lives of a people whose cultural milieu was that of the ancient Near East. . . .
   3. The Mosaic corpus was intended to regulate the lives of people whose religious milieu was that of the ancient Near Eastern world (particularly Canaan) and would be more or less inapplicable outside that world. . . .
   4. The code of laws was issued by God to lay the detailed groundwork for and regulate the various affairs of an actual politically- and geographically-defined nation. . . .
   5. The corpus was formulated to establish and maintain a cultic regime that has been discontinued with the Church (see Hebrews 8:18).
      Dorsey then reaches this succinct conclusion:
      "In sum, the Sinaitic law code was very specifically designed by God to regulate the lives of the West Semitic inhabitants of the southern Levant. Nearly all the regulations of the corpus—over ninety-five percent—are so culturally specific, geographically limited, and so forth that they would be completely inapplicable, and in fact unfulfillable, to Christians living throughout the world today. This fact alone should suggest that the corpus is not legally binding upon Christians and that it cannot possibly represent the

marching orders of the Church" (p. 329).
6. Some divide the Mosaic Law into the three divisions of civil, ceremonial, and moral laws. There is no argument that the civil laws governing the theocracy of Israel and the ceremonial laws governing the worship of God in Israel are not binding for Christians among these advocates. However, they argue that the "moral laws" (like the Ten Commandments) are still binding. In response to this reasoning, David A. Dorsey ("The Law of Moses and the Christian") makes these three points (pp. 329-331):

1. The scheme of a tripartite [threefold] division is unknown both in the Bible and in early rabbinic literature.
2. The categorizing of certain selected laws as "moral" is methodologically questionable.
3. The attempt to formulate this special category in order to "save" for New Testament Christians a handful of apparently universally-applicable laws—particularly the ones quoted in the New Testament—is an unnecessary effort.

7. Dorsey, p. 333.

Chapter Seven: Souls That Sing: The Psalms

1. Eugene Peterson, *Living the Message* (San Francisco: Harper, 1996), p. 277.
2. See Derek Kidner, *Psalms 1–72,* Tyndale Old Testament Commentaries (Downers Grove, Ill.: InterVarsity, 1973), pp. 1-46, for an excellent introduction to the Psalms. See also his companion volume, *Psalms 73–150,* Tyndale Old Testament Commentaries (Downers Grove, Ill.: InterVarsity, 1975).
3. A helpful book that strikes this dynamic balance is Tremper Longman III, *How to Read the Psalms* (Downers Grove, Ill.: InterVarsity, 1988).
4. The line breaks of these poetic passages have been altered from their placement in the NIV to more clearly demonstrate poetic parallelism. For a very helpful discussion of poetry in the Old Testament and its various kinds of parallelism, see William W. Klein, Craig L. Blomberg, and Robert L. Hubbard, Jr., *Introduction to Biblical Interpretation* (Dallas: Word, 1993), chap. 7, "General Rules of Hermeneutics—Old Testament Poetry," and James L. Kugel, *The Idea of Biblical Poetry* (New Haven, Conn.: Yale University Press, 1981).
5. Used with permission.
6. I am indebted to Kidner, *Psalms 1–72,* pp. 65-68, for much of this wording and insight.

Chapter Eight: To Be Wise: Proverbs and the Wisdom Books

1. Particularly helpful in understanding the genre and message of Job are the following: Francis I. Andersen, *Job: An Introduction and Commentary,* Tyndale Old Testament Commentaries (Downers Grove, Ill.: InterVarsity, 1976); Derek Kidner, *The Wisdom of Proverbs, Job, and Ecclesiastes* (Downers Grove, Ill.: InterVarsity, 1985); Leland Ryken, *Words of Delight: A Literary Introduction to the Bible* (Grand Rapids: Baker, 1987), especially chap. 15, "Drama"; and Roy Zuck, *Job,* Everyman's Bible Commentary (Chicago: Moody, 1978).
2. Bruce K. Waltke, "The Book of Proverbs and Ancient Wisdom Literature," *Bibliotheca Sacra* 136 (1979): pp. 233-234. See also by the same author, "The Book of Proverbs and Old Testament Theology," *Bibliotheca Sacra* 136 (1979): pp. 302-317. I am deeply indebted to Dr. Waltke for his rich insights into all of Wisdom Literature, but especially into the book of Proverbs.
3. Waltke, "The Book of Proverbs and Ancient Wisdom Literature," pp. 236-238.
4. This is the view of Gordon D. Fee and Douglas Stuart, *How to Read the Bible for All Its Worth,* 2nd ed. (Grand Rapids: Zondervan, 1993), pp. 212-215.
5. This is close to the perspective of Ryken, pp. 319-328, and Kidner, chaps. 6–7.
6. I am especially indebted in my understanding to J. Stafford Wright, "The

Interpretation of Ecclesiastes," in *Classical Evangelical Essays in Old Testament Interpretation,* compiled and edited by Walter C. Kaiser, Jr. (Grand Rapids: Baker, 1972), pp. 133-150.

7. Ryken, pp. 320-321.
8. Ryken, p. 276. Ryken's treatment of the Song of Solomon (chap. 11) is one of the most helpful I have read.
9. Waltke, "The Book of Proverbs and Ancient Wisdom Literature," pp. 230-232.
10. Derek Kidner, *The Proverbs,* Tyndale Old Testament Commentaries (Downers Grove, Ill.: InterVarsity, 1964), p. 69. This is an extremely helpful and edifying commentary. The eight subject studies at the beginning of the commentary are invaluable on topics like wisdom, the fool, friends, words, and so on.
11. My translation.

Chapter Nine: Heart for God: The Prophets

1. Gordon D. Fee and Douglas Stuart, *How to Read the Bible for All Its Worth,* 2nd ed. (Grand Rapids: Zondervan, 1993), p. 166.
2. Fee and Stuart's specific term for the prophets is "covenant enforcement mediators" (p. 167).
3. These insights are from Richard D. Patterson, "The Psalm of Habakkuk," *Grace Theological Journal* 8 (1987): 163-194.
4. William W. Klein, Craig L. Blomberg, and Robert L. Hubbard, Jr., *Introduction to Biblical Interpretation* (Dallas: Word, 1993), pp. 292-302.
5. Fee and Stuart, pp.176-177.

Chapter Ten: Discipleship 101: The Gospels

1. John Blanchard, *Gathered Gold* (Durham, England: Evangelical Press, 1984), p. 174.
2. These are quoted from the very helpful article by Renald Showers, "Why Did Jesus Perform Miracles?" *Israel My Glory* (December 1975-January 1976): pp. 17-20.
3. Showers, p. 17.
4. This is why Jesus fulfills His responsibility as firstborn son to make provisions for His mother Mary's care even while He is dying on the cross (see John 19:26-27)!
5. Two books should prove to be very helpful in this regard: for culture, see Bruce J. Malina, *The New Testament World: Insights from Cultural Anthropology,* rev. ed. (Louisville: Westminster/John Knox, 1993); for history, see Joel B. Green, Scot McKnight, and I. Howard Marshall, eds., *Dictionary of Jesus and the Gospels* (Downers Grove, Ill.: InterVarsity, 1992).
6. Nevertheless, there is great value in studying Gospel "harmonies." These are particularly helpful in sketching a full account of Jesus' life and ministry. However, they do obscure each Gospel's distinctions in the process.
7. The best work done on discipleship is by Michael J. Wilkins, *In His Image: Reflecting Christ in Everyday Life* (Colorado Springs, Colo.: NavPress, 1997), and also by Wilkins, *Following the Master: Discipleship in the Steps of Jesus* (Grand Rapids: Zondervan, 1992).

Chapter Eleven: Our Purpose: The Acts of the Apostles

1. George Santayana, *The Life of Reason* (Amherst, NY: Prometheus Books, 1998; reprint), Vol. 1, p. 13.
2. Gordon D. Fee and Douglas Stuart, *How to Read the Bible for All Its Worth,* 2nd ed. (Grand Rapids: Zondervan, 1993), p. 106, emphasis in original.
3. This date and all of the following ones are from Harold W. Hoehner, "A Chronological Table of the Apostolic Age," from "Chronology of the Apostolic Age" (diss., Dallas Theological Seminary, 1965; revised April 1972 and July 1989).
4. See Richard N. Longenecker, *Acts of the Apostles,* The Expositor's Bible Commentary,

vol. 9 (Grand Rapids: Zondervan, 1981), pp. 403-404, for these citations.

5. The most helpful work that I have ever read on this dynamic is by my colleague at Biola University, Harold Dollar, *St. Luke's Missiology: A Cross-Cultural Challenge* (Pasadena, Calif.: William Carey Library, 1996).

6. For a fuller development of this point, see Walt Russell, "The Anointing with the Holy Spirit in Luke-Acts," *Trinity Journal*, n.s., 7 (Spring 1986): pp. 47-63.

Chapter Twelve: Community: The Epistles

1. Quoted in Lewis B. Smedes, "Telling the Truth" in *Discernment: A Newsletter of the Center for Applied Christian Ethics*, Vol. 1, No. 1 (Winter, 1992), p. 2.

2. E. D. Hirsch, Jr., *Validity in Interpretation* (New Haven, Conn.: Yale University Press, 1967), p. 8.

3. For an excellent guide, see especially Stanley K. Stowers, *Letter Writing in Greco-Roman Antiquity, Library of Early Christianity*, vol. 5 (Philadelphia: Westminster, 1986).

Chapter Thirteen: Living Expectantly: Revelation

1. "Eight Compelling Reasons Why Christ Is Coming 'Very, Very Soon,'" *Orange County Register,* December 7, 1998, "Metro" section, p. 2.

2. Essentially reviving this ancient view is the major work by G. K. Beale, *The Book of Revelation,* New International Greek Testament Commentary (Grand Rapids: Eerdmans, 1998).

3. Generally preterist in perspective is the massive work by David Aune, *Revelation,* 3 vols., Word Biblical Commentary 52 A, B, and C (Dallas: Word, 1997-1998).

4. The most thorough commentary is by E. B. Elliott, *Horae Apocalypticae,* 4 vols., 3rd ed. (Seely's, 1847).

5. Although containing some preterist elements, the most balanced futurist work is by Robert H. Mounce, *The Book of Revelation,* rev. ed., New International Commentary on the New Testament (Grand Rapids: Eerdmans, 1998).

6. Gordon D. Fee and Douglas Stuart, *How to Read the Bible for All Its Worth,* 2nd ed. (Grand Rapids: Zondervan, 1993), p. 243.

7. William W. Klein, Craig L. Blomberg, and Robert L. Hubbard, Jr., *Introduction to Biblical Interpretation* (Dallas: Word, 1993), p. 369.

8. See the discussion of these parallels in J. Ramsey Michaels, *Revelation,* IVP New Testament Commentary Series, vol. 20 (Downers Grove, Ill.: InterVarsity, 1997), pp. 216-217.

Author

WALT RUSSELL teaches the principles of *Playing with Fire* to students in his biblical interpretation classes at Talbot School of Theology. He is professor of Bible at Talbot and chairman of biblical studies and theology at Biola University. Walt has written numerous articles on related subjects in both scholarly journals and popular magazines including *Christianity Today*. Russell has been ministering in various churches and teaching the Bible for more than twenty years. His love for teaching the Bible on college campuses and in churches throughout the United States has spanned thirty years. He is a sought-after as a speaker who equips others to be spiritually formed by God's Word. He and his family live in Yorba Linda, California.

General Editor

DALLAS WILLARD is a professor in the school of philosophy at the University of Southern California in Los Angeles. He has been at USC since 1965, where he was director of the school of philosophy from 1982 to 1985. He has also taught at the University of Wisconsin (Madison), where he received his Ph.D. in 1964, and has held visiting appointments at UCLA (1969) and the University of Colorado (1984).

His philosophical publications are mainly in the areas of epistemology, the philosophy of mind and of logic, and on the philosophy of Edmund Husserl, including extensive translations of Husserl's early writings from German into English. His *Logic and the Objectivity of Knowledge*, a study on Husserl's early philosophy, appeared in 1984.

Dr. Willard also lectures and publishes in religion. *In Search of Guidance* was published in 1984 (second edition in 1993), and *The Spirit of the Disciplines* was released in 1988.

He is married to Jane Lakes Willard, a marriage and family counselor with offices in Van Nuys and Canoga Park, California. They have two children, John and Rebecca, and live in Chatsworth, California.

MORE PATHS TO A FULFILLING RELATIONSHIP WITH GOD.

Reading the Bible with Heart and Mind

The Bible isn't an ordinary book—it can change your life! Renew your passion for Scripture and learn how it can mold you into the image of Christ.

Reading the Bible with Heart and Mind
(Tremper Longman III) $14

Love Your God with All Your Mind

Have you really thought about your faith? This book examines the role of reason in faith, helping you use your intellect to further God's kingdom.

Love Your God with All Your Mind
(J. P. Moreland) $14

Spiritual Disciplines for the Christian Life

Drawn from the church's rich heritage, this book will guide you through disciplines that can deepen your walk with God including Scripture reading, evangelism, fasting, journaling, and stewardship.

Spiritual Disciplines for the Christian Life
(Donald S. Whitney) $13

Get your copies today at your local bookstore, or call (800) 366-7788 and ask for offer **#6042**.

NAVPRESS
BRINGING TRUTH TO LIFE
w w w . n a v p r e s s . c o m

Prices subject to change.